GENERAL TABLE OF CONTENTS.

STATUTES COMPRISED.

This compilation comprises the following statutes so far as they relate to internal revenue, in whole or in part, those sections being omitted which cease to be in force after the act of July 13, 1866, takes full effect:

AN ACT to provide internal revenue to support the government, and to pay interest on the public debt, approved July 1, 1862.—*Statutes at Large, vol. XII, pages* 432—489, *Chap. CXIX.*

AN ACT to amend an act entitled "An act to provide internal revenue to support the government, and to pay interest on the public debt, approved July 1, 1862," and for other purposes, approved March 3, 1863.—*Ibid., vol. XII, pages* 713—731, *Chap. LXXIV.*

AN ACT to provide internal revenue to support the government, to pay interest on the public debt, and for other purposes, approved June 30, 1864.—*Ibid., vol. XIII, pages* 223—306, *Chap. CLXXIII.*

AN ACT to amend an act entitled "An act to provide internal revenue to support the government, to pay interest on the public debt, and for other purposes, approved June 30, 1864," approved March 3, 1865.

AN ACT authorizing the Secretary of the Treasury to appoint assistant assessors of internal revenue, approved January 15, 1866.

AN ACT to declare the meaning of certain parts of the internal revenue act, approved June 30, 1864, and for other purposes, approved March 10, 1866.

AN ACT to reduce internal taxation, and to amend an act entitled "An act to provide internal revenue to support the government, to pay the interest on the public debt, and for other purposes, approved June 30, 1864," and acts amendatory thereof, approved July 13, 1866.

AN ACT to authorize the refunding of certain taxes, approved July 27, 1866.

AN ACT amendatory of section thirteen of an act entitled "An act to amend an act entitled 'An act to provide internal revenue to support the government, to pay interest on the public debt, and for other purposes,' approved June 30, 1864," approved March 3, 1865, approved July 27, 1866.

Also the following, relating to the care of the public moneys, viz:

AN ACT to provide for the better organization of the treasury, and for the collection, safe-keeping, transfer and disbursement of the public revenue, approved August 6, 1861.

AN ACT to provide more effectually for the settlement of accounts between the United States and receivers of public money, approved March 3, 1797:

The appendix containing the following joint resolutions, viz:

JOINT RESOLUTION imposing a special income duty, approved July 4, 1864, public resolution No. 59.

JOINT RESOLUTION to prevent the further enforcement of the Joint Resolution (No. 77) approved July 4, 1864, against officers and soldiers of the United States who have been honorably discharged, so as to relieve them from the further payment of the special five per cent. income tax imposed thereby, approved July 28, 1866.

TABLE

SHOWING THE

ARRANGEMENT OF THE SEVERAL SECTIONS OF THE DIFFERENT ACTS COMPRISED IN THIS COMPILATION.

Act	Section	Compilation No.
1 July, 1862, §	1	1
Do	2	10
3 March, 1863, §	4, (tariff act)	75
Do	19	5
Do	20	7
30 June, 1864, §	1	2
Do	2	3
Do	3	5
Do	4	8
Do	5	9
Do	7	10
Do	8	11
Do	9	13
Do	10	14
Do	11	29
Do	12	30
Do	13	31
Do	14	32
Do	15	219
Do	16	33
Do	17	34
Do	18	35
Do	19	37
Do	20	38
Do	21	25
Do	22	17
Do	23	27
Do	24	18
Do	25	19
Do	26	20
Do	27	39
Do	28	40
Do	29	41
Do	30	44
Do	31	45
Do	32	46
Do	33	47
Do	34	48
Do	35	49
Do	36	26
Do	37	50
Do	38	51
Do	39	15
Do	40	16
Do	41	52
Do	42	220
Do	43	24
Do	44	54
Do	45	42
Do	46	235
Do	48	224
Do	49	223
Do	51	23
Do	52	22
Do	58	242
Do	60	127
Do	61	136
Do	71	56
Do	72	57
Do	73	58
Do	74	59
Do	75	60
Do	76	61
Do	77	62
Do	78	63
Do	79	64
Do	80	65
Do	81	67
30 June, 1864, §	82	97
Do	83	106
Do	84	108
Do	85	103
Do	86	100
Do	87	98
Do	88	99
Do	89	107
Do	90	101
Do	91	104
Do	92	105
Do	93	93
Do	94	94
Do	95	96
Do	96	92
Do	97	89
Do	98	69
Do	99	70
Do	100	157
Do	103	74
Do	104	76
Do	105	77
Do	106	81
Do	107	78
Do	108	79
Do	109	80
Do	110	71
Do	111	82
Do	112	83
Do	113	84
Do	114	86
Do	115	87
Do	116	158
Do	117	159
Do	118	160
Do	119	161
Do	120	162
Do	121	163
Do	122	164
Do	123	165
Do	124	167
Do	125	168
Do	126	169
Do	127	170
Do	128	171
Do	129	172
Do	130	173
Do	131	174
Do	132	175
Do	133	178
Do	134	180
Do	135	181
Do	136	179
Do	137	189
Do	138	176
Do	139	177
Do	140	182
Do	141	183
Do	142	190
Do	143	188
Do	144	187
Do	145	191
Do	146	186
Do	147	184
Do	148	192
Do	149	185
Do	151, (Schedule B)	193
Do	152	197

Act	§	Compilation No.
30 June, 1864,	§ 153	199
Do	154	195
Do	155	203
Do	156	201
Do	157	202
Do	158	204
Do	159	194
Do	160	196
Do	161	205
Do	162	200
Do	163	198
Do	164, (Schedule C)	206
Do	165	211
Do	166	212
Do	167	213
Do	168	208
Do	169	210
Do	170	214
Do	171	215
Do	172	218
Do	173	240
Do	174	241
Do	176	53
Do	177	116
Do	178	166
Do	179	227
Do	180	226
Do	182	237
3 March, 1865,	§ 1	8, 11, 16, 19, 20, 32, 40, 51, 59, 67, 70, 71, 74, 77, 80, 92, 94, 98, 100, 101, 104, 105, 106, 108, 136, 156, 158, 159, 160, 161, 162, 168, 178, 181, 185, 193, 196, 204, 206, 208, 210, 211, 213, 215, 227.
3 March, 1865,	§ 3	4
Do	6	72
Do	11	209
Do	13	85
Do	14	73
Do	15	217
Do	16	239
Do	17	90
15 Jan'y, 1866,	§ 1	12
10 March, 1866,	§ 3, 4, 5	36
13 July, 1866,	§ 1	109
Do	2	110
Do	3	111
Do	4	112
Do	5	113
Do	6	216
Do	7	114
Do	8	115
Do	9	9, 11, 17, 18, 20, 25, 32, 37, 38, 40, 41, 44, 48, 52, 54, 56, 57, 58, 59, 60, 61, 62, 63, 64, 65, 67, 69, 70, 71, 74, 78, 82, 86, 93. 94, 98, 99, 100, 101, 104, 105, 107, 157, 158, 161, 162, 164, 165, 167, 168, 176, 184, 189, 191, 192, 193, 195, 197, 198, 203, 204, 206, 210, 211, 215, 224, 227.
13 July, 1866,	§ 9, bis	36, 72, 73
Do	10	91
Do	11	102

Act	§	Compilation No.
13 July, 1866,	§ 12	66
Do	13	207
Do	14	225
Do	15	229
Do	16	222
Do	17	43
Do	18	88
Do	19	55
Do	20	217
Do	21	119
Do	22	120
Do	23	121
Do	24	122
Do	25	123
Do	26	140
Do	27	126
Do	28	128
Do	29	129
Do	30	130
Do	31	124
Do	32	117
Do	33	118
Do	34	125
Do	35	138
Do	36	95
Do	37	132
Do	38	131
Do	39	139
Do	40	135
Do	41	133
Do	42	137
Do	43	142
Do	44	141
Do	45	134
Do	46	144
Do	47	145
Do	48	143
Do	49	146
Do	50	147
Do	51	151
Do	52	148
Do	53	149
Do	54	152
Do	55	150
Do	56	153
Do	57	155
Do	58	154
Do	59	28
Do	60	233
Do	61	156
Do	62	221
Do	63	228
Do	64	6
Do	65	21
Do	66	234
Do	67	230
Do	68	231
Do	69	232
Do	70	238
Do	71	236
27 July, 1866,	authorizing to refund certain taxes	68
Do	amending sec. 13, Act March 3, 1865	85

Sections relating to the care of public moneys:

6 August, 1846, § 16.
3 March, 1797, § 1, 2, 3, 4, 5, 6, 7. } Follow 23.

Sections relating to special income tax for 1863:

4 July, 1864, (joint resolution.)
28 July, 1866, do. } May be found in the appendix.

LIST

OF

ACTS OF CONGRESS RELATING TO INTERNAL REVENUE

ENACTED SINCE JULY 4, 1861.*

An act to provide increased revenue from imports to pay interest on the public debt, and for other purposes, approved August 5, 1861; Chap. XLV, vol. 12; 292. Sections 49, 50, and 51 imposed an income tax, and so far were repealed July 1, 1862.

An act to provide internal revenue to support the government and to pay interest on the public debt, approved July 1, 1862; Chap. CXIX, vol. 12; 432, 489. Section 89 repealed portions of act August 5, 1861, as above. Repealed June 30, 1864, except sections 115 and 119; section 115 was repealed in effect March 3, 1865. Section 119 is omitted from this compilation as relating wholly to direct tax.

An act increasing temporarily the duties on imports, and for other purposes, approved July 14, 1862; Chap. CLXIII, vol. 12; 560, 1. Sections 24 and 25 amended section 95 act July 1, 1862, and provided when provisions relating to stamp duties should take effect. Repealed June 30, 1864.

An act to impose an additional duty on sugars produced in the United States, approved July 16, 1862; Chap. CLXXXVII, vol 12; 588. Repealed June 30, 1864.

Joint resolution to amend section 77 of "An act to provide internal revenue to support the government and to pay interest on the public debt," and for other purposes, approved July 17, 1862; No. 64, page 627. Provided when act of July 1, 1862, should take effect. Limited in itself.

An act to amend an act entitled "An act to provide internal revenue to support the government and to pay interest on the public debt," approved December 25, 1862; Chap. V, vol. 12; 632. Amended act of July 1, 1862. Repealed by act of June 30, 1864.

An act to amend an act entitled "An act to provide internal revenue to support the government and pay interest on the public debt," approved July 1, 1862, and for other purposes, approved March 3, 1863; Chap. LXXIV, vol. 12; 713, 731. Repealed by act of June 30, 1864, except as relates to appointment of deputy commissioner and cashier of internal revenue, sections 19 and 21.

An act to prevent and punish frauds upon the revenue, and for other purposes, approved March 3, 1863; Chap. LXXVI, vol. 12; 737. Section 2 referred to "revenue." This section was repealed June 30, 1864, "so far as the same applies to officers of internal revenue."

An act to increase the internal revenue, and for other purposes, approved March 7, 1864; Chap. XX, vol. 12; 14, 17. Repealed June 30, 1864.

Joint resolution to provide for the printing annually of the report of the Commissioner of Internal Revenue; No. 4, page 400. Approved January 13, 1864.

An act to provide internal revenue to support the government, to pay interest on the public debt, and for other purposes, approved June 30, 1864; Chap. CLXXIII, vol. 13; 223, 306. For repeal of former acts see section 173. Sections 6, 50, 53, 54, 55, 56, 57, 59, 62, 63, 64, 65, 66, 67, 68, 69, and 70; and parts of sections 83, 101, 102, 150, 177, were repealed July 13, 1866. Sections 47, relating to direct tax, and 131, making an annual appropriation, are omitted.

An act to amend an act entitled "An act to provide," &c., approved December 22, 1864; Chap. VIII, vol. 13; 420; as to when tax on whiskey, provided in section 55 of above act, should be increased. Limited in itself.

Joint resolution imposing a special income duty for the year ending December 31 next preceding October 1, 1864, approved July 4, 1864; No. 77, page 417. Limited in itself.

An act to amend an act entitled, &c., approved June 30, 1864, approved March 3, 1865; Chap. LXXVIII, vol. 13; 469. Section 16 repealed "all provisions of any former act inconsistent with the provisions of this act;" sections 2, 5, 8, 9, 10, and 12, repealed July 13, 1866.

---

* "This being the date of the assembling of the Thirty-seventh Congress in its first (extra) session, when, among other measures made necessary by the existing rebellion and war, was commenced the legislation which has since produced the present system of internal taxation."

ARRANGEMENT OF SUBJECTS.

VI.

VII.

VIII.

IX.

X.

XI.

XII.

APPENDIX.

INTERNAL REVENUE LAWS.

8. The Congress shall have power to lay and collect taxes, duties, imposts, and excises, to pay the debts, and provide for the common defence and general welfare of the United States; but all duties, imposts, and excises shall be uniform throughout the United States.—*Constitution of the United States, article* 1.

I.

OFFICE OF INTERNAL REVENUE.

OFFICERS—APPOINTMENTS—DUTIES—COMPENSATION—PROHIBITIONS.

1 July, 1862, § 1.

Office of Commissioner of Internal Revenue created.

1. That, for the purpose of superintending the collection of internal duties, stamp duties, licenses, or taxes imposed by this act, or which may be hereafter imposed, and of assessing the same, an office is hereby created in the Treasury Department to be called the office of the Commissioner of Internal Revenue; and the President of the United States is hereby authorized to nominate, and, with the advice and consent of the Senate, to appoint, a Commissioner of Internal Revenue. * * * * *

30 June, 1864, § 1.

Commissioner of Internal Revenue.

Duties and powers.

2. That, for the purpose of superintending the collection of internal duties, stamp duties, licenses, or taxes imposed by this act, or which may hereafter be imposed, and of assessing the same, the Commissioner of Internal Revenue * * * * shall be charged, under the direction of the Secretary of the Treasury, with preparing all the instructions, regulations, directions, forms, blanks, stamps, and licenses, and distributing the same, or any part thereof, and all other matters pertaining to the assessment and collection of the duties, stamp duties, licenses, and taxes which may be necessary to carry this act into effect, and with the general superintendence of his office, as aforesaid, and shall have authority, and hereby is authorized and required, to provide cotton marks, hydrometers, and proper and sufficient adhesive stamps, and stamps or dies for expressing and denoting the several stamp duties, or the amount thereof in the case of percentage duties, imposed by this act, and to alter and renew or replace such stamps, from time to time, as occasion shall require. He may also contract for or procure the printing of requisite forms, decisions, regulations, and advertisements; but the printing of such forms, decisions, and regulations shall be done at the public printing office, unless the public printer shall be unable to perform the work. * * * And the privilege of franking all letters and documents pertaining to the duties of his office, and of receiving free of postage all such letters and documents, is hereby extended to said Commissioner.

Commissioner may frank letters pertaining to the business of the office.

30 June, 1864, § 2.

Commissioner to pay over moneys daily.

Accounts to be rendered monthly of all moneys received or paid out.

3. That it shall be the duty of the Commissioner of Internal Revenue to pay over daily to the Treasurer of the United States all public moneys which may come into his possession, for which the Treasurer shall give proper receipts and keep a faithful account; and at the end of each month the said Commissioner shall render true and faithful accounts of all public moneys received or paid out, or paid to the Treasurer of the United States, exhibiting

Auditing of accounts.

proper vouchers therefor, and the same shall be received and examined by the Fifth Auditor of the Treasury, who shall thereafter certify the balance, if any, and transmit the accounts, with the vouchers and certificate, to the First Comptroller for his decision thereon; and the said Commissioner, when such accounts are settled as herein provided for, shall transmit a copy thereof to the Secretary of the Treasury. He shall at all times submit to the Secretary of the Treasury and the Comptroller, or either of them, the inspection of moneys in his hands, and shall, prior to the entering upon the duties of his office, execute a bond, with sufficient sureties, to be approved by the Secretary of the Treasury and by the First Comptroller, in a sum of not less than one hundred thousand dollars, payable to the United States, conditioned that said Commissioner shall faithfully perform the duties of his office according to law, and shall justly and faithfully account for and pay over to the United States, in obedience to law and in compliance with the order or regulations of the Secretary of the Treasury, all public moneys which may come into his hands or possession, and for the safe-keeping and faithful account of all stamps, adhesive stamps, or vellum, parchment or paper bearing a stamp denoting any duty thereon, which bond shall be filed in the office of the First Comptroller of the Treasury. And such Commissioner shall, from time to time, renew, strengthen, and increase his official bond as the Secretary of the Treasury may direct.

Copy of each account when settled to be sent to Secretary.

Secretary and Comptroller may inspect moneys in Commissioner's hands.

Commissioner to give bond.

3 March, 1865, § 3.

4. That from and after the thirtieth day of June, eighteen hundred and sixty-five, the gross amount of all duties, taxes, and revenues received or collected by virtue of the several acts to provide internal revenue to support the government and to pay the interest on the public debt, and of any other act or acts that may now or hereafter be in force connected with the internal revenues, shall be paid by the officers, collectors, or agents receiving or collecting the same daily into the treasury of the United States, under the instructions of the Secretary of the Treasury, without any abatement or deduction on account of salary, compensation, fees, costs, charges, expenses, or claims of any description whatever, anything in any law to the contrary notwithstanding. And all moneys now directed by law to be paid to the Commissioner of Internal Revenue, including those derived from the sale of stamps, shall be paid into the treasury of the United States by the party making such payment; and a certificate of such payment, stating the name of the depositor, and the specific account on which the deposit was made, signed by the treasurer, assistant treasurer, designated depositary or proper officer of a deposit bank, and transmitted to and received by the Commissioner of Internal Revenue, shall be deemed a compliance with the law requiring payment to be made to the Commissioner, any law to the contrary notwithstanding: *Provided*, That in districts where, from the distance of the officer, collector, or agent receiving or collecting such duties, taxes, and revenues from a proper government depository, the Secretary of the Treasury may deem it proper, he may extend the time for making such payment, not exceeding, however, in any case, a period of one month.

All duties to be paid daily into the treasury after June 30, 1865.

Certificate of deposit to be return d to Commissioner.

Secretary may extend time in certain cases.

5. That the President shall appoint in the Department of the Treasury, by and with the advice and consent of the Senate, a competent person, who shall be called the Deputy Commissioner of Internal Revenue, * * * * * who shall be charged with such duties in the Bureau of Internal Revenue as may be prescribed by the Secretary of the Treasury, or as may be required by law, and who shall act as Commissioner of Internal Revenue in the absence of that officer, and exercise the privilege of franking all letters and documents pertaining to the office of Internal Revenue.

3 March, 1863, § 19. 30 June, 1864, § 3. Deputy Commissioner. Duties and powers.

6. That the office of the Commissioner of Internal Revenue be reorganized so as to include—

13 July, 1866, § 64. Reorganization of the office of Internal Revenue.

One Commissioner of Internal Revenue, with a salary of six thousand dollars, and one Deputy Commissioner, with a salary of three thousand five hundred dollars; which offices are already created, and the duties thereof defined by law; and to authorize, under the direction of the Secretary of the Treasury, the employment of the following additional officers and clerks, and with the salaries hereinafter specified, namely:

Officers, clerks, employés, and their salaries.

Two Deputy Commissioners, each with a salary of three thousand dollars;

One Solicitor, with a salary of four thousand dollars;

Seven heads of divisions, each with a salary of two thousand five hundred dollars.

Thirty-four clerks of class four; forty-five clerks of class three; fifty clerks of class two; and thirty-seven clerks of class one;

Fifty-five female clerks;

Five messengers, three assistant messengers, and fifteen laborers. And a sum sufficient to pay the additional salaries of officers, clerks, and employés herein authorized is hereby appropriated out of any money in the treasury not otherwise appropriated; and this section shall take effect from and after the thirtieth day of June, eighteen hundred and sixty-six.

7. That the Secretary of the Treasury may appoint not exceeding three revenue agents, whose duties shall be, under the direction of the Secretary of the Treasury, to aid in the prevention, detection, and punishment of frauds upon the revenue, who shall be paid such compensation as the Secretary of the Treasury may deem just and reasonable, not exceeding two thousand dollars per annum. The above salaries to be paid in the same manner as are other expenses for collecting the revenue.

3 March, 1863, § 20. Revenue agents.

8. That the Secretary of the Treasury may appoint not exceeding ten revenue agents, whose duties shall be, under the direction of the Secretary of the Treasury, to aid in the prevention, detection, and punishment of frauds upon the internal revenue, and in the enforcement of the collection thereof, who shall be paid, in addition to the expenses necessarily incurred by them, such compensation as the Secretary of the Treasury may deem just and reasonable, not exceeding two thousand dollars per annum. The above salaries to be paid in the same manner as are other expenses for collecting the revenue.

30 June, 1864, § 4. 3 March, 1865, § 1. Revenue agents. Duties. Compensation.

9. That the Secretary of the Treasury may appoint inspectors in any assessment district where in his judgment it may be necessary for the purposes of a proper enforcement of the internal revenue laws or the detection of frauds; and such inspectors and revenue agents aforesaid shall be subject to the rules and regulations of the said Secretary, and have all the powers conferred upon any other officers of internal revenue in making any examination

30 June, 1864, § 6. Inspectors. Duties.

of persons, books, and premises which may be necessary in the discharge of the duties of their office; and the compensation of such inspectors shall be fixed and paid for such time as they may be actually employed, not exceeding four dollars per day, and their just and proper travelling expenses. And any inspector or revenue agent, or any special agent appointed by the Secretary of the Treasury, who shall demand or receive any compensation, fee, or reward, other than such as are provided by law for or in regard to the performance of his official duties, or shall be guilty of any extortion or wilful oppression in the discharge of such duties, shall, upon conviction thereof in any circuit or district court of the United States having jurisdiction thereof, be subject to a fine of not exceeding one thousand dollars, or to imprisonment for not exceeding one year, or both, at the discretion of the court, and shall be dismissed from office, and shall be forever disqualified from holding any office under the government of the United States. And one-half of the fine so imposed shall be for the use of the United States, and the other half for the use of the person, to be ascertained by the judgment of the court, who shall first give the information whereby any such fine may be imposed.

Compensation.

13 July, 1866, § 9.

Punishment for receiving unlawful compensation and for extortion.

10. That, for the purpose of assessing, levying, and collecting the duties or taxes hereinafter prescribed by this act, the President of the United States be, and he is hereby, authorized to divide, respectively, the States and Territories of the United States and the District of Columbia into convenient collection districts, and to nominate, and, by and with the advice and consent of the Senate, to appoint an assessor and a collector for each such district, who shall be residents within the same: *Provided*, That any of said States and Territories and the District of Columbia may, if the President shall deem it proper, be erected into and included in one district: *Provided*, That the number of districts in any State shall not exceed the number of representatives to which such State shall be entitled in the present Congress, except in such States as are entitled to an increased representation in the thirty-eighth Congress, in which States the number of districts shall not exceed the number of representatives to which any such State may be so entitled: *And provided further*, That in the State of California the President may establish a number of districts not exceeding the number of senators and representatives to which said State is entitled in the present Congress. And the President is hereby authorized to alter the respective collection districts provided for in said section as the public interests may require.

1 July, 1862, § 2.

Collection districts.

Assessor and collector appoint'd for each district.

Limitation of the number of districts

Additional districts in California.

30 June, 1864, § 7.*

Districts may be altered.

11. That each assessor shall divide his district into a convenient number of assessment districts, which may be changed as often as may be deemed necessary, subject to such regulations and limitations as may be imposed by the Commissioner of Internal Revenue, within each of which [the assessor, whenever there shall be a vacancy, shall appoint, with the approval of said Commissioner,] one or more assistant assessors, who shall be a resident of such assessment district; and in case of a vacancy occurring in the office of assessor by reason of death or any other cause, the assistant assessor of the assessment district in which the assessor resided at the time of the vacancy occurring shall act as assessor until an appointment filling the vacancy shall be made.

30 June, 1864, § 8.
3 March, 1865, § 1.
13 July, 1866, § 9.

Assessors to divide their districts into assessment districts.

In case of vacancy in the office of assessor.

*The remaining portion of this section is as follows:

Sec. 7. *And be it further enacted*, That the second section of an act entitled "An act to provide internal revenue to support the government and to pay interest on the public debt," approved July one, eighteen hundred and sixty-two, shall remain and continue in full force.

12. That the Secretary of the Treasury is hereby authorized to appoint any assistant assessors of internal revenue now provided by law. 15 Jan., 1866, § 1.

13. That before any collector shall enter upon the duties of his office, he shall execute a bond for such amount as shall be prescribed by the Commissioner of Internal Revenue, under the direction of the Secretary of the Treasury, with not less than five sureties to be approved by the Solicitor of the Treasury, conditioned that said collector shall faithfully perform the duties of his office according to law, and shall justly and faithfully account for and pay over to the United States, in compliance with the order or regulations of the Secretary of the Treasury, all public moneys which may come into his hands or possession; which bond shall be filed in the office of the First Comptroller of the Treasury. And such collector shall, from time to time, renew, strengthen, and increase his official bond, as the Secretary of the Treasury may direct, with such further conditions as the said Commissioner shall prescribe. 30 June, 1864, § 9. Collectors to give bonds. Conditions thereof. Bond may be renewed.

14. That each collector shall be authorized to appoint, by an instrument of writing under his hand, as many deputies as he may think proper, to be by him compensated for their services, and also to revoke any such appointment, giving such notice thereof as the Commissioner of Internal Revenue shall prescribe; and may require bonds or other securities, and accept the same, from such deputy; and each such deputy shall have the like authority, in every respect, to collect the duties and taxes levied or assessed within the portion of the district assigned to him which is by this act vested in the collector himself; but each collector shall, in every respect, be responsible both to the United States and to individuals, as the case may be, for all moneys collected, and for every act done by any of his deputies whilst acting as such, and for every omission of duty. 30 June, 1864, § 10. Deputy collectors. Bonds may be required. Duties and powers. Collector responsible for acts of deputies.

15. That in case of the sickness or temporary disability of a collector to discharge such of his duties as cannot under existing laws be discharged by a deputy, they may be devolved by him upon one of his deputies; and for the official acts and defaults of such deputy the collector or his sureties shall be held responsible to the United States. 30 June, 1864, § 39. Collector may devolve his duties upon a deputy in case of sickness.

16. That in case a collector shall die, resign, or be removed, the deputies of such collector shall continue to act until his successor is appointed; and the deputy of such collector longest in service at the time immediately preceding shall, until a successor shall be appointed, discharge all the duties of said collector; and for the official acts and defaults of such deputy a remedy shall be had on the official bond of the collector, as in other cases; and of two or more deputy collectors appointed on the same day, the one residing nearest the residence of the collector at the time of his death, resignation, or removal, shall discharge the said duties until the appointment of a successor: *Provided*, That in case it shall appear to the Secretary of the Treasury that the interest of the government shall so require, he may, by his order, direct said duties to be performed by such other one of the said deputies as he may in such order designate. And any bond or security taken from a deputy by such collector, pursuant to this act, shall be available to his legal representatives and sureties to indemnify them for loss or damage accruing from any act of the deputy so continuing or succeeding to the duties of such collector. 30 June, 1864, § 40. 3 March, 1865, § 1. Oldest deputy collector to act in case of vacancy. Secretary may designate deputies in certain cases. Bond of deputy available to heirs, &c., in case of loss.

30 June, 1864, § 22.
13 July, 1866, § 9.

Compensation of assessors.
Salary.
Commissions.

17. That there shall be allowed and paid to the several assessors a salary of fifteen hundred dollars per annum, payable quarterly; and, in addition thereto, where the receipts of the collection district shall exceed the sum of one hundred thousand dollars, and shall not exceed the sum of four hundred thousand dollars annually, one-half of one per centum upon the excess of receipts over one hundred thousand dollars. Where the receipts of a collection district shall exceed four hundred thousand dollars, and shall not exceed six hundred thousand, one-fifth of one per centum upon the excess of receipts over four hundred thousand dollars. Where the receipts shall exceed six hundred thousand dollars, one-tenth of one per centum upon such excess; but the salary of no assessor shall in any case exceed the sum of four thousand dollars. And the several assessors shall be allowed and paid the sums actually and necessarily expended, with the approval of the Commissioner of Internal Revenue, for office rent; but no account of such rent shall be allowed or paid until it shall have been verified in such manner as the Commissioner shall require, and shall have been audited and approved by the proper officers of the Treasury Department. And the several assessors shall be paid, after the account thereof shall have been rendered to and approved by the proper officers of the treasury, their necessary and reasonable charges for clerk-hire; but no such account shall be approved unless it shall state the name or names of the clerk or clerks employed and the precise periods of time for which they were respectively employed, and the rate of compensation agreed upon, and shall be accompanied by an affidavit of the assessor stating that such service was actually required by the necessities of his office, and was actually rendered, and also by the affidavit of each clerk, stating that he has rendered the service charged in such account on his behalf, the compensation agreed upon, and that he has not paid, deposited, or assigned, or contracted to pay, deposit, or assign any part of such compensation to the use of any other person, or in any way, directly or indirectly, paid or given, or contracted to pay or give, any reward or compensation for his office or employment, or the emoluments thereof; and the chief clerk of any such assessor is hereby authorized to administer, in the absence of the assessor, such oaths or affirmations as are required by this act. And there shall be allowed and paid to each assistant assessor four dollars for every day actually employed in collecting lists and making valuations, the number of days necessary for that purpose to be certified by the assessor, and three dollars for every hundred persons assessed contained in the tax list, as completed and delivered by him to the assessor, and twenty-five cents for each permit granted for making tobacco, snuff, or cigars; and assistant assessors may be allowed, in the settlement of their accounts, such sum as the Commissioner of Internal Revenue shall approve, not exceeding three hundred dollars per annum, for office rent; but no account for such rent shall be allowed or paid until it shall have been verified in such manner as the Commissioner of Internal Revenue may require, and shall have been audited and approved by the proper officers of the Treasury Department; and assistant assessors, when employed outside of the town in which they reside, in addition to the compensation now allowed by law, shall, during such time so employed, receive one dollar per day; and the said assessors and

Not to exceed $4,000.
Office rent.
Clerk hire.
Chief clerk may administer oaths in the absence of assessor.
Compensation of assistant assessors.

assistant assessors, respectively, shall be paid, after the account thereof shall have been rendered to and approved by the proper officers of the treasury, their necessary and reasonable charges for stationery and blank books used in the discharge of their duties, and for postage actually paid on letters and documents received and sent, and relating exclusively to official business, and for money actually paid for publishing notices required by this act: *Provided*, That no such account shall be approved unless it shall state the date and the particular item of every such expenditure, and shall be verified by the oath or affirmation of such assessor or assistant assessor; and the compensation herein specified shall be in full for all expenses not otherwise particularly authorized: *Provided further*, That the Commissioner of Internal Revenue may, under such regulations as may be established by the Secretary of the Treasury, after due public notice, receive bids and make contracts for supplying stationery, blank books, and blanks to the assessors, assistant assessors, and collectors in the several collection districts: *Provided further*, That the Secretary of the Treasury shall be, and he is hereby, authorized to fix such additional rates of compensation to be made to assessors and assistant assessors in cases where a collection district embraces more than a single congressional district, and to assessors and assistant assessors, revenue agents, and inspectors in Louisiana, Georgia, South Carolina, Alabama, Florida, Texas, Arkansas, North Carolina, Mississippi, Tennessee, California, Nevada, and Oregon, and the Territories, as may appear to him to be just and equitable, in consequence of the greater cost of living and travelling in those States and Territories, and as may, in his judgment, be necessary to secure the services of competent officers; but the compensation thus allowed shall not exceed the rate of five thousand dollars per annum. Collectors of internal revenue acting as disbursing officers shall be allowed all bills of assistant assessors heretofore paid by them in pursuance of the directions of the Commissioner of Internal Revenue, notwithstanding the assistant assessor did not certify to hours therein, or that two dollars per diem was deducted from his salary or compensation before computation of the tax thereon.

Stationery, blank books, postage, and publication.

Accounts to be verified by oath.

Commissioner may contract for stationery, &c.

Secretary may allow additional compensation in certain cases.

Limit of compensation.

Collectors shall be allowed bills of assistant assessors heretofore paid, notwithstanding informality.

18. That assistant assessors shall make out their accounts for pay and charges allowed by law monthly, specifying each item and including the date of each day of service, and shall transmit the same, verified by oath or affirmation, to the assessor of the district, who shall thereupon examine the same, and, if it appear just and in accordance with law, he shall indorse his approval thereon, but otherwise shall return the same with objections. Any such account so approved may be presented by the assistant assessor to the collector of the district for payment, who shall thereupon pay the same, and, when receipted by the assistant assessor, be allowed therefor upon presentation to the Commissioner of Internal Revenue. Where any account, so transmitted to the assessor, shall be objected to, in whole or in part, the assistant assessor may appeal to the Commissioner of Internal Revenue, whose decision on the case shall be final. And should it appear at any time that any assessor has knowingly or negligently approved any account, as aforesaid, allowing any assistant assessor a sum larger than was due according to law, it shall be the duty of the Commissioner of Internal Revenue, upon proper proof thereof, to deduct the sum so allowed from

30 June, 1864, § 24.

Assistant assessors to make out accounts.

Account to be approved by assessor.

And paid by collectors.

Assistant assessor may appeal to Commissioner.

Amount negligently approved by assessor to be deducted from his pay.

any pay which may be due to such assessor; or the Commissioner, as aforesaid, may direct a suit to be brought in any court of competent jurisdiction against the assessor or assistant assessor in default for the recovery of the amount knowingly or negligently allowed, as hereinbefore mentioned: *Provided*, That in calculating the commissions of assessors and collectors of internal revenue in districts whence cotton or distilled spirits are shipped in bond to be sold in another district, one-half the amount of tax received on the quantity of cotton or spirits so shipped shall be added to the amount on which the commissions of such assessors and collectors are calculated, and a corresponding amount shall be deducted from the amount on which the commissions of the assessors and collectors of the districts to which such cotton or spirits are shipped are calculated.

13 July, 1866, § 9.

Taxes received on cotton and distilled spirits shipped in bond to be divided in calculating commissions.

30 June, 1864, § 25.
3 March, 1865, § 1.

Compensation of collectors.
Salary.
Commissions.

19. That there shall be allowed to collectors, in full compensation for their services and that of their deputies, a salary of fifteen hundred dollars per annum, to be paid quarterly, and in addition thereto a commission of three per centum upon the first hundred thousand dollars, and a commission of one per centum upon all sums above one hundred thousand dollars and not exceeding four hundred thousand dollars, and a commission of one-half of one per centum on all sums above four hundred thousand dollars and not exceeding one million of dollars, and one-eighth of one per centum on all sums above one million of dollars, such commissions to be computed upon the amounts by them respectively collected and paid over and accounted for under the instructions of the Treasury Department. And there shall be further paid, after the account thereof has been rendered to and approved by the proper officers of the treasury, to each collector his necessary and reasonable charges for advertising, stationery, and blank books used in the performance of his official duties, and for postage actually paid on letters and documents received or sent, and exclusively relating to official business; but no such account shall be approved unless it shall state the date and the particular items of every such expenditure, and shall be verified by the oath or affirmation of the collector: *And provided*, That the Secretary of the Treasury be authorized to make such further allowances, from time to time, as may be reasonable in cases in which, from the territorial extent of the district, or from the amount of internal duties collected, or from other circumstances, it may seem just to make such allowances.

Stationery, blank books, and postage.

Secretary may make further allowance in certain cases.

30 June, 1864, § 26.
3 March, 1865, § 1.
13 July, 1866, § 9.

Fiscal year to be observed in adjusting accounts.
Commissions to be apportioned in case of two officers in same year.

20. That in the adjustment of the accounts of assessors and collectors of internal revenue which shall accrue after the thirtieth of June, eighteen hundred and sixty-four, and in the payment of their compensation for services after that date, the fiscal year of the treasury shall be observed; and where such compensation, or any part of it, shall be by commissions upon assessments or collections, and shall during any year, in consequence of a new appointment, be due to more than one assessor or collector in the same district, such commissions shall be apportioned between such assessors or collectors; but in no case shall a greater amount of the commissions be allowed to two or more assessors or collectors in the same district than is or may be authorized by law to be allowed to one assessor or collector. And the salary and commissions of assessors and collectors heretofore earned and accrued shall be adjusted, allowed, and paid in conformity to the provisions of this section, and not

Salaries and commissions heretofore earned.

otherwise; but no payment shall be made to assessors or collectors on account of salaries or commissions without the certificate of the Commissioner of Internal Revenue that all reports required by law or regulation have been received, or that a satisfactory explanation has been rendered to him of the cause of the delay.

No payment of salary or commissions to be made without certificate of Commissioner.

21. That all official communications made by assessors to collectors, assessors to assessors or by collectors to collectors, or by collectors to assessors, or by assessors to assistant assessors, or by assistant assessors to assessors, or by collectors to their deputies, or by deputy collectors to collectors, may be officially franked by the writers thereof, and shall, when so franked, be transmitted by mail free of postage.

13 July, 1866, § 65.

Official communications of certain revenue officers to be free of postage

22. That all assessors and their assistants, all collectors and their deputies, revenue agents and all inspectors, are hereby authorized to administer oaths and take evidence touching any part of the administration of this law with which they are respectively charged, or where such oaths and evidence are by law authorized to be taken; and any perjury therein shall be punished in the like manner, and to the same degree, as in the case of perjury committed in proceedings in the courts of the United States.

30 June, 1864, § 52.

Assessors and their assistants, collectors and their deputies, revenue agents and inspectors, authorized to administer oaths.

23. That the provisions of the sixteenth section of the act approved August sixth, eighteen hundred and forty-six, entitled "An act to provide for the better organization of the treasury, and for the collection, safe-keeping, transfer, and disbursement of the public revenue," are hereby applied to, and shall be construed to include, all officers of the internal revenue charged with the safe-keeping, transfer, or disbursement of the public moneys arising therefrom, and to all other persons having actual charge, custody, or control of moneys or accounts arising from the administration of the internal revenue.

30 June, 1864, § 51.

Section 16, act of August 6, 1846, applied to internal revenue officers.

[SEC. 16. ***And be it further enacted,*** That all officers and other persons charged by this act, or any other act, with the safe-keeping, transfer, and disbursement of the public moneys, other than those connected with the Post Office Department, are hereby required to keep an accurate entry of each sum received, and of each payment or transfer; and that if any one of the said officers, or of those connected with the Post Office Department, shall convert to his own use, in any way whatever, or shall use, by way of investment in any kind of property or merchandise, or shall loan, with or without interest, or shall deposit in any bank, or shall exchange for other funds, except as allowed by this act, any portion of the public moneys intrusted to him for safe-keeping, disbursement, transfer, or for any other purpose, every such act shall be deemed and adjudged to be an embezzlement of so much of the said moneys as shall be thus taken, converted, invested, used, loaned, deposited, or exchanged, which is hereby declared to be a felony; and any failure to pay over or to produce the public moneys intrusted to such person shall be held and taken to be *prima facie* evidence of such embezzlement; and if any officer charged with the disbursements of public moneys shall accept, or receive, or transmit to the Treasury Department to be allowed in his favor, any receipt or voucher from a creditor of the United States, without having paid to such creditor, in such funds as the said officer may have received for disbursement, or such other funds as he may be authorized by this act to take in exchange, the full amount specified in such receipt or voucher, every such act shall be deemed to be a conversion by such officer to his own use of the amount specified in such receipt or voucher; and any officer or agent of the United States, and all persons advising or participating in such act, being convicted thereof before any court of the United States of competent jurisdiction, shall be sentenced to imprisonment for a term of not less than six months nor more than ten years, and to a fine equal to the amount of the money embezzled. And upon the trial of any indictment against any person for embezzling public money under the provisions of this act, it shall be sufficient evidence, for the purpose of showing a balance against such person, to produce a transcript from the books and proceedings of the treasury, as required in civil cases, under the provisions of the act entitled "An act to provide more effectually

6 August, 1846, § 16.

Entries to be made of the public moneys other than those of the Post Office Departm't.

Felony to use, loan, or deposit in a bank, &c., public money.

Evidence of embezzlement.

Payment in other funds to be deemed a conversion.

Punishment.

What shall be sufficient evidence to show a balance on a charge of embezzlement.

1797, ch. 20.

for the settlement of accounts between the United States and receivers of public money," approved March third, one thousand seven hundred and ninety-seven; and the provisions of this act shall be so construed as to apply to all persons charged with the safe-keeping, transfer, or disbursement of the public money, whether such persons be indicted as receivers or depositaries of the same; and the refusal of such person, whether in or out of office, to pay any draft, order, or warrant which may be drawn upon him by the proper officer of the Treasury Department, for any public money in his hands belonging to the United States, no matter in what capacity the same may have been received or may be held, or to transfer or disburse any such money promptly, upon the legal requirement of any authorized officer of the United States, shall be deemed and taken, upon the trial of any indictment against such person for embezzlement, as prima facie evidence of such embezzlement.]

3 March, 1797, § 1.

Revenue officer or other person not paying public money to be sued, to forfeit commissions, and to pay interest.

[SEC. 1. *Be it enacted by the Senate and House of Representatives of the United States of America in Congress assembled,* That when any revenue officer, or other person accountable for public money, shall neglect or refuse to pay into the treasury the sum or balance reported to be due to the United States upon the adjustment of his account, it shall be the duty of the Comptroller, and he is hereby required, to institute suit for the recovery of the same, adding to the sum stated to be due on such account the commissions of the delinquent, which shall be forfeited in every instance where suit is commenced and judgment obtained thereon, and an interest of six per cent. per annum from the time of receiving the money until it shall be repaid into the treasury.]

3 March, 1797, § 2.

A transcript of the books of the treasury to be evidence.

[SEC. 2. *And be it further enacted,* That in every case of delinquency, where suit has been or shall be instituted, a transcript from the books and proceedings of the treasury, certified by the register and authenticated under the seal of the department, shall be admitted as evidence, and the court trying the cause shall be thereupon authorized to grant judgment and award execution accordingly. And all copies of bonds, contracts, or other papers relating to or connected with the settlement of any account between the United States and an individual, when certified by the register to be true copies of the originals on file, and authenticated under the seal of the department, as aforesaid, may be annexed to such transcripts, and shall have equal validity and be entitled to the same degree of credit which would be due to the original papers if produced and authenticated in court: *Provided,* That where suit is brought upon a bond, or other sealed instrument, and the defendant shall plead "non est factum," or upon motion to the court, such plea or motion being verified by the oath or affirmation of the defendant, it shall be lawful for the court to take the same into consideration and (if it shall appear to be necessary for the attainment of justice) to require the production of the original bond, contract, or other paper specified in such affidavit.]

Original contract to be produced in certain cases.

3 March, 1797, § 3.

Judgment to be rendered at return term, except in certain cases.

[SEC. 3. *And be it further enacted,* That where suit shall be instituted against any person or persons indebted to the United States, as aforesaid, it shall be the duty of the court where the same may be pending to grant judgment at the return term, upon motion, unless the defendant shall, in open court, (the United States attorney being present,) make oath or affirmation that he is equitably entitled to credits which had been, previous to the commencement of the suit, submitted to the consideration of the accounting officers of the treasury, and rejected; specifying each particular claim so rejected in the affidavit, and that he cannot then come safely to trial. Oath or affirmation to this effect being made, subscribed, and filed, if the court be thereupon satisfied, a continuance until the next succeeding term may be granted, but not otherwise, unless as provided in the preceding section.]

3 March, 1797, § 4.

No credit to be admitted unless presented to the treasury, or out of the power of the party to present it.

[SEC. 4. *And be it further enacted,* That in suits between the United States and individuals no claim for a credit shall be admitted upon trial but such as shall appear to have been presented to the accounting officers of the treasury for their examination and by them disallowed, in whole or in part, unless it should be proved to the satisfaction of the court that the defendant is, at the time of trial, in possession of vouchers not before in his power to procure, and that he was prevented from exhibiting a claim for such credit at the treasury by absence from the United States or some unavoidable accident.]

3 March, 1797, § 5.

In all cases of insolvency, the debt due to the United States shall be first paid.

[SEC. 5. *And be it further enacted,* That where any revenue officer, or other person hereafter becoming indebted to the United States by bond or otherwise, shall become insolvent, or where the estate of any deceased debtor in the hands of executors or administrators shall be insufficient to pay all the debts due from the deceased, the debt due to the United States shall be first satisfied, and the priority hereby established shall be deemed to extend as well to cases in which a debtor not having sufficient property to pay all his debts shall make a voluntary assignment thereof, or in which the estate and effects of an absconding, concealed, or absent debtor shall be attached by process of law, as to cases in which an act of legal bankruptcy shall be committed.]

[SEC. 6. *And be it further enacted*, That all writs of execution upon any judgment obtained for the use of the United States in any of the courts of the United States in one State may run and be executed in any other State, or in any of the Territories of the United States, but shall be issued from and made returnable to the court where the judgment was obtained, any law to the contrary notwithstanding.]

3 March, 1797, § 6.

Writs of execution may be executed in any State.

[SEC. 7. *And be it further enacted*, That nothing in this act shall be construed to repeal, take away, or impair any legal remedy or remedies for the recovery of debts now due, or hereafter to be due, to the United States, in law or equity, from any person or persons whatsoever, which remedy or remedies might be used if this act was not in force.]

3 March, 1797, § 7.

Prior legal remedies not to be impaired.

SEC. 24. That separate accounts shall be kept at the treasury of all moneys received from internal duties or taxes in each of the respective States, Territories, and collection districts; and that separate accounts shall be kept of the amount of each species of duty or tax that shall accrue, so as to exhibit, as far as may be, the amount collected from each source of revenue, with the moneys paid as compensation and for allowances to the collectors and deputy collectors, assessors and assistant assessors, inspectors, and other officers employed in each of the respective States, Territories, and collection districts, an abstract in tabular form, of which accounts it shall be the duty of the Secretary of the Treasury annually, in the month of December, to lay before Congress.

30 June 1864, § 43.

Separate accounts to be kept of moneys receiv'd from the several districts, and the several sources of revenue.

Abstract to be laid before Congress.

25. That every assessor or assistant assessor who shall enter upon and perform the duties of his office without having taken the oath or affirmation prescribed by law, or who shall wilfully neglect to perform any of the duties prescribed by this act at the time and in the manner herein designated, or who shall knowingly make any false or fraudulent list or valuation or assessment, or shall demand or receive any compensation, fee, or reward other than those provided for herein for the performance of any duty, or shall be guilty of extortion or wilful oppression in office, shall, upon conviction thereof in any circuit or district court of the United States having jurisdiction thereof, be subject to a fine of not exceeding one thousand dollars, or to imprisonment for not exceeding one year, or both, at the discretion of the court, and shall be dismissed from office, and shall be forever disqualified from holding any office under the government of the United States. And one-half of the fine so imposed shall be for the use of the United States, and the other half for the use of the informer, who shall be ascertained by the judgment of the court; and the said court shall also render judgment against the said assessor or assistant assessor for the amount of damages sustained in favor of the party injured, to be collected by execution.

30 June, 1864, § 21.
13 July, 1866, § 9.

Penalty for misconduct on part of assessor or assistant.

Disposition of penalties.

26. That each and every collector, or his deputy, who shall be guilty of any extortion or wilful oppression, under color of law, or shall knowingly demand other or greater sums than shall be authorized by law, or shall receive any fee, compensation, or reward, except as herein prescribed, for the performance of any duty, or shall wilfully neglect to perform any of the duties enjoined by this act, shall, upon conviction, be subject to a fine of not exceeding one thousand dollars, or to be imprisoned for not exceeding one year, or both, at the discretion of the court, and be dismissed from office, and be forever thereafter incapable of holding any office under the government; and one-half of the fine so imposed shall be for the use of the United States, and the other half for the use of the informer, who shall be ascertained by the judgment of the court; and the said court shall also render judg-

30 June, 1864, § 36.

Penalty upon collectors for extortion or oppression.

Disposal of fines.

ment against said collector or deputy collector for the amount of damages accruing to the party injured, to be collected by execution. And each and every collector, or his deputies, shall give receipts for all sums by them collected.

30 June, 1864, § 23. Fraud in appointment of assistant assessor. Penalty.

27. That if any assessor shall demand of, or receive directly or indirectly from, any assistant assessor, as a condition of his appointment to or continuance in his said office of assistant assessor, any portion of the compensation herein allowed such assistant assessor, or any other consideration, such assessor so offending shall be summarily dismissed from office, and shall be liable to a fine of not less than five hundred dollars upon conviction of said offence in any district or circuit court of the United States of the district in which such offence may be committed.

13 July, 1866, § 59. Certain revenue officers not to be interested in certain manufactures.

28. That any inspector or revenue agent who shall hereafter become interested, directly or indirectly, in the manufacture of tobacco, snuff, or cigars, and any assessor, collector, inspector, or revenue agent, who shall hereafter become interested, directly or indirectly, in the production, by distillation or by other process, of spirits, ale, or beer, or other fermented liquors, shall, on conviction before any court of the United States of competent jurisdiction, pay a penalty not less than five hundred dollars nor more than five thousand dollars, in the discretion of the court. And any such officer interested as aforesaid in any such manufacture at the time this act takes effect, who shall fail to divest himself of such interest within sixty days thereafter, shall be held and declared to have become so interested after this act takes effect.

II.

30 June, 1864, § 11.

ASSESSMENT AND COLLECTION OF TAXES IN GENERAL.

Persons liable to taxation to make list of returns. Return to be made on oath. Nature of return.

29. That it shall be the duty of any person, partnership, firm, association, or corporation, made liable to any duty, license, stamp, or tax imposed by law, when not otherwise provided for, on or before the first Monday of May in each year, and in other cases before the day of levy, to make a list or return, verified by oath or affirmation, to the assistant assessor of the district where located, of the amount of annual income, the articles or objects charged with a special duty or tax, the quantity of goods, wares, and merchandise made or sold, and charged with a specific or ad valorem duty or tax, the several rates and aggregate amount, according to the respective provisions of this act, and according to the forms and regulations to be prescribed by the Commissioner of Internal Revenue, under the direction of the Secretary of the Treasury, for which such person, partnership, firm, association, or corporation is liable to be assessed.

30 June, 1864, § 12. Regulations of Commiss'ner binding on all persons. Assistant assessors to canvass districts. Duties of assistant assessors.

30. That the instructions, regulations, and directions, as hereinbefore mentioned, shall be binding on each assessor and his assistants, and on each collector and his deputies, and on all other persons, in the performance of the duties enjoined by or under this act; pursuant to which instructions the said assessors shall, on the first Monday of May in each year, and from time to time thereafter, in accordance with this act, direct and cause the several assistant assessors to proceed through every part of their respective districts and inquire after and concerning all persons being within the assessment districts where they respectively reside, owning, possessing, or having the care or management of any property, goods, wares, and merchandise, articles or objects liable to pay

any duty, stamp, or tax, including all persons liable to pay a license or other duty under the provisions of this act, and to make a list of the owners, and to value and enumerate the said objects of taxation respectively, by reference to any lists of assessment or collection taken under the laws of the respective States, to any other records or documents, to the written list, schedule, or return required to be made out and delivered to the assistant assessor, and by all other lawful ways and means, in the manner prescribed by this act, and in conformity with the regulations and instructions before mentioned.

30 June, 1864, § 13.

Assistant assessor to make list for person disclosing.

31. That if any person liable to pay any duty or tax, or owning, possessing, or having the care or management of property, goods, wares, and merchandise, articles or objects liable to pay any duty, tax, or license, shall fail to make and exhibit a list or return required by law, but shall consent to disclose the particulars of any and all the property, goods, wares, and merchandise, articles and objects liable to pay any duty or tax, or any business or occupation liable to pay any license, as aforesaid, then and in that case it shall be the duty of the officer to make such list or return, which, being distinctly read, consented to, and signed and verified by oath or affirmation by the person so owning, possessing, or having the care and management as aforesaid, may be received as the list of such person.

List to be read to and consented to by the person liable to tax.

To be signed and verified by oath or affirmation.

30 June, 1864, § 14. 3 March, 1865, § 1. 13 July, 1866, § 9.

Notice to be left for absent persons.

32. That in case any person shall be absent from his or her residence or place of business at the time an assistant assessor shall call for the annual list or return, and no annual list or return has been rendered by such person to the assistant assessor as required by law, it shall be the duty of such assistant assessor to leave at such place of residence or business, with some one of suitable age and discretion, if such be present, otherwise to deposit in the nearest post office, a note or memorandum, addressed to such person, requiring him or her to render to such assistant assessor the list or return required by law within ten days from the date of such note or memorandum, verified by oath or affirmation. And if any person, on being notified or required as aforesaid, shall refuse or neglect to render such list or return within the time required as aforesaid, or if any person without notice, as aforesaid, shall not deliver a monthly or other list or return at the time required by law, or if any person shall deliver or disclose to any assessor or assistant assessor any list, statement, or return which, in the opinion of the assessor, is false or fraudulent, or contains any understatement or undervaluation, it shall be lawful for the assessor to summon such person, his agent, or other person having possession, custody, or care of books of account containing entries relating to the trade or business of such person, or any other person he may deem proper, to appear before such assessor and produce such book, at a time and place therein named, and to give testimony or answer interrogatories under oath or affirmation respecting any objects liable to tax as aforesaid, or the lists, statements, or returns thereof, or any trade, business, or profession liable to any tax as aforesaid. And the assessor may summon, as aforesaid, any person residing or found within the State in which his district is situated. And when the person intended to be summoned does not reside and cannot be found within such State, the assessor may enter any collection district where such person may be found, and there make the examination hereinbefore authorized. And to this end he shall there have and may exercise all the power

Persons neglecting to make return.

Or making fraudulent return.

May be summoned before the assessor.

Power of assessor.

and authority he has or may lawfully exercise in the district for which he is commissioned. The summons authorized by this section shall in all cases be served by an assistant assessor of the district where the person to whom it is directed may be found, by an attested copy delivered to such person in hand or left at his last and usual place of abode, allowing such person at the rate of one day for each twenty-five miles he may be required to travel, computed from the place of service to the place of examination; and the certificate of service signed by such assistant assessor shall be evidence of the facts it states on the hearing of an application for an attachment; and when the summons requires the production of books, it shall be sufficient if such books are described with reasonable certainty. In case any person so summoned shall neglect or refuse to obey such summons, or to give testimony, or to answer interrogatories as required, it shall be lawful for the assessor to apply to the judge of the district court or to a commissioner of the circuit court of the United States for the district within which the person so summoned resides for an attachment against such person as for a contempt. It shall be the duty of such judge or commissioner to hear such application, and, if satisfactory proof be made, to issue an attachment, directed to some proper officer, for the arrest of such person, and upon his being brought before him to proceed to a hearing of the case; and upon such hearing the judge or commissioner shall have power to make such order as he shall deem proper, not inconsistent with the provisions of existing laws for the punishment of contempts, to enforce obedience to the requirements of the summons and punish such person for his default or disobedience. It shall be the duty of the assessor or assistant assessor of the district within which such person shall have taxable property to enter into and upon the premises, if it be necessary, of such person so refusing or neglecting, or rendering a false or fraudulent list or return, and to make, according to the best information which he can obtain, including that derived from the evidence elicited by the examination of the assessor, and on his own view and information, such list or return, according to the form prescribed, of the property, goods, wares, and merchandise, and all articles or objects liable to tax, owned or possessed or under the care or management of such person, and assess the tax thereon, including the amount, if any, due for special or income tax; and in case of the return of a false or fraudulent list or valuation, he shall add one hundred per centum to such tax; and in case of a refusal or neglect, except in cases of sickness or absence, to make a list or return, or to verify the same as aforesaid, he shall add fifty per centum to such tax; and in case of neglect occasioned by sickness or absence as aforesaid, the assessor may allow such further time for making and delivering such list or return as he may judge necessary, not exceeding thirty days; and the amount so added to the tax shall, in all cases, be collected by the collector at the same time and in the same manner as the tax; and the list or return so made and subscribed by such assessor or assistant assessor shall be taken and reputed as good and sufficient for all legal purposes.

Service of summons. Travel. Summons to produce books. Proceedings in case of failure to obey summons. Authority and duty of judge or commissioner. Assessors may enter premises. May make list or return. Penalties to be assessed. In case of sickness or absence, further time. Collection of assessed penalties. Return of assessor good.

30 June, 1864, § 16.

Taxable property owned by non-resident.

33. That whenever there shall be in any assessment district any property, goods, wares, and merchandise, articles or objects, not owned or possessed by, or under the care or management of, any person within such district, and liable to be taxed as aforesaid, and no list of which shall have been transmitted to the assistant assessor in the manner provided by this act, it shall be the duty of the assistant

assessor for such district to enter into and upon the premises where such property is situated, and take such view thereof as may be necessary, and to make lists of the same, according to the form prescribed, which lists, being subscribed by the said assessor, shall be taken and reputed as good and sufficient lists of such property, goods, wares, and merchandise, articles or objects, as aforesaid, for all legal purposes.

30 June, 1864. § 17.

Person having taxable property in another district may make return in the district where he resides.

34. That any owner or person having the care or management of property, goods, wares, and merchandise, articles or objects, not lying or being within the assessment district in which he resides, shall be permitted to make out and deliver the lists thereof required by this act (provided the assessment district in which the said objects of duty or taxation are situated is therein distinctly stated) at the time and in the manner prescribed to the assistant assessor of the assessment district wherein such person resides. And it shall be the duty of the assistant assessor who receives any such list to transmit the same to the assistant assessor where such objects of taxation are situated, who shall examine such lists; and if he approves the same, he shall return it to the assistant assessor from whom he received it, with his approval thereof; and if he fails to approve the same, he shall make such alterations therein and additions thereto as he may deem to be just and proper, and shall then return the said list to the assistant assessor from whom it was received, who shall proceed, in making the assessment of the tax upon the list by him so received, in all respects as if the said list had been made out by himself.

List to be transmitted to other district for examination.

30 June, 1864, § 18.

Annual, monthly, and special lists.

35. That the lists aforesaid shall, where not otherwise specially provided for, be taken with reference to the day fixed for that purpose by this act as aforesaid; and where duties accrue at other and different times, the list shall be taken with reference to the time when said duties become due, and shall be denominated annual, monthly, and special lists. And the assistant assessors, respectively, after collecting the said lists, shall proceed to arrange the same, and to make two general lists, the first of which shall exhibit, in alphabetical order, the names of all persons, firms, companies, or corporations liable to pay any duty, tax, or license under this act, residing within the assessment district, together with the value and assessment or enumeration, as the case may require, of the objects liable to duty or taxation within such districts for which each such person is liable, or for which any firm, company, or corporation is liable, with the amount of duty or tax payable thereon; and the second list shall exhibit, in alphabetical order, the names of all persons residing out of the collection district who own property within the district, together with the value and assessment or enumeration thereof, as the case may be, with the amount of duty or tax payable thereon as aforesaid. The forms of the said general list shall be devised and prescribed by the assessor, under the direction of the Commissioner of Internal Revenue, and lists taken according to such forms shall be made out by the assistant assessors and delivered to the assessor within thirty days after the day fixed by this act as aforesaid, requiring lists from individuals; or where duties, licenses, or taxes accrue at other and different times, the lists shall be delivered from time to time as they become due.

Two general lists to be made.

Alphabetical list of residents.

And of non-residents.

Form to be prescribed by Commissioner.

Lists to be returned by assistant within thirty days.

Other lists to be deliver'd from time to time.

10 March, 1866.
13 July, 1866, § 9, (bis.)

Returns must show whether made in legal tender currency or coined money.

36. That it shall be the duty of all persons required to make returns or lists of income and articles or objects charged with an internal tax, to declare in such returns or lists whether the several rates and amounts therein contained are stated according to their values

Penalty for refusal or neglect.

in legal tender currency or according to their values in coined money; and in case of neglect or refusal so to declare to the satisfaction of the assistant assessor receiving such returns or lists, such assistant assessor is hereby required to make returns or lists for such persons so neglecting or refusing, as in cases of persons neglecting or refusing to make the returns or lists required by the acts aforesaid, and to assess the tax thereon, and to add thereto the amount of penalties imposed by law in cases of such neglect or refusal.

Returns stated in coin to be reduced to legal tender currency

And whenever the rates and amounts contained in the returns or lists as aforesaid shall be stated in coined money, it shall be the duty of each assessor receiving the same to reduce such rates and amounts to their equivalent in legal tender currency, according to the value of such coined money in said currency for the time covered by such returns.

Lists returned to collectors to be in legal tender currency

And the lists required by law to be furnished to collectors by assessors shall in all cases contain the several amounts of taxes assessed, estimated, or valued in legal tender currency only.

30 June, 1864, § 19.
13 July, 1866, § 9.

Annual assessments to be advertised.

37. That the assessor for each collection district shall give notice by advertisement in one newspaper published in each county within said district, and if there be none published in the district, then in a newspaper published in the collection district adjoining thereto, and shall post notices in at least four public places within each assessment district, and shall mail a copy of such notice to each postmaster in his district, to be posted in his office, stating the time and place within said collection district when and where appeals will be received and determined relative to any erroneous or excessive valuations, assessments, or enumerations by the assessor or assistant assessor returned in the annual list, and such notice shall be advertised and posted by the assessor and mailed as aforesaid at least ten days before the time appointed for hearing said appeals.

Assessor to hold appeals.

Lists to be submitted to the inspection of any & all persons.

And it shall be the duty of the assessor for each collection district, at the time fixed for hearing such appeals as aforesaid, to submit the proceedings of the assessor and assistant assessor, and the annual lists taken and returned as aforesaid, to the inspection of any and all persons who may apply for that purpose. And such assessor is hereby authorized at any time to hear and determine in a summary way, according to law and right, upon any and all appeals which may be exhibited against the proceedings of the said assessor or assistant assessors, and the office or principal place of business of the said assessor shall be open during the business hours of each day for the hearing of appeals by parties who shall appear voluntarily before him:

Appeals to be made in writing.

Provided, That no appeal shall be allowed to any party after he shall have been duly assessed, and the annual list containing the assessment has been transmitted to the collector of the district. And all appeals to the assessor as aforesaid shall be made in writing, and shall specify the particular cause, matter, or thing respecting which a decision is requested, and shall, moreover, state the ground or principle of error complained of.

Assessor to re-examine and correct assessments.

Assessment not to be increased without five days' notice.

And the assessor shall have power to re-examine and determine upon the assessments and valuations, and rectify the same as shall appear just and equitable; but such valuation, assessment, or enumeration shall not be increased without a previous notice of at least five days to the party interested to appear and object to the same if he judge proper, which notice shall be in writing and left at the dwelling-house, office, or place of business of the party by such assessor, assistant assessor, or other person, or sent by mail to the nearest or usual post office address of said party: *Provided further*, That on the hearing of appeals it shall be lawful for the assessor to require by summons the attendance of witnesses and the production of books of account in the same manner and under the same penalties as are provided in cases of refusal or neglect to furnish lists or returns. The costs for the attendance and mileage of said witnesses shall be taxed by the assessor and paid by the delinquent parties, or by the disbursing agent for the district, on certificate of the assessor, at the rates allowed to witnesses in the district courts of the United States.

Witnesses may be summoned.

Fees of witnesses.

38. That the assessor of each collection district shall, immediately after the expiration of the time for hearing appeals concerning taxes returned in the annual list, and from time to time, as taxes become liable to be assessed, make out lists containing the sums payable according to law upon every subject of taxation for each collection district; which list shall contain the name of each person residing within the said district, or owning or having the care or superintendence of property lying within the said district, or engaged in any business or pursuit which is liable to any tax, when such person or persons are known, together with the sums payable by each; and where there is any property within any collection district liable to tax, not owned or occupied by or under the superintendence of any person resident therein, there shall be a separate list of such property, specifying the sum payable, and the names of the respective proprietors when known. And the assessor making out any such separate list shall transmit to the assessor of the district where the persons liable to pay such tax reside, or shall have their principal place of business, copies of the list of property held by persons so liable to pay such tax, to the end that the taxes assessed under the provisions of this act may be paid within the collection district where the persons liable to pay the same reside, or may have their principal place of business. And in all other cases the said assessor shall furnish to the collectors of the several collection districts, respectively, within ten days after the time of hearing appeals concerning taxes returned in the annual list, and from time to time thereafter as required, a certified copy of such list or lists for their proper collection districts. And in case it shall be ascertained that the annual list, or any other list, which may have been, or which shall hereafter be, delivered to any collector, is imperfect or incomplete in consequence of the omission of the names of any persons or parties liable to tax, or in consequence of any omission, or understatement, or undervaluation, or false or fraudulent statement contained in any return or returns made by any persons or parties liable to tax, the said assessor may, from time to time, or at any time within fifteen months from the time of the passage of this act or from the time of the delivery of the list to the collector as aforesaid, enter on any monthly or special list the names of such persons or parties so omitted, together with the amount of tax for which they may have been or shall become liable, and also the names of the persons or parties in respect to whose returns, as aforesaid, there has been or shall be any omission, under valuation, understatement, or false or fraudulent statement, together with the amounts for which such persons or parties may be liable, over and

30 June, 1864, § 20. 13 July, 1866, § 9.

Assessors to make lists.

Contents of lists.

List of property owned by non-residents.

To be transmitted to assessor of district where person liable resides or has his place of business.

Annual lists to be sent to collector within ten days after hearing appeals.

When list is imperfect or incomplete.

Reassessment may be made within fifteen months.

above the amount for which they may have been, or shall be, assessed upon any return or returns made as aforesaid, and shall certify or return said list to the collector as required by law. And all provisions of law for the ascertainment of liability to any tax, or the assessment or collection thereof, shall be held to apply, as far as may be necessary to the proceedings herein authorized and directed. And wherever the word "duty" is used in this act, or the acts to which this is an amendment, it shall be construed to mean "tax" whenever such construction shall be necessary in order to effect the purposes of said acts.

Further proceedings regulated.

30 June, 1864, § 27.

Collector to sign triplicate receipts of lists received from assessor.

39. That each collector, on receiving, from time to time, lists and returns from the said assessors, shall subscribe three receipts, one of which shall be made upon a full and correct copy of each list or return, and be delivered by him to, and shall remain with, the assessor of his collection district, and shall be open to the inspection of any person who may apply to inspect the same, and the other two shall be made upon aggregate statements of the lists or returns aforesaid, exhibiting the gross amount of taxes to be collected in his collection district, one of which aggregate statements and receipts shall be transmitted to the Commissioner of Internal Revenue, and the other to the First Comptroller of the Treasury.

30 June, 1864, § 28.
3 March 1865, § 1.
13 July, 1866, § 9.

Collectors to give notice to tax payers within twenty days thereafter.

40. That each of said collectors shall, within twenty days after receiving his annual collection list from the assessors, give notice, by advertisement in one newspaper published in each county in his collection district, if there be any, and if not, then in a newspaper published in an adjoining county, and by notifications to be posted in at least four public places in each county in his collection district, that the said taxes have become due and payable, and state the time and place within said county at which he or his deputy will attend to receive the same, which time shall not be less than ten days after the date of such notification, and shall send a copy of such notice by mail to each postmaster in the county, to be posted in his office. And if any person shall neglect to pay, as aforesaid, for more than ten days, it shall be the duty of the collector or his deputy to issue to such person a notice, to be left at his dwelling or usual place of business, or be sent by mail, demanding the payment of said taxes, stating the amount thereof, with a fee of twenty cents for the issuing and service of such notice, and with four cents for each mile actually and necessarily travelled in serving the same. And if such persons shall not pay the duties or taxes, and the fee of twenty cents and mileage as aforesaid, within ten days after the service or the sending by mail of such notice, it shall be the duty of the collector or his deputy to collect the said taxes and fee of twenty cents and mileage, with a penalty of ten per centum additional upon the amount of taxes. And with respect to all such taxes as are not included in the annual lists aforesaid, [and] all taxes the collection of which is not otherwise provided for in this act, it shall be the duty of each collector, in person or by deputy, to give notice and demand payment thereof, in the manner last mentioned, within ten days from and after receiving the list thereof from the assessor, or within twenty days from and after the expiration of the time within which such tax should have been paid; and if the annual or other taxes shall not be paid within ten days from and after such notice and demand, it shall be lawful for such collector, or his deputies, to proceed to collect the said taxes, with ten per centum additional

In case of neglect, collector to give notice personally or by mail.

If taxes are not paid within ten days after demand penalty of ten per cent. to be added.

Taxes not included in annual lists.

Collectors to demand payment, when.

Upon non-payment, collector to make distraint.

thereto, as aforesaid, by distraint and sale of the goods, chattels, or effects, including stocks, securities, and evidences of debt, of the persons delinquent as aforesaid. And in case of distraint, it shall be the duty of the officer charged with the collection to make, or cause to be made, an account of the goods or effects distrained, a copy of which, signed by the officer making such distraint, shall be left with the owner or possessor of such goods or effects, or at his or her dwelling or usual place of business, with some person of suitable age and discretion, if any such can be found, with a note of the sum demanded, and the time and place of sale; and the said officer shall forthwith cause a notification to be published in some newspaper within the county wherein said distraint is made, if there is a newspaper published in said county, or to be publicly posted at the post office, if there be one within five miles, nearest to the residence of the person whose property shall be distrained, and in not less than two other public places, which notice shall specify the articles distrained, and the time and place for the sale thereof, which time shall not be less than ten nor more than twenty days from the date of such notification to the owner or possessor of the property and the publication or posting of such notice as herein provided, and the place proposed for sale shall not be more than five miles distant from the place of making such distraint. And said sale may be adjourned from time to time by said officer, if he shall think it advisable to do so, but not for a time to exceed in all thirty days. And if any person, bank, association, company, or corporation, liable to pay any tax, shall neglect or refuse to pay the same after demand, the amount shall be a lien in favor of the United States from the time it was due until paid, with the interest, penalties, and costs that may accrue in addition thereto, upon all property and rights to property belonging to such person, bank, association, company, or corporation; and the collector, after demand, may levy, or by warrant may authorize a deputy collector to levy upon all property and rights to property belonging to such person, bank, association, company, or corporation, or on which the said lien exists, for the payment of the sum due as aforesaid, with interest and penalty for non-payment, and also of such further sum as shall be sufficient for the fees, costs, and expenses of such levy. And in all cases of sale, as aforesaid, the certificate of such sale shall transfer to the purchaser all right, title, and interest of such delinquent in and to the property sold; and where such property shall consist of stocks, said certificate shall be notice, when received, to any corporation, company, or association of said transfer, and shall be authority to such corporation, company, or association to record the same on their books and records, in the same manner as if transferred or assigned by the person or party holding the same, in lieu of any original or prior certificates, which shall be void, whether cancelled or not. And said certificates, where the subject of sale shall be securities or other evidences of debt, shall be good and valid receipts to the person holding the same, as against any person holding, or claiming to hold, possession of such securities or other evidences of debt. And all persons, and officers of companies or corporations, are required, on demand of a collector or deputy collector about to distrain, or having distrained on any property or rights of property, to exhibit all books containing evidence or statements relating to the

Proceedings in case of distraint.

Length of notice previous to sale.

Adjournment of sale.

Anything unpaid to be a lien from the time it was due.

Collector may distrain, upon what.

Effect of certificate of sale.

In case stocks are sold.

Books relating to subject of distraint.

subject or subjects of distraint, or the property or rights of property liable to distraint for the tax so due as aforesaid: *Provided*, That in any case of distraint for the payment of the taxes aforesaid, the goods, chattels, or effects so distrained shall and may be restored to the owner or possessor, if prior to the sale payment of the amount due shall be made to the proper officer charged with the collection, together with the fees and other charges; but in case of non-payment as aforesaid, the said officers shall proceed to sell the said goods, chattels, or effects at public auction, and shall retain from the proceeds of such sale the amount demandable for the use of the United States, and a commission of five per centum thereon for his own use, with the fees and charges for distraint and sale, rendering the overplus, if any there be, to the person who may be entitled to receive the same: *Provided further*, That there shall be exempt from distraint and sale, if belonging to the head of a family, the school books and wearing apparel necessary for such family; also arms for personal use, one cow, two hogs, five sheep and the wool thereof, provided the aggregate market value of said sheep shall not exceed fifty dollars; the necessary food for such cow, hogs, and sheep for a period not exceeding thirty days; fuel to an amount not greater in value than twenty-five dollars; provisions to an amount not greater than fifty dollars; household furniture kept for use to an amount not greater than three hundred dollars; and the books, tools, or implements of a trade or profession to an amount not greater than one hundred dollars shall also be exempt; and the officer making the distraint shall summon three disinterested householders of the vicinity, who shall appraise and set apart to the owner the amount of property herein declared to be exempt.

Goods to be restored on payment before sale.

Otherwise to be sold.

Property exempt from distraint.

30 June, 1864, § 29.
13 July, 1866, § 9.

41. That in all cases where property liable to distraint for taxes may not be divisible, so as to enable the collector by a sale of part thereof to raise the whole amount of the tax, with all costs, charges, and commissions, the whole of such property shall be sold, and the surplus of the proceeds of the sale, after satisfying the tax, costs, and charges, shall be paid to the person legally entitled to receive the same; or if he cannot be found, or refuse to receive the same, then such surplus shall be deposited in the treasury of the United States, to be there held for the use of the person legally entitled to receive the same, until he shall make application therefor to the Secretary of the Treasury, who, upon such application and satisfactory proofs in support thereof, shall, by warrant on the treasury, cause the same to be paid to the applicant. And if any of the property advertised for sale as aforesaid is of a kind subject to tax, and such tax has not been paid, and the amount bid for such property is not equal to the amount of such tax, the collector may purchase the same in behalf of the United States for an amount not exceeding the said tax. And in all cases where property subject to tax, but upon which the tax has not been paid, shall be seized upon distraint and sold, the amount of such tax shall, after deducting the expenses of such sale, be first appropriated out of the proceeds thereof to the payment of said tax. And if no assessment of tax has been made upon such property, the collector shall make a return thereof in the form required by law, and the assessor shall assess the tax thereon. And all property so purchased may be sold by said collector, under such regulations as may be prescribed by the

Property indivisible the whole to be sold.

Disposition of surplus proceeds.

Property may be purchased for the United States.

Tax on property sold.

How assessed.

Property purchased by collector may be sold.

Commissioner of Internal Revenue. And the collector shall render a distinct account of all charges incurred in the sale of such property to the Commissioner of Internal Revenue, who shall by regulation determine the fees and charges to be allowed in all cases of distraint and other seizures; or where necessary expenses for making such distraint or seizure have been incurred, and in case of sale, the said collector shall pay into the treasury the surplus, if any there be, after defraying such fees and charges.

Fees in cases of seizures.

42. That in all cases of distraint and sale of goods or chattels for non-payment of taxes, duties, or licenses, as provided for, the bill of sale of such goods or chattels given by the officer making such sale, to the purchaser thereof, shall be prima facie evidence of the right of the officer to make such sale, and conclusive evidence of the regularity of his proceedings in selling the same.

30 June, 1864, § 45.

Bill of sale given by collector to be prima facie evidence of right to make sale, and conclusive evidence of regularity of his proceedings.

43. That where any whiskey, oil, tobacco, or other articles of manufacture or produce requiring brands, stamps, or marks of whatever kind to be placed thereon, shall be sold upon distraint, forfeiture, or other process provided by law, the same not having been branded, stamped, or marked as required by law, the officer selling the same shall, upon sale thereof, fix or cause to be fixed the brands, stamps, or marks so required, and deduct the expense thereof from the proceeds of such sale.

13 July, 1866, § 17.

Articles requiring brands, &c., sold for want thereof, shall be properly marked by the officer making sale.

44. That in any case where goods, chattels, or effects sufficient to satisfy the taxes imposed by law upon any person liable to pay the same shall not be found by the collector or deputy collector whose duty it may be to collect the same, he is hereby authorized to collect the same by seizure and sale of real estate; and the officer making such seizure and sale shall give notice to the person whose estate is proposed to be sold, by giving him in hand, or leaving at his last or usual place of abode, if he has any such within the collection district where said estate is situated, a notice, in writing, stating what particular estate is proposed to be sold, describing the same with reasonable certainty, and the time when and place where said officer proposes to sell the same; which time shall not be less than twenty nor more than forty days from the time of giving said notice. And the said officer shall also cause a notification to the same effect to be published in some newspaper within the county where such seizure is made, if any such there be, and shall also cause a like notice to be posted at the post office nearest to the estate to be seized, and in two other public places within the county; and the place of said sale shall not be more than five miles distant from the estate seized, except by special order of the Commissioner of Internal Revenue. At the time and place appointed, the officer making such seizure shall proceed to sell the said estate at public auction, offering the same at a minimum price, including the expense of making such levy, and all charges for advertising and an officer's fee of ten dollars. And in case the real estate so seized, as aforesaid, shall consist of several distinct tracts or parcels, the officer making sale thereof shall offer each tract or parcel for sale separately, and shall, if he deem it advisable, apportion the expenses, charges, and fees, aforesaid, to such several tracts or parcels, or to any of them, in estimating the minimum price aforesaid. And if no person offers for said estate the amount of said minimum price, the officer shall declare the same to be purchased by him for the United States, and shall deposit with the district attorney of the United States a deed

30 June, 1864, § 30.
16 July, 1866, § 9.

Personal property not sufficient, real estate may be seized and sold.
Notice.

Time of.
To be advertised.

Place of sale.

Mode of sale.

Mode of sale in case of several parcels.

In a certain case, estate may be purchased for the United States.

thereof, as hereinafter specified and provided; otherwise, the same shall be declared to be sold to the highest bidder. And said sale may be adjourned from time to time by said officer for not exceeding thirty days in all, if he shall think it advisable so to do. If the amount bid shall not be then and there paid, the officer shall forthwith proceed to again sell said estate in the same manner; and upon any sale and the payment of the purchase money shall give to the purchaser a certificate of purchase, which shall set forth the real estate purchased, for whose taxes the same was sold, the name of the purchaser, and the price paid therefor; and if the said real estate be not redeemed in the manner and within the time hereinafter provided, then the said collector or deputy collector shall execute to the said purchaser, upon his surrender of said certificate, a deed of the real estate purchased by him as aforesaid, reciting the facts set forth in said certificate, and in accordance with the laws of the State in which such real estate is situate upon the subject of sales of real estate under execution, which said deed shall be prima facie evidence of the facts therein stated; and if the proceedings of the officer as set forth have been substantially in accordance with the provisions of law, shall be considered and operate as a conveyance of all the right, title, and interest the party delinquent had in and to the real estate thus sold at the time the lien of the United States attached thereto. Any person, whose estate may be proceeded against as aforesaid, shall have the right to pay the amount due, together with the costs and charges thereon, to the collector or deputy collector at any time prior to the sale thereof, and all further proceedings shall cease from the time of such payment. The owners of any real estate sold as aforesaid, their heirs, executors, or administrators, or any person having any interest therein, or a lien thereon, or any person in their behalf, shall be permitted to redeem the land sold as aforesaid, or any particular tract thereof, at any time within one year after the sale thereof, upon payment to the purchaser, or, in case he cannot be found in the county in which the land to be redeemed is situate, then to the collector of the district in which the land is situate, for the use of the purchaser, his heirs or assigns, the amount paid by the said purchaser and interest thereon at the rate of twenty per centum per annum. And any collector or deputy collector may, for the collection of taxes imposed upon any person, or for which any person may be liable, and committed to him for collection, seize and sell the lands of such person situated in any other collection district within the State in which said officer resides; and his proceedings in relation thereto shall have the same effect as if the same were had in his proper collection district. And it shall be the duty of every collector to keep a record of all sales of land made in his collection district, whether by himself or his deputies, or by another collector, in which shall be set forth the tax for which any such sale was made, the dates of seizure and sale, the name of the party assessed, and all proceedings in making said sale, the amount of fees and expenses, the name of the purchaser, and the date of the deed; which record shall be certified by the officer making the sale. And it shall be the duty of any deputy making sale, as aforesaid, to return a statement of all his proceedings to the collector, and to certify the record thereof. And in case of the death or removal of the collector or the expiration

Adjournment.

Amount bid not paid, estate to be resold.

Certificate of purchase.

To be surrendered, and deed given, if estate not redeemed.

Deed in accordance with State laws.

Effect of deed.

Owner may redeem before sale.

After sale, when and how

Collector may seize and sell lands in any other district in the State.

Record of sales.

Return by deputy.

of his term of office from any other cause, said record shall be delivered to his successor in office; and a copy of every such record, certified by the collector, shall be evidence in any court of the truth of the facts therein stated. And when any lands sold, as aforesaid, shall be redeemed as hereinbefore provided, the collector shall make an entry of the fact upon the record aforesaid, and the said entry shall be evidence of such redemption. And when any property, personal or real, seized and sold by virtue of the foregoing provisions, shall not be sufficient to satisfy the claim of the United States for which distraint or seizure may be made against any person whose property may be so seized and sold, the collector may, thereafter, and as often as the same may be necessary, proceed to seize and sell, in like manner, any other property liable to seizure of such person until the amount due from him, together with all expenses, shall be fully paid: *Provided,* That the word "county," wherever the same occurs in this act, or the acts of which this is amendatory, shall be construed to mean also a parish or any other equivalent subdivision of a State or Territory.

Record to be delivered to successor.

To be evidence in any court.

Record of redemption.

Tax not satisfied, other property may be seized and sold.

Word "county" defined.

45. That if any collector shall find, upon any list of taxes returned to him for collection, property lying within his district which is charged with any specific or ad valorem tax or duty, but which is not owned, occupied, or superintended by some person known to such collector to reside or to have some place of business within the United States, and upon which the duty or tax has not been paid within the time required by law, such collector shall forthwith take such property into his custody, and shall advertise the same, and the tax charged upon the same, in some newspaper published in his district, if any shall be published therein, otherwise in some newspaper in an adjoining district, for the space of thirty days; and if the taxes thereon, with all charges for advertising, shall not be paid within the said thirty days, such collector shall proceed to sell the same, or so much as is necessary, in the manner provided for the sale of other goods distrained for the non-payment of taxes, and out of the proceeds shall satisfy all taxes charged upon such property, with the costs of advertising and selling the same. And like proceedings to those provided in the preceding section for the purchase and resale of property which cannot be sold for the amount of duty or tax due thereon shall be had with regard to property sold under the provisions of this section. And any surplus arising from any sale herein provided for shall be paid into the treasury, for the benefit of the owner of the property. And the Secretary of the Treasury is authorized, in any case where money shall be paid into the treasury for the benefit of any owner of property sold as aforesaid, to repay the same, on proper proof being furnished that the person applying therefor is entitled to receive the same.

30 June, 1864, § 31

Taxes returned against non-residents.

How collected.

46. That whenever a collector shall have on any list duly returned to him the name of any person not within his collection district who is liable to tax, or of any person so liable to tax who shall have, in the collection district in which he resides, no sufficient property subject to seizure or distraint from which the money due for duties or tax can be collected, it shall and may be lawful for such collector to transmit a copy or statement containing the name of the person liable to such duty or tax aforesaid, with the amount and nature thereof, duly certified under his hand, to the collector of any district to which said person shall have removed, or in which

30 June, 1864, § 32.

Collector may transmit list to another district where person liable resides, or where he has property.

Duty of collector receiving such list.

he shall have property, real or personal, liable to be seized and sold for duty or tax; and the collector of the district to whom the said certified copy or statement shall be transmitted shall proceed to collect the said duty or tax in the same way as if the name of the person and objects of tax contained in the said certified copy or statement were on any list furnished to him by the assessor of his own collection district; and the said collector, upon receiving said certified copy or statement as aforesaid, shall transmit his receipt for it to the collector sending the same to him.

30 June, 1864, § 33.
3 March, 1865, § 3.

Collect'rs to transmit monthly statements of collections to Commissioner, and pay over moneys collected at such places as he may designate.

Final account to be rendered as often as required.

Depositories.

47. That the several collectors shall, at the expiration of each and every month after they shall, respectively, commence their collections, transmit to the Commissioner of Internal Revenue a statement of the collections made by them, respectively, within the month, and pay over * * * the moneys by them respectively collected, * * * at such places as may be designated and required by the Commissioner of Internal Revenue; and each of the said collectors shall complete the collection of all sums assigned to him for collection, as aforesaid, shall pay over the same into the treasury, and shall render his accounts to the Treasury Department as often he as may be required. And the Secretary of the Treasury is authorized to designate one or more depositories in each State for the deposit and safe-keeping of the money collected by virtue of this act; and the receipt of the proper officer of such depository to a collector for the money deposited by him shall be a sufficient voucher for such collector in the settlement of his accounts at the Treasury Department. And the Commissioner of Internal Revenue may, under the direction of the Secretary of the Treasury, prescribe such regulations with reference to such deposits as he may deem necessary.

Regulations in reference to deposits to be prescribed.

30 June, 1864, § 34.
13 July, 1866, § 9.

Collectors shall be charged with what.

48. That each collector shall be charged with the whole amount of taxes, whether contained in lists delivered to him by the assessors, respectively, or delivered or transmitted to him by assistant assessors from time to time, or by other collectors, or by his predecessor in office, and with the additions thereto, with the par value of all stamps deposited with him, and with all moneys collected for passports, penalties, forfeitures, fees, or costs, and he shall be credited with all payments into the treasury made as provided by law, with all stamps returned by him uncancelled to the treasury, and with the amount of taxes contained in the lists transmitted in the manner above provided to other collectors, and by them receipted as aforesaid; and also with the amount of the taxes of such persons as may have absconded, or become insolvent, prior to the day when the tax ought, according to the provisions of law, to have been collected, and with all uncollected taxes transferred by him or by his deputy acting as collector to his successor in office: *Provided*, That it shall be proved to the satisfaction of the Commissioner of Internal Revenue that due diligence was used by the collector, who shall certify the facts to the First Comptroller of the Treasury. And each collector shall also be credited with the amount of all property purchased by him for the use of the United States, provided he shall faithfully account for and pay over the proceeds thereof upon a resale of the same as required by law. In case of the death, resignation, or removal of the collector, all lists and accounts of taxes uncollected shall be transferred to his successor in office as soon as such successor shall be appointed and qualified, and it shall be the duty of such successor to collect the same.

Credited with what.

Lists & accounts of taxes uncollected to be transfer'd to successor for collection.

49. That if any collector shall fail either to collect or to render his account, or to pay over in the manner or within the times hereinbefore provided, it shall be the duty of the First Comptroller of the Treasury, and he is hereby authorized and required, immediately after evidence of such deliquency, to report the same to the Solicitor of the Treasury, who shall issue a warrant of distress against such delinquent collector, directed to the marshal of the district, therein expressing the amount with which the said collector is chargeable, and the sums, if any, which have been paid over by him, so far as the same are ascertainable. And the said marshal shall, himself or by his deputy, immediately proceed to levy and collect the sum which may remain due, with five per centum thereon, and all the expenses and charges of collection, by distress and sale of the goods and chattels or any personal effects of the delinquent collector, giving at least five days' notice of the time and place of sale, in the manner provided by law for advertising sales of personal property on execution in the State wherein such collector resides. And the bill of sale of the officer of any goods, chattels, or other personal property distrained and sold as aforesaid, shall be conclusive evidence of title to the purchaser, and prima facie evidence of the right of the officer to make such sale, and of the correctness of his proceedings in selling the same. And for want of goods and chattels, or other personal effects of such collector, sufficient to satisfy any warrant of distress, issued pursuant to the preceding section of this act, the lands and real estate of such collector, or so much thereof as may be necessary for satisfying the said warrant, after being advertised for at least three weeks, in not less than three public places in the collection district, and in one newspaper printed in the county or district, if any there be, prior to the proposed time of sale, shall be sold at public auction by the marshal or his deputy, who, upon such sale, shall, as such marshal or deputy marshal, make and deliver to the purchaser of the premises so sold a deed of conveyance thereof, to be executed and acknowledged in the manner and form prescribed by the laws of the State in which said lands are situated, which said deed so made shall invest the purchaser with all the title and interest of the defendant or defendants named in said warrant existing at the time of the seizure thereof. And all moneys that may remain of the proceeds of such sale after satisfying the said warrant of distress, and paying the reasonable costs and charges of sale, shall be returned to the proprietor of the lands or real estate sold as aforesaid.

30 June, 1864, § 35.

Collectors failing to account for taxes due.

Duty of the First Comptroller thereon.

Solicitor of the Treasury to issue a warrant.

Marshal to levy on the property of the collector.

Bill of sale to be conclusive evidence of title, and prima facie evidence of right of officer to make sale.

Levy on real estate.

Notice of sale.

Marshal to execute deed.

Surplus to be returned to proprietor of lands sold.

50. That a collector or deputy collector, assessor, assistant assessor, revenue agent, or inspector, shall be authorized to enter, in the daytime, any brewery, distillery, manufactory, building, or place where any property, articles, or objects, subject to duty or taxation under the provisions of this act, are made, produced, or kept, within his district, so far as it may be necessary for the purpose of examining said property, articles, or objects, or inspecting the accounts required by this act from time to time to be made or kept by any manufacturer or producer, relating to such property, articles, or objects. And every owner of such brewery, distillery, manufactory, building, or place, or persons having the agency or superintendence of the same, who shall refuse to admit such officer, or to suffer him to examine said property, articles, or objects, or to inspect said accounts, shall, for every such refusal, forfeit and

30 June, 1864, § 37.

Revenue officers may enter brewery, &c., in the daytime.

Penalty for refusing to admit officers.

And at night when premises are open.

pay the sum of five hundred dollars: *Provided, however,* That when such premises shall be open at night, such officers may enter while so open in the performance of their official duties.

30 June, 1864, § 38. 3 March, 1865, § 1.

Penalty for obstructing revenue officer.

51. That if any person shall forcibly obstruct or hinder any assessor or assistant assessor, or any collector or deputy collector, revenue agent or inspector, in the execution of this act, or of any power and authority hereby vested in him, or shall forcibly rescue, or cause to be rescued, any property, articles, or objects, after the same shall have been seized by him, or shall attempt or endeavor so to do, the person so offending shall, upon conviction thereof, for every such offence, forfeit and pay the sum of five hundred dollars, or double the value of property so rescued, or be imprisoned for a term not exceeding two years, at the discretion of the court: *Provided,* That if any such officer shall divulge to any party, or make known in any manner other than as provided in this act, the operations, style of work or apparatus of any manufacturer or producer visited by him in the discharge of his official duties, he shall be subject to the penalties prescribed in section thirty-six of this act.

Penalty for officer divulging the operations of any person visited.

30 June, 1864, § 41. 13 July, 1866, § 9.

Collectors to collect taxes, and sue for fines and penalties.

52. That it shall be the duty of the collectors aforesaid, or their deputies, in their respective districts, and they are hereby authorized, to collect all the taxes imposed by law, however the same may be designated, and to prosecute for the recovery of any sum or sums which may be forfeited by law; and all fines, penalties, and forfeitures which may be incurred or imposed by law, shall be sued for and recovered, in the name of the United States, in any proper form of action, or by any appropriate form of proceeding, *qui tam* or otherwise, before any circuit or district court of the United States for the district within which said fine, penalty, or forfeiture may have been incurred, or before any other court of competent jurisdiction. And taxes may be sued for and recovered, in the name of the United States, in any proper form of action before any circuit or district court of the United States for the district within which the liability to such tax may have been or shall be incurred, or where the party from whom such tax is due may reside at the time of the commencement of said action. But no such suit shall be commenced unless the Commissioner of Internal Revenue shall authorize or sanction the proceedings: *Provided,* That in case of any suit for penalties or forfeitures brought upon information received from any person, other than a collector, deputy collector, assessor, assistant assessor, revenue agent, or inspector of internal revenue, the United States shall not be subject to any costs of suit, nor shall the fees of any attorney or counsel employed by any such officer be allowed in the settlement of his account, unless the employment of such attorney or counsel shall be authorized by the Commissioner of Internal Revenue, either expressly or by general regulations.

Suits to be in name of the United States.

Taxes may be sued for.

But not without sanction of the Commissioner.

United States not subject to costs in certain cases.

Counsel fees not to be paid unless employment authorized.

30 June, 1864, § 176.

Secretary of the Treasury may establish regulations for certain cases.

53. That when any tax or duty is imposed by law, and the mode or time of assessment or collection is not therein provided, the same shall be established by regulation of the Secretary of the Treasury.

30 June, 1864, § 44. 13 July, 1866, § 9.

Commissioner authorized to refund taxes illegally collected, &c.

54. That the Commissioner of Internal Revenue, subject to regulations prescribed by the Secretary of the Treasury, shall be, and is hereby, authorized, on appeal to him made, to remit, refund, and pay back all taxes erroneously or illegally assessed or collected, all penalties collected without authority, and all taxes that shall appear to be unjustly assessed or excessive in amount

or in any manner wrongfully collected, and also repay to collectors or deputy collectors the full amount of such sums of money as shall or may be recovered against them, or any of them, in any court, for any internal taxes or licenses collected by them, with the costs and expenses of suit, and all damages and costs recovered against assessors, assistant assessors, collectors, deputy collectors, and inspectors, in any suit which shall be brought against them, or any of them, by reason of anything that shall or may be done in the due performance of their official duties; and all judgments and moneys recovered or received for taxes, costs, forfeitures, and penalties, shall be paid to the collector as internal taxes are required to be paid: *Provided*, That where a second assessment may have been made in case of a list, statement, or return which in the opinion of the assessor or assistant assessor was false or fraudulent, or contained any understatement or undervaluation, such assessment shall not be remitted, nor shall taxes collected under such assessment be recovered, refunded, or paid back, unless it is proved that said list, statement, or return was not false or fraudulent, and did not contain any understatement or undervaluation.

May repay to collectors & other officers money recovered of them for acts done in performance of duties.

Moneys recovered or received to be paid to collectors.

When second assessment may be set aside.

55. That no suit shall be maintained in any court for the recovery of any tax alleged to have been erroneously or illegally assessed or collected, until appeal shall have been duly made to the Commissioner of Internal Revenue, according to the provisions of law in that regard, and the regulations of the Secretary of the Treasury established in pursuance thereof, and a decision of said commissioner be had thereon, unless such suit shall be brought within six months from the time of said decision, or within six months from the time this act takes effect: *Provided*, That if said decision shall be delayed more than six months from the date of said appeal, then said suit may be brought at any time within twelve months from the date of such appeal.

13 July, 1866, § 19.

No suit to be maintained for illegal taxes until appeal is made to the Commissioner.

When to be brought.

III.

SPECIAL TAXES.

56. That no person, firm, company, or corporation shall be engaged in, prosecute, or carry on any trade, business, or profession, hereinafter mentioned and described, until he or they shall have paid a special tax therefor in the manner hereinafter provided.

30 June, 1864, § 71.
13 July, 1866, § 9.

Trades and occupations to pay a special tax.

57. That every person, firm, company, or corporation engaged in any trade, business, or profession, on which a special tax is imposed by law, shall register with the assistant assessor of the assessment district, first, his or their name or style, and in case of a firm or company, the names of the several persons constituting such firm or company, and their places of residence; second, the trade, business, or profession, and the place where such trade, business, or profession is to be carried on; third, if a rectifier, the number of barrels he designs to rectify; if a peddler, whether he designs to travel on foot, or with one, two, or more horses or mules; if an inn-keeper, the yearly rental value of the house and property to be occupied for said purpose. All of which facts shall be returned duly certified by such assistant assessor, to both the assessor and collector of the district; and the special tax shall be paid to the collector or deputy collector of the district as hereinafter provided for such trade, business, or profession, who shall give a receipt therefor.

30 June, 1864, § 72.
13 July, 1866, § 9.

To be registered.

Tax to be paid and receipt given therefor.

30 June, 1864, § 73. 13 July, 1866, § 9.

Penalty for not paying special tax.

58. That any one who shall exercise or carry on any trade, business, or profession, or do any act hereinafter mentioned, for the exercising, carrying on, or doing of which a special tax is imposed by law, without payment thereof as in that behalf required, shall, for every such offence, besides being liable to the payment of the tax, be subject to imprisonment for a term not exceeding two years, or a fine not exceeding five hundred dollars, or both, and such fine shall be distributed between the United States and the informer, if there be any, as provided by law.

Distribution of fines.

30 June, 1864, § 74. 3 March, 1865, § 1. 13 July, 1866, § 9.

Form of receipt.

59. That the receipt for the payment of any special tax shall contain and set forth the purpose, trade, business, or profession for which such tax is paid, and the name and place of abode of the person or persons paying the same; if by a rectifier, the quantity of spirits intended to be rectified; if by a peddler, whether for travelling on foot or with one, or two, or more horses or mules, the time for which payment is made, the date or time of payment, and (except in case of auctioneers, produce brokers, commercial brokers, patent-right dealers, photographers, builders, insurance agents, insurance brokers, and peddlers) the place at which the trade, business, or profession for which the tax is paid shall be carried on: *Provided*, That the payment of the special tax herein imposed shall not exempt from an additional special tax the person or persons, (except lawyers, physicians, surgeons, dentists, cattle brokers, horse dealers, peddlers, produce brokers, commercial brokers, patent-right dealers, photographers, builders, insurance agents, insurance brokers, and auctioneers,) or firm, company, or corporation doing business in any other place than that stated; but nothing herein contained shall require a special tax for the storage of goods, wares, or merchandise in other places than the place of business, nor for the sale by manufacturers or producers of their own goods, wares, and merchandise, at the place of production or manufacture, and at their principal office or place of business, provided no goods, wares, or merchandise shall be kept except as samples, at said office or place of business. And every person exercising or carrying on any trade, business, or profession, or doing any act for which a special tax is imposed, shall, on demand of any officer of internal revenue, produce and exhibit the receipt for payment of the tax, and unless he shall do so may be taken and deemed not to have paid such tax. And in case any peddler shall refuse to exhibit his or her receipt, as aforesaid, when demanded by any officer of internal revenue, said officer may seize the horse or mule, wagon, and contents, or pack, bundle, or basket of any person so refusing, and the assessor of the district in which the seizure has occurred may, on ten days' notice, published in any newspaper in the district, or served personally on the peddler, or at his dwelling-house, require such peddler to show cause, if any he has, why the horses or mules, wagon, and contents, pack, bundle, or basket so seized shall not be forfeited; and in case no sufficient cause is shown, the assessor may direct a forfeiture, and issue an order to the collector or to any deputy collector of the district for the sale of the property so forfeited; and the same, after payment of the expenses of the proceedings, shall be paid to the collector for the use of the United States. And all such special taxes shall become due on the first day of May in each year, or on commencing any trade, business, or profession upon which such tax is by law imposed. In the former case the tax shall be reckoned for one year;

Proviso against carrying on business in any other place than described in receipt.

Shall produce receipt on demand of officer

Penalty.

Disposition of goods seized in hands of peddler.

Special taxes due May 1, each year.

and in the latter case, proportionately for that part of the year from the first day of the month in which the liability to a special tax commenced, to the first day of May following.

60. That upon the death of any person having paid the special tax for any trade, business, or profession, it may and shall be lawful for the executors or administrators, or the wife or child, or the legal representatives of such deceased person to occupy the house or premises, and in like manner to exercise or carry on, for the residue of the term for which the tax shall have been paid, the same trade, business, or profession, as the deceased before exercised or carried on, in or upon the same houses or premises, without payment of any additional tax. And in case of the removal of any person or persons from the house or premises for which any trade, business, or profession was taxed, it shall be lawful for the person or persons so removing to any other place to carry on the trade, business, or profession specified in the tax receipt at the place to which such person or persons may remove without payment of any additional tax: *Provided*, That all cases of death, change, or removal, as aforesaid, shall be registered with the assistant assessor, and with the collector, together with the name or names of the person or persons making such change or removal, or successor to any person deceased, under regulations to be prescribed by the Commissioner of Internal Revenue.

30 June, 1864, § 75.
13 July, 1866, § 9.

Removals authorized.

Executors, &c., may carry on business.

Change or removal to be registered with the assistant assessor and collector.

61. That in every case where more than one of the pursuits, employments, or occupations, hereinafter described, shall be pursued or carried on in the same place by the same person at the same time, except as hereinafter provided, the tax shall be paid for each according to the rates severally prescribed: *Provided*, That in cities and towns having a less population than six thousand persons according to the last preceding census, one special tax shall be held to embrace the business of land warrant brokers, claim agents, and real estate agents, upon payment of the highest rate of tax applicable to either one of said pursuits.

30 June, 1864, § 76.
13 July, 1866, § 9.

Special tax to be paid for each pursuit, &c.

Proviso.

62. That no auctioneer shall, by virtue of having paid the special tax as an auctioneer, sell any goods or other property at private sale, nor shall he employ any other person to act as auctioneer in his behalf, except in his own store or warehouse or in his presence; and any auctioneer who shall sell goods or commodities otherwise than by auction, without having paid the special tax imposed upon such business, shall be subject and liable to the penalty imposed upon persons dealing in or retailing, trading or selling goods or commodities without payment of the special tax for exercising or carrying on such trade or business; and where goods or commodities are the property of any person or persons taxed to deal in or retail, or trade in or sell the same, it shall and may be lawful for any person exercising or carrying on the trade or business of an auctioneer to sell such goods or commodities for and on behalf of such person or persons in said house or premises.

30 June, 1864, § 77.
13 July, 1866, § 9.

Auctioneers not to employ other persons, nor to sell at private sale.

Penalty.

Licensed auctioneer may sell goods of licensed dealer on premises.

63. That any number of persons, except lawyers, conveyancers, claim agents, patent agents, physicians, surgeons, dentists, cattle brokers, horse dealers, and peddlers, doing business in copartnership at any one place, shall be required to pay but one special tax for such copartnership.

30 June, 1864, § 78.
13 July, 1866, § 9.

Business may be carried on in copartnership, except by lawyers, &c.

64. That a special tax shall be, and hereby is, imposed as follows, that is to say:

30 June, 1864, § 79.
13 July, 1866, § 9.

One. Banks chartered or organized under a general law, with

Bankers, $100.

a capital not exceeding fifty thousand dollars, and bankers using or employing a capital not exceeding the sum of fifty thousand dollars, shall pay one hundred dollars; when exceeding fifty thousand dollars, for every additional thousand dollars in excess of fifty thousand dollars, two dollars. Every incorporated or other bank, and every person, firm, or company having a place of business where credits are opened by the deposit or collection of money or currency, subject to be paid or remitted upon draft, check, or order, or where money is advanced or loaned on stocks, bonds, bullion, bills of exchange, or promissory notes, or where stocks, bonds, bullion, bills of exchange, or promissory notes are received for discount or for sale, shall be regarded as a bank or as a banker: *Provided*, That any savings bank having no capital stock, and whose business is confined to receiving deposits and loaning or investing the same for the benefit of its depositors, and which does no other business of banking, shall not be subject to this tax.

For every $1,000 in excess of $50,000, $2.

Definition of.

Savings banks exempted in certain cases.

Two. Wholesale dealers, whose annual sales do not exceed fifty thousand dollars, shall pay fifty dollars; and if their annual sales exceed fifty thousand dollars, for every additional thousand dollars in excess of fifty thousand dollars, they shall pay one dollar; and the amount of all sales within the year beyond fifty thousand dollars shall be returned monthly to the assistant assessor, and the tax on sales in excess of fifty thousand dollars shall be assessed by the assessors and paid monthly as other monthly taxes are assessed and paid. Every person shall be regarded as a wholesale dealer whose business it is, for himself or on commission, to sell or offer to sell any goods, wares, or merchandise of foreign or domestic production, not including wines, spirits, or malt liquors, whose annual sales exceed twenty-five thousand dollars. And the payment of the special tax as a wholesale dealer shall not exempt any such person acting as a commercial broker from the payment of the special tax imposed upon commercial brokers: *Provided*, That no person paying the special tax as a wholesale dealer in liquors shall be required to pay an additional special tax on account of the sale of other goods, wares, or merchandise on the same premises: *And provided further*, That, in estimating the amount of sales for the purposes of this section, any sales made by or through another wholesale dealer on commission shall not be again estimated and included as sold by the party for whom the sale was made.

Wholesale dealers, $50.

For every $1,000 in excess of $50,000, $1.

Definition.

Cannot act as commercial broker.

Three. Retail dealers shall pay ten dollars. Every person whose business or occupation it is to sell or offer for sale any goods, wares, or merchandise of foreign or domestic production, not including spirits, wines, ale, beer, or other malt liquors, and whose annual sales exceed one thousand and do not exceed twenty-five thousand dollars, shall be regarded as a retail dealer.

Retail dealers, $10.

Definition of.

Four. Wholesale dealers in liquors whose annual sales do not exceed fifty thousand dollars shall pay one hundred dollars, and if exceeding fifty thousand dollars, for every additional one thousand dollars in excess of fifty thousand dollars, they shall pay one dollar, and such excess shall be assessed and paid in the same manner as required of wholesale dealers. Every person who shall sell or offer for sale any distilled spirits, fermented liquors, or wines of any kind in quantities of more than three gallons at one time to the same purchaser, or whose annual sales, including sales

Wholesale liquor dealers, $50.

For every $1,000 in excess of $50,000, $1.

Definition of.

of other merchandise, shall exceed twenty-five thousand dollars, shall be regarded as a wholesale dealer in liquors.

Five. Retail dealers in liquors shall pay twenty-five dollars. Every person who shall sell or offer for sale foreign or domestic spirits, wines, ale, beer, or other malt liquors in quantities of three gallons or less, and whose annual sales, including all sales of other merchandise, do not exceed twenty-five thousand dollars, shall be regarded as a retail dealer in liquors.

Retail liquor dealers, $25. Definition of.

Six. Lottery ticket dealers shall pay one hundred dollars. Every person, association, firm, or corporation who shall make, sell, or offer to sell lottery tickets or fractional parts thereof, or any token, certificate, or device representing or intending to represent a lottery ticket or any fractional part thereof, or any policy of numbers in any lottery, or shall manage any lottery, or prepare schemes of lotteries, or superintend the drawing of any lottery, shall be deemed a lottery ticket dealer: *Provided,* That the managers of any lottery shall give bond in the sum of one thousand dollars that the person paying such tax shall not sell any tickets or supplementary ticket of such lottery which has not been duly stamped according to law, and that he will pay the tax imposed by law upon the gross receipts of his sales.

Lottery ticket dealers, $100. Definition of.

Proviso.

Seven. Horse dealers shall pay ten dollars. Any person whose business it is to buy or sell horses or mules shall be regarded a horse dealer: *Provided,* That one special tax having been paid, no additional tax shall be imposed upon any horse dealer for keeping a livery stable, nor upon any livery stable keeper for dealing in horses.

Horse dealers, $10. Definition of.

Eight. Livery stable keepers shall pay ten dollars. Any person whose business it is to keep horses for hire, or to let, or to keep, feed, or board horses for others, shall be regarded as a livery stable keeper.

Livery stable keepers, $10. Definition of.

Nine. Brokers shall pay fifty dollars. Every person, firm, or company, whose business it is to negotiate purchases or sales of stocks, bonds, exchange, bullion, coined money, bank notes, promissory notes, or other securities, for themselves or others, shall be regarded as a broker: *Provided,* That any person having paid the special tax as a banker shall not be required to pay the special tax as a broker.

Brokers, $50. Definition of.

Bankers not subject to license as brokers.

Ten. Pawnbrokers using or employing a capital of not exceeding fifty thousand dollars shall pay fifty dollars; and when using or employing a capital exceeding fifty thousand dollars, for every additional thousand dollars in excess of fifty thousand dollars, shall pay two dollars. Every person whose business or occupation it is to take or receive, by way of pledge, pawn, or exchange, any goods, wares, or merchandise, or any kind of personal property whatever, as security for the repayment of money lent thereon, shall be deemed a pawnbroker.

Pawnbrokers, $50.

For every $1,000 in excess of $50,000, $2. Definition of.

Eleven. Land-warrant brokers shall pay twenty-five dollars. Any person shall be regarded as a land-warrant broker who makes a business of buying and selling land warrants or of furnishing them to settlers or other persons.

Land warrant brokers, $25. Definition of.

Twelve. Cattle brokers, whose annual sales do not exceed ten thousand dollars, shall pay ten dollars; and if exceeding the sum of ten thousand dollars, one dollar for each additional thousand dollars; and such excess shall be assessed and paid in the same manner as required of wholesale dealers. Any person whose busi-

Cattle brokers, $10. For every $1,000 in excess of $10,000, $1.

Definition of.

ness it is to buy or sell or deal in cattle, hogs, or sheep, shall be considered as a cattle broker.

Produce brokers $10. Definition of.

Thirteen. Produce brokers, whose annual sales do not exceed the sum of ten thousand dollars, shall pay ten dollars. Every person other than one having paid the special tax as a commercial broker or cattle broker, or wholesale or retail dealer, or peddler, whose occupation it is to buy or sell agricultural or farm products, and whose annual sales do not exceed ten thousand dollars, shall be regarded as a produce broker.

Commercial brokers, $20 Definition of.

Fourteen. Commercial brokers shall pay twenty dollars. Any person or firm whose business it is, as a broker, to negotiate sales or purchases of goods, wares, or merchandise, or to negotiate freights and other business for the owners of vessels, or for the shippers, or consignors, or consignees of freight carried by vessels, shall be regarded a commercial broker.

Custom-house brokers, $10. Definition of.

Fifteen. Custom-house brokers shall pay ten dollars. Every person whose occupation it is, as the agent of others, to arrange entries and other custom-house papers, or transact business at any port of entry relating to the importation or exportation of goods, wares, or merchandise, shall be regarded a custom-house broker.

Distillers, $100. Definition of. Vide post, "DISTILLED SPIRITS."

Distillers making less than 150 barrels per year, $50; less than 50 barrels, $20. Distillers of apples, grapes, and peaches, making less than 150 barrels per year, $12 50.

Sixteen. Distillers shall pay one hundred dollars. Every person, firm, or corporation, who distils or manufactures spirits, or who brews or makes mash, wort, or wash for distillation or the production of spirits, shall be deemed a distiller: *Provided,* That distillers of apples, grapes, or peaches, distilling or manufacturing fifty and less than one hundred and fifty barrels per year from the same, shall pay fifty dollars; and those distilling or manufacturing less than fifty barrels per year from the same shall pay twenty dollars: *And provided further,* That no tax shall be imposed for any still, stills, or other apparatus used by druggists and chemists for the recovery of alcohol for pharmaceutical and chemical or scientific purposes which has been used in those processes.

Brewers, $100. Definition of.

Brewers making less than 500 barrels per year, $50.

Seventeen. Brewers shall pay one hundred dollars. Every person, firm, or corporation who manufactures fermented liquors of any name or description, for sale, from malt, wholly or in part, or from any substitute therefor, shall be deemed a brewer: *Provided,* That any person, firm, or corporation, who manufactures less than five hundred barrels per year, shall pay the sum of fifty dollars.

Rectifiers, $25.

For every additional 500 barrels, $25. Definition of. Vide post, "DISTILLED SPIRITS."

Eighteen. Rectifiers who shall rectify any quantity of spirituous liquors, not exceeding five hundred barrels, packages, or casks, containing not more than forty gallons to each barrel, package, or cask, shall pay twenty-five dollars; and twenty-five dollars additional for each additional five hundred such barrels, packages, or casks, or any fractional part thereof. Every person, firm, or corporation, who rectifies, purifies, or refines distilled spirits or wines by any process, or who, by mixing distilled spirits or wine with any materials, manufactures any spurious, imitation, or compound liquors for sale, under the name of whiskey, brandy, gin, rum, wine, "spirits," or "wine bitters," or any other name, shall be regarded as a rectifier.

Coal oil distillers, $50. Definition of.

Nineteen. Coal oil distillers and distillers of burning fluid and camphene shall pay fifty dollars. Any person, firm, or corporation, who shall refine, produce, or distil petroleum, or rock oil or oil made of coal, asphaltum, shale, peat, or other bituminous substances, or shall manufacture illuminating oil, shall be regarded as a coal oil distiller.

Hotels, inns, and taverns.

Where the yearly rental does not exceed $200, $10.

For every additional $100, $5.

Definition of.

Keepers of hotels, taverns, and eating-houses, selling liquors, must pay additional tax.

Steamers and vessels, $25.

Penalty in case of fraud.

Twenty. Keepers of hotels, inns, or taverns, shall be classified and rated according to the yearly rental, or, if not rented, according to the estimated yearly rental of the house and property intended to be so occupied, as follows, to wit: when the rent or valuation of the yearly rental of said house and property shall be two hundred dollars, or less, they shall pay ten dollars; and if exceeding two hundred dollars, for any additional one hundred dollars or fractional part thereof in excess of two hundred dollars, five dollars: *Provided*, That a payment of such special tax shall be construed to permit the person so keeping a hotel, inn, or tavern, to furnish the necessary food for the animals of such travellers or sojourners without the payment of an additional special tax as a livery stable keeper. Every place where food and lodging are provided for and furnished to travellers and sojourners for pay shall be regarded as a hotel, inn, or tavern: *Provided*, That keepers of hotels, taverns, and eating-houses, in which liquors are sold by retail, to be drank upon the premises, shall pay an additional tax of twenty-five dollars. The yearly rental shall be fixed and established by the assistant assessor of the proper assessment district at its proper value; but if rented, at not less than the actual rent agreed on by the parties. All steamers and vessels, upon waters of the United States, on board of which passengers or travellers are provided with food or lodgings, shall be subject to and required to pay twenty-five dollars: *Provided*, That any person who shall make a false or fraudulent return concerning the actual rent mentioned in this paragraph shall be subject to a penalty therefor of double the amount of the tax.

Eating-houses, $10.

Definition of.

No additonal tax for selling tobacco, &c.

Twenty-one. Keepers of eating-houses shall pay ten dollars. Every place where food or refreshments of any kind, not including spirits, wines, ale, beer, or other malt liquors, are provided for casual visitors and sold for consumption therein, shall be regarded as an eating-house. But the keeper of an eating-house, having paid the tax therefor, shall not be required to pay a special tax as a confectioner, anything in this [act] to the contrary notwithstanding. And keepers of hotels, inns, taverns, and eating-houses, having paid the special tax therefor, shall not be required to pay additional tax for selling tobacco, snuff, or cigars on the same premises, anything in this act to the contrary notwithstanding.

Confectioners, $10.

Definition of.

Twenty-two. Confectioners shall pay ten dollars. Every person who sells at retail confectionery, sweetmeats, comfits, or other confects, in any building, shall be regarded as a confectioner. But wholesale and retail dealers, having paid the special tax therefor, shall not be required to pay the special tax as a confectioner, anything in this act to the contrary notwithstanding.

Claim agents, $10.

Definition of.

Twenty-three. Claim agents and agents for procuring patents shall pay ten dollars. Every person whose business it is to prosecute claims in any of the executive departments of the federal government, or procure patents, shall be deemed a claim or patent agent, as the case may be.

Patent-right dealers, $10.

Definition of.

Twenty-four. Patent-right dealers shall pay ten dollars. Every person whose business it is to sell, or offer for sale, patent rights, shall be regarded as a patent-right dealer.

Real-estate agents, $10. Definition of.

Twenty-five. Real-estate agents shall pay ten dollars. Every person whose business it is to sell or offer for sale real estate for others, or to rent houses, stores, or other buildings or real estate, or to collect rent for others, except lawyers paying a special tax as such, shall be regarded as a real-estate agent.

Conveyancers, $10. Definition of.

Twenty-six. Conveyancers shall pay ten dollars. Every person, other than one having paid the special tax as a lawyer or claim agent, whose business it is to draw deeds, bonds, mortgages, wills, writs, or other legal papers, or to examine titles to real estate, shall be regarded as a conveyancer.

Intelligence office keepers, $10. Definition of.

Twenty-seven. Intelligence office keepers shall pay ten dollars. Every person whose business it is to find or furnish places of employment for others, or to find or furnish servants upon application in writing or otherwise, receiving compensation therefor, shall be regarded as an intelligence office keeper.

Insurance agents, $10. Definition of.

Twenty-eight. Insurance agents shall pay ten dollars. Any person who shall act as agent of any fire, marine, life, mutual, or other insurance company or companies, or any person who shall negotiate or procure insurance for which he receives any commission or other compensation, shall be regarded as an insurance agent: *Provided*, That if the annual receipts of any person as such agent shall not exceed one hundred dollars, he shall pay five dollars only: *And provided further*, That no special tax shall be imposed upon any person for selling tickets or contracts of insurance against injury to persons while travelling by land or water.

$5.

Travelling insurance exempt.

Foreign insurance agents, $50. Definition of.

Twenty-nine. Foreign insurance agents shall pay fifty dollars. Every person who shall act as agent of any foreign fire, marine, life, mutual or other insurance company or companies shall be regarded as a foreign insurance agent.

Auctioneers whose annual sales do not exceed $10,000, $10. Annual sales exceeding $10,000, $20. Definition of. Exemption.

Thirty. Auctioneers, whose annual sales do not exceed ten thousand dollars, shall pay ten dollars, and if exceeding ten thousand dollars shall pay twenty dollars. Every person shall be deemed an auctioneer whose business it is to offer property at public sale to the highest or best bidder: *Provided*, That the provisions of this paragraph shall not apply to judicial or executive officers making auction sales by virtue of any judgment or decree of any court, nor public sales made by or for executors, administrators, or guardians of any estate held by them as such.

Manufacturers, $10. Definition of.

Thirty-one. Manufacturers shall pay ten dollars. Any person, firm, or corporation who shall manufacture by hand or machinery any goods, wares, or merchandise, not otherwise provided for, exceeding annually the sum of one thousand dollars, or who shall be engaged in the manufacture or preparation for sale of any articles or compounds, or shall put up for sale in packages with his own name or trade-mark thereon any articles or compound, shall be regarded as a manufacturer.

Peddlers.

1st class, $50.

2d class, $25.

3d class, $15.

4th class, $10. Definition of.

Thirty-two. Peddlers shall be classified and rated as follows, to wit: When travelling with more than two horses, or mules, the first class, and shall pay fifty dollars; when travelling with two horses, or mules, the second class, and shall pay twenty-five dollars; when travelling with one horse, or mule, the third class, and shall pay fifteen dollars; when travelling on foot, or by public conveyance, the fourth class, and shall pay ten dollars. Any person, except persons peddling only charcoal, newspapers, magazines, Bibles, religious tracts, or the products of his farm or garden, who sells or offers to sell, at retail, goods, wares, or other commodities, travelling from place to place in the town or through the country, shall be regarded a peddler: *Provided*, That any peddler who sells, or offers to sell, distilled spirits, fermented liquors or wines, dry-goods, foreign or domestic, by one or more original packages or pieces, at one time, to the same person or persons, or who peddles jewelry, shall pay fifty dollars: *Provided further*, That manufacturers and producers of agricultural tools and implements, garden seeds, fruit and ornamental trees, stoves and hollow ware, brooms, wooden ware, charcoal, and gunpowder, delivering and selling at wholesale any of said articles, by themselves or their authorized agents, at places other than the place of manufacture, shall not therefor be required to pay any special tax: *Provided further*, That persons who shall sell shell or other fish, or both, travelling from place to place, and not from any shop or stand, shall be required to pay five dollars only; and no special tax shall be imposed for selling shell or other fish from hand-carts or wheelbarrows.

Peddlers of distilled spirits, fermented liquors or wines, dry goods, and jewelry, $50.

Exemption.

Travelling peddlers of fish, $5.

Thirty-three. Apothecaries shall pay ten dollars. Every person who keeps a shop or building where medicines are compounded or prepared according to prescriptions of physicians, or where medicines are sold, shall be regarded as an apothecary. But wholesale and retail dealers, who have paid the special tax therefor, shall not be required to pay a tax as an apothecary; nor shall apothecaries who have paid the special tax be required to pay the tax as retail dealers in liquor in consequence of selling alcohol, or of selling or of dispensing, upon physicians' prescriptions, the wines and spirits officinal in the United States and other national pharmacopœias, in quantities not exceeding half a pint of either at any one time, nor exceeding in aggregate cost value the sum of three hundred dollars per annum.

Apothecaries, $10. Definition of.

Thirty-four. Photographers shall pay ten dollars. Any person who makes for sale photographs, ambrotypes, daguerreotypes, or pictures, by the action of light, shall be regarded a photographer.

Photographers, $10. Definition of.

Thirty-five. Tobacconists shall pay ten dollars. Any person, firm, or corporation whose business it is to manufacture cigars, snuff, or tobacco in any form, shall be regarded a tobacconist.

Tobacconists, $10. Definition of.

Thirty-six. Butchers shall pay ten dollars. Every person whose business it is to sell butchers' meat at retail shall be regarded as a butcher: *Provided*, That no butcher having paid the special tax therefor shall be required to pay the special tax as a retail dealer on account of selling other articles at the same store, stall, or premises: *Provided further*, That butchers who sell butchers' meat exclusively by themselves or agents, travelling from place to place, and not from any shop or stand, shall be required to pay five dollars only, any existing law to the contrary notwithstanding.

Butchers, $10. Definition of.

Travelling, $5.

Thirty-seven. Proprietors of theatres, museums, and concert halls, shall pay one hundred dollars. Every edifice used for the purpose of dramatic or operatic or other representations, plays, or performances, for admission to which entrance money is received, not including halls rented or used occasionally for concerts or theatrical representations, shall be regarded as a theatre: *Provided*, That when any such edifice is under lease at the passage of this act the tax shall be paid by the lessee, unless otherwise stipulated between the parties to said lease.

Theatres, museums, and concert halls, $100. Definition of.

Thirty-eight. The proprietor or proprietors of circuses shall pay [one] hundred dollars. Every building, tent, space, or area,

Circuses, $100. Definition of.

where feats of horsemanship or acrobatic sports or theatrical performances are exhibited, shall be regarded as a circus: *Provided*, That no special tax paid in one State shall exempt exhibitions from the tax in another State. And but one special tax shall be imposed for exhibitions within any one State.

Jugglers, $20. Definition of.

Thirty-nine. Jugglers shall pay twenty dollars. Every person who performs by sleight of hand shall be regarded as a juggler.

Exhibitions or shows, $10.

The proprietors or agents of all other public exhibitions or shows for money, not enumerated in this section, shall pay ten dollars: *Provided*, That a special tax paid in one State shall not exempt exhibitions from the tax in another State. And but one special tax shall be required for exhibitions within any one State.

Bowling alleys and billiard rooms, for each alley or table, $10. Definition of.

Forty. Proprietors of bowling alleys and billiard rooms shall pay ten dollars for each alley or table. Every place or building where bowls are thrown or billiards played, and open to the public with or without price, shall be regarded as a bowling alley or billiard room, respectively.

Gift enterprises, $150. Definition of.

Forty-one. Proprietors of gift enterprises shall pay one hundred and fifty dollars. Every person, firm, or corporation who shall sell or offer for sale any real estate or article of merchandise of any description whatsoever, or any ticket of admission to any exhibition or performance, with a promise, express or implied, to give or bestow, or in any manner hold out the promise of gift or bestowal of any article or thing for and in consideration of the purchase by any person of any other article or thing, shall be regarded as a proprietor of a gift enterprise: *Provided*, That no such proprietor, in consequence of being thus taxed, shall be exempt from paying any other tax imposed by law, and the special tax herein required shall be in addition thereto.

Stallions and jacks, $10. Persons liable to pay.

Forty-two. Owners of stallions and jacks shall pay ten dollars. Every person who keeps a horse or a jack for the use of mares, requiring or receiving pay therefor, shall be regarded as the owner thereof, and shall furnish a statement to the assessor or assistant assessor, which shall contain a brief description of the animal, its age, and place or places where used or to be used: *Provided*, That all accounts, notes, or demands for the use of any such horse or jack, the owner or keeper thereof not having paid the tax as aforesaid, shall be void.

Lawyers, $10. Definition of.

Forty-three. Lawyers shall pay ten dollars. Every person who for fee or reward shall prosecute or defend causes in any court of record or other judicial tribunal of the United States or of any of the States, or whose business it is to give legal advice in relation to any cause or matter whatever, shall be deemed to be a lawyer.

Physicians, surgeons, and dentists, $10. Definition of.

Forty-four. Physicians, surgeons, and dentists shall pay ten dollars. Every person (except apothecaries) whose business it is, for fee and reward, to prescribe remedies or perform surgical operations for the cure of any bodily disease or ailing, shall be deemed a physician, surgeon, or dentist.

Architects and civil engineers, $10. Definition of.

Forty-five. Architects and civil engineers shall pay ten dollars. Every person whose business it is to plan, design, or superintend the construction of buildings, or ships, or of roads, or bridges, or canals, or railroads, shall be regarded as an architect and civil

Exemption.

engineer: *Provided*, That this shall not include a practical carpenter who labors on a building.

Forty-six. Builders and contractors shall pay ten dollars. Every person whose business it is to construct buildings, or vessels, or bridges, or canals, or railroads, by contract, whose receipts from building contracts exceed two thousand five hundred dollars in any one year, shall be regarded as a builder and contractor.

Builders and contractors, $10. Definition of.

Forty-seven. Plumbers and gas-fitters shall pay ten dollars. Every person, firm, or corporation, whose business it is to fit, furnish, or sell plumbing materials, gas-pipes, gas-burners, or other gas-fixtures, shall be regarded a plumber and gas-fitter.

Plumbers and gas-fitters, $10. Definition of.

Forty-eight. Assayers, assaying gold and silver, or either, of a value not exceeding in one year two hundred and fifty thousand dollars, shall pay one hundred dollars, and two hundred dollars when the value exceeds two hundred and fifty thousand dollars and does not exceed five hundred thousand dollars, and five hundred dollars when the value exceeds five hundred thousand dollars. Any person or persons or corporation whose business or occupation it is to separate gold and silver from other metals or mineral substances with which such gold or silver, or both, are alloyed, combined, or united, or to ascertain or determine the quantity of gold or silver in any alloy or combination with other metals, shall be deemed an assayer.

Assayers, not exceeding $250,000, $100. Exceeding $250,000 and not exceeding $500,000, $200. Exceeding $500,000, $500. Definition of.

Forty-nine. Miners shall pay ten dollars. Every person, firm, or company, who shall employ others in the business of mining for coal, or for gold, silver, copper, lead, iron, zinc, spelter, or other minerals, not having paid the tax therefor as a manufacturer, and no other, shall be regarded as a miner: *Provided*, That this shall not apply to any miner whose receipts as such shall not exceed, annually, one thousand dollars.

Miners, $10. Definition of.

Fifty. Express carriers and agents shall pay ten dollars. Every person, firm, or company, engaged in the carrying or delivery of money, valuable papers, or any articles for pay, or doing an express business, whose gross receipts therefrom exceed the sum of one thousand dollars per annum, shall be regarded as an express carrier: *Provided*, That but one special tax of ten dollars shall be imposed upon any one person, firm, or company, in respect to all the business to be done by such person, firm, or company, on a continuous route, and the payment of such tax shall cover all business done upon such route by such person, firm, or company, anywhere in the United States; and such tax shall be required only from the principal in such business, and not from any subordinate: *Provided further*, That draymen and teamsters owning only one dray or team shall not be required to pay such tax.

Express carriers, $10. Definition of.

Proviso.

Fifty-one. Grinders of coffee or spices shall pay one hundred dollars. Any person who manufactures or prepares for use and sale, by grinding or other process, coffee, spices, or mustard, or adulterated coffee, spices, or mustard, or any article or compound intended for use in the adulteration of or as substitutes for coffee, spices, or mustard, shall be regarded as a grinder of coffee or spices: *Provided*, That any person who shall roast coffee for use and sale shall be required to pay the special tax herein imposed upon grinders of coffee or spices.

Grinders of coffee or spices, $100. Definition of.

*[*And provided further*, That all boats, barges and flats not used for carrying passengers, nor propelled by steam or sails, which are floated or towed by tug-boats or horses, and used exclusively for carrying coal, oil, minerals, or agricultural products to market, shall be re-

Proviso to § 103, June 30, 1864. 13 July, 1866, vide § 74, post.

Boats, &c., to pay $5; over one hundred tons, $10.

* Reprinted here for convenience.

quired hereafter, in lieu of enrolment fees or tonnage tax, to pay an annual special tax for each and every such boat of a capacity exceeding twenty-five tons, and not exceeding one hundred tons, five dollars; and when exceeding one hundred tons, as aforesaid, shall be required to pay ten dollars; and said tax shall be assessed and collected as other special taxes provided for in this act.]

30 June, 1864, § 80. 13 July, 1866, § 9.

No special tax in certain cases, unless gross receipts exceed $1,000 per annum.

How annual receipts are to be estimated.

65. That the special tax shall not be imposed upon apothecaries, confectioners, butchers, keepers of eating-houses, hotels, inns, or taverns, or retail dealers, except retail dealers in spirituous and malt liquors when their annual gross receipts shall not exceed the sum of one thousand dollars, any provision of law to the contrary notwithstanding; the amount of such annual receipts to be ascertained or estimated in such manner as the Commissioner of Internal Revenue shall prescribe, as well as the amount of all other annual sales or receipts where the tax is graduated by the amount of sales or receipts; and where the amount of the tax has been increased by law above the amount paid by any person, firm, or company, or has been understated or underestimated, such person, firm, or company shall be again assessed, and pay the amount of such increase: *Provided*, That when any person, before the passage of this act, has been assessed for a license, the amount thus assessed being equal to the tax herein imposed for the business covered by such license, no special tax shall be assessed until the expiration of the period for which such license was assessed.

Proviso in regard to licenses.

13 July, 1866, § 12.

Certain apothecaries not regarded as manufacturers.

66. That apothecaries who manufacture, for their own dispensation and sales to consumers and to physicians, the medicines compounded according to the United States or other national pharmacopœias, or of which the full and proper formula is published in any of the dispensatories now or hitherto in common use among physicians or apothecaries, or in any pharmaceutical journal now issued by any incorporated college of pharmacy, shall not be regarded as manufacturers under this act. But apothecaries and all other persons who manufacture for the dispensing and sales of others, or who make and advertise any article, medicinal or otherwise, simple or compound, with any special proprietary claim to merit, or to special advantage in use or effect, whether such claim be based on the properties, qualities, price, or any other distinctive or distinguishing characteristic, whether real or pretended, of the articles so made and advertised, whether such article be or be not made according to the authorities above cited in this section, shall be regarded as manufacturers under this act.

Certain other apothecaries and persons regarded as manufturers.

30 June, 1864, § 81. 3 March, 1865, § 1. 13 July, 1866, § 9.

Special tax not imposed upon vintners in certain cases.

Nor upon apothecaries.

Nor upon physicians.

Nor upon farmers.

Proviso.

67. That nothing contained in the preceding sections of this act shall be construed to impose a special tax upon vintners who sell wine of their own growth at the place where the same is made; nor upon apothecaries, as to wines or spirituous liquors which they use exclusively in the preparation or making up of medicines; nor shall physicians be taxed for keeping on hand medicines solely for the purpose of making up their own prescriptions for their own patients; nor shall farmers be taxed as manufacturers or producers for making butter or cheese, with milk from their own cows, or for any other farm products: *Provided*, That the payment of any tax imposed by law shall not be held or construed to exempt any person carrying on any trade, business or profession, from any penalty or punishment provided by the laws of any State for carrying on such trade, business or profession within such State, or in any manner to authorize the commencement or continuance of

such trade, business, or profession contrary to the laws of such State, or in places prohibited by municipal law; nor shall the payment of any tax herein provided be held or construed to prohibit or prevent any State from placing a duty or tax for State or other purposes on any trade, business, or profession, upon which a tax is imposed by law.

27 July, 1866, § 1.

Amount paid by wholesale dealer for license in excess of actual sales may be refunded.

68. That where the license tax imposed upon any wholesale dealer has been calculated upon the amount of such dealer's sales for the previous year, in accordance with the terms of the seventy-ninth section of an act approved June thirtieth, eighteen hundred and sixty-four, and it shall be proved to the satisfaction of the Commissioner of Internal Revenue that the sales made under such license did not equal in amount the sales of such previous year, it shall be lawful for said Commissioner to refund to such wholesale dealer so much of the amount paid for such license as may be in excess of the proper tax chargeable upon the amount of sales actually made under such license during the year for which the same was issued.

IV.

MISCELLANEOUS SUBJECTS OF TAXATION.

AUCTION SALES—BROKERS—BANKS—RAILROADS—STEAMBOATS, ETC.—EXPRESS COMPANIES—INSURANCE COMPANIES—TELEGRAPH COMPANIES—THEATRES, ETC.—PASSPORTS—LOTTERIES—ADVERTISEMENTS.

30 June, 1864, § 98.
13 July, 1866, § 9.

Auction sales.

No duty levied on sales by judicial officers, &c.

69. That there shall be levied and collected and paid monthly on all sales of real estate, goods, wares, merchandise, articles, or things at auction, including all sales of stocks, bonds, and other securities, a duty of one-tenth of one per centum on the gross amount of such sales: *Provided*, That no tax shall be levied under the provisions of this section upon any sales by or for judicial or executive officers making auction sales by virtue of a judgment or decree of any court, nor to public sales made by guardians, executors, or administrators.

30 June, 1864, § 99.
3 March, 1865, § 1.
13 July, 1866, § 9.

Brokers.
Per centum on sales.

Sale to be made by bill or memorandum, and stamps to be affixed thereto equal in value to amount of tax.

70. That there shall be paid on all sales made by brokers, banks or bankers, whether made for the benefit of others or on their own account, the following taxes, that is to say: Upon all sales and contracts for the sale of stocks, bonds, gold and silver bullion and coin, promissory notes or other securities, a tax at the rate of one cent for every hundred dollars of the amount of such sales or contracts; and on all sales and contracts for sale negotiated and made by any person, firm or company not paying a special tax as a broker, bank or banker, of any gold or silver bullion, coin, promissory notes, stocks, bonds, or other securities, not his or their own property, there shall be paid a tax at the rate of five cents for every hundred dollars of the amount of such sales or contracts; and on every sale and contract for sale, as aforesaid, there shall be made and delivered by the seller to the buyer a bill or memorandum of such sale or contract, on which there shall be affixed a lawful stamp or stamps in value equal to the amount of tax on such sale, to be determined by the rates of tax before mentioned; and in computing the amount of the stamp tax in any case herein provided for, any fractional part of one hundred dollars of value or amount on which tax is computed shall be accounted at one hundred dollars. And every bill or memorandum of sale, or contract of sale, before mentioned, shall show the date thereof, the name of the seller, the amount of the sale or contract, and the matter or thing to which

Penalty.

it refers. And any person or persons liable to pay the tax as herein provided, or any one who acts in the matter as agent or broker for such person or persons, who shall make any such sale or contract, or who shall, in pursuance of any sale or contract, deliver or receive any stocks, bonds, bullion, coin, promissory notes, or other securities, without a bill or memorandum thereof as herein required, or who shall deliver or receive such bill or memorandum without having the proper stamps affixed thereto, shall forfeit and pay to the United States a penalty of five hundred dollars for each and every offence where the tax so evaded, or attempted to be evaded, does not exceed one hundred dollars, and a penalty of one thousand dollars when such tax shall exceed one hundred dollars, which may be recovered with costs in any court of the United States of competent jurisdiction, at any time within one year after the liability to such penalty shall have been incurred; and the

To be distributed between United States and the informer.

penalty recovered shall be awarded and distributed by the court between the United States and the informer, if there be any, as provided by law, who, in the judgment of the court, shall have first given the information of the violation of the law for which re-

Proviso.

covery is had: *Provided*, That where it shall appear that the omission to affix the proper stamp was not with intent to evade the provisions of this section, said penalty shall not be incurred.

Law in relation to stamp duties in schedule B to apply.

And the provisions of law in relation to stamp duties in schedule B of this act shall apply to the stamp taxes herein imposed upon sales and contracts of sales made by brokers, banks or bankers, and

Commercial brokers—per centum on sales.

others as aforesaid. And there shall be paid monthly on all sales by commercial brokers of any goods, wares, or merchandise, a tax of one-twentieth of one per centum upon the amount of such sales;

Returns to be made monthly to assistant assessor.

and on or before the tenth day of each month, every commercial broker shall make a list or return to the assistant assessor of the district of the gross amount of such sales as aforesaid for the preceding month, in form and manner as may be prescribed by the

Proviso.

Commissioner of Internal Revenue: *Provided*, That in estimating sales of goods, wares, and merchandise for the purposes of this sec-

30 June, 1864, § 110.
3 March, 1865, § 1.
13 July, 1866, § 9.

tion, any sales made by or through another broker upon which a tax has been paid shall not be estimated and included as sold by the broker for whom the sale was made.

Monthly tax of one twenty-fourth of one per cent. upon deposits in banks or with any person engaged in banking.

Monthly tax of one twenty-fourth of one per cent. upon the capital of banks and persons engaged in banking.

Amount invested in United States bonds exempted.

Monthly tax of one-twelfth of one per cent. upon average amount of circulation issued by any bank.

Additional monthly tax of one-sixth of one per cent. upon average amount of circulation beyond ninety per cent. of capital.

71. That there shall be levied, collected, and paid a tax of one twenty-fourth of one per centum each month upon the average amount of the deposits of money, subject to payment by check or draft, or represented by certificates of deposit or otherwise, whether payable on demand or at some future day, with any person, bank, association, company, or corporation engaged in the business of banking; and a tax of one twenty-fourth of one per centum each month, as aforesaid, upon the capital of any bank, association, company, or corporation, and on the capital employed by any person in the business of banking beyond the average amount invested in United States bonds; and a tax of one-twelfth of one per centum each month upon the average amount of circulation issued by any bank, association, corporation, company, or person, including as circulation all certified checks and all notes and other obligations calculated or intended to circulate or to be used as money, but not including that in the vault of the bank, or redeemed and on deposit for said bank; and an additional tax of one-sixth of one per centum, each month, upon the average amount of such circulation, issued as aforesaid, beyond

the amount of ninety per centum of the capital of any such bank, association, corporation, company, or person. And a true and accurate return of the amount of circulation, of deposit and of capital, as aforesaid, and of the amount of notes of persons, State banks or State banking associations paid out by them for the previous month, shall be made and rendered monthly by each of such banks, associations, corporations, companies, or persons to the assessor of the district in which any such bank, association, corporation, or company may be located, or in which such person has his place of business, with a declaration annexed thereto, and the oath or affirmation of such person, or of the president or cashier of such bank, association, corporation, or company, in such form and manner as may be prescribed by the Commissioner of Internal Revenue, that the same contains a true and faithful statement of the amounts subject to tax as aforesaid; and for any refusal or neglect to make or to render return and payment, any such bank, association, corporation, company, or person so in default shall be subject to and pay a penalty of two hundred dollars, besides the additional penalty and forfeitures in other cases provided by law; and the amount of circulation, deposit, capital, and notes of persons, State banks and banking associations paid out, as aforesaid, in default of the proper return, shall be estimated by the assessor or assistant assessor of the district as aforesaid, upon the best information he can obtain; and every such penalty may be recovered for the use of the United States in any court of competent jurisdiction. And in the case of banks with branches, the tax herein provided for shall be assessed upon the circulation of each branch, severally, and the amount of capital of each branch shall be considered to be the amount allotted to such branch; and so much of an act entitled "An act to provide ways and means for the support of the government," approved March three, eighteen hundred and sixty-three, as imposes any tax on banks, their circulation, capital, or deposits, other than is herein provided, is hereby repealed: *Provided*, That this section shall not apply to associations which are taxed under and by virtue of the act "to provide a national currency secured by a pledge of United States bonds, and to provide for the circulation and redemption thereof." And the deposits in associations or companies known as Provident Institutions, Savings Banks, Savings Funds, or Savings Institutions, having no capital stock and doing no other business than receiving deposits to be loaned or invested for the sole benefit of the parties making such deposits, without profit or compensation to the association or company, shall be exempt from tax on so much of their deposits as they have invested in securities of the United States, and on all deposits less than five hundred dollars made in the name of any one person; and the returns required to be made by such Provident Institutions and Savings Banks after July, eighteen hundred and sixty-six, shall be made on the first Monday of January and July of each year, in such form and manner as may be prescribed by the Commissioner of Internal Revenue.

Additional monthly tax of one-sixth of one per cent. upon amount of circulation beyond the average for the six months preceding July 1, 1864.

Return to be made monthly to the assessor of the district.

Return to be verified by the oath of the president or cashier in the form prescribed by the Commissioner.

Penalty for neglect.

Proceedings in case of neglect.

Banks with branches.

This section not to apply to national banks.

Deposits in savings institutions having no capital stock, &c., exempt where invested in securities of the United States.

Deposits less than $500, in the name of any one person, exempt.

Returns to be made semi-annually.

72. That every national banking association, State bank, or State banking association, shall pay a tax of ten per centum on the amount of notes of any person, State bank, or State banking association, used for circulation and paid out by them after the first day of August, eighteen hundred and sixty-six, and such tax shall be assessed and paid in such manner as shall be prescribed by the Commisssioner of Internal Revenue.

3 March, 1865, § 6. 13 July, 1866, § 9 bis.

Tax of 10 per cent. upon circulation of State banks, &c., after August 1, 1866.

3 March, 1865, § 14. 13 July, 1866, § 9 bis.

Capital of State banks converted into national bank to be considered the same as before conversion.

When circulation does not exceed 5 per cent. of capital to be exempt from tax.

National banks to be held for the tax due from the State bank.

73. That the capital of any State bank or banking association which has ceased or shall cease to exist, or which has been or shall be converted into a national bank, shall be assumed to be the capital as it existed immediately before such bank ceased to exist or was converted as aforesaid; and whenever the outstanding circulation of any bank, association, corporation, company, or person shall be reduced to an amount not exceedingfive per centum of the chartered or declared capital existing at the time the same was issued, said circulation shall be free from taxation; and whenever any bank which has ceased to issue notes for circulation shall deposit in the treasury of the United States, in lawful money, the amount of its outstanding circulation, to be redeemed at par, under such regulations as the Secretary of the Treasury shall prescribe, it shall be exempt from any tax upon such circulation; and whenever any State bank or banking association has been converted into a national banking association, and such national banking association has assumed the liabilities of such State bank or banking association, including the redemption of its bills, by any agreement or understanding whatever with the representatives of such State bank or banking association, such national banking association shall be held to make the required return and payment on the circulation outstanding, so long as such circulation shall exceed five per centum of the capital before such conversion of such State bank or banking association.

30 June, 1864, § 103. 3 March, 1865, § 1. 13 July, 1866, § 9.

Tax of 2½ per centum upon the gross receipts of railroads, canals, steamboats, ships, barges, canal boats, vessels, stage coaches, and vehicles transporting passengers or property for hire.

Not chargeable upon steamers and vessels plying between the United States and foreign ports.

Tax of three per centum on ferries and bridges receiving tolls for passengers and freight, on gross receipts.

Not taxable when receipts are less than expenses of repairs.

74. That every person, firm, company, or corporation owning or possessing or having the care or management of any railroad, canal, steamboat, ship, barge, canal-boat, or other vessel, or any stage coach or other vehicle, except hacks or carriages not running on continuous routes, engaged or employed in the business of transporting passengers for hire, or in transporting the mails of the United States upon contracts made prior to August first, eighteen hundred and sixty-six, shall be subject to and pay a tax of two and one-half per cent. of the gross receipts from passengers and mails of such railroad, canal, steamboat, ship, barge, canal-boat, or other vessel, or such stage coach or other vehicle: *Provided*, That the tax hereby imposed shall not be assessed upon receipts for the transportation of persons or mails between the United States and any foreign port; but such tax shall be assessed upon the transportation of persons from a port within the United States through a foreign territory to a port within the United States, and shall be assessed upon and collected from persons, firms, companies, or corporations within the United States, receiving hire or pay for such transportation of persons or mails; and so much of section one hundred and nine as requires returns to be made of receipts hereby exempted from tax when derived from transporting property for hire is hereby repealed: *Provided also*, That any person or persons, firms, companies, or corporations owning, possessing, or having the care or management of any toll-road, ferry, or bridge, authorized by law to receive toll for the transit of passengers, beasts, carriages, teams, and freight of any description, over such toll-road, ferry, or bridge, shall be subject to and pay a tax of three per centum of the gross amount of all their receipts of every description; but when the gross receipts of any such bridge or toll-road, for and during any term of twelve consecutive calendar months, shall not exceed the amount necessarily expended during said term to keep such bridge or road in repair, no tax shall be

assessed upon such receipts during the month next following any such term: *Provided further*, That all such persons, companies, and corporations shall, until the thirtieth day of April, eighteen hundred and sixty-seven, have the right to add the tax imposed hereby to their rates of fare whenever their liability thereto may commence, any limitations which may exist by law or by agreement with any person or company which may have paid or be liable to pay such fare to the contrary notwithstanding. And whenever the addition to any fare shall amount only to the fraction of one cent, any person, or company, liable to the tax of two and a half per centum, may add to such fare one cent, in lieu of such fraction, and such person or company shall keep for sale, at convenient points, tickets in packages of twenty and multiples of twenty, to the price of which, only an amount equal to the revenue tax, shall be added: *And provided further*, That no tax under the foregoing provisions of this section shall be assessed upon any person, firm, company, or corporation, whose gross receipts do not exceed one thousand dollars per annum: *And provided further*, That all boats, barges, and flats not used for carrying passengers, nor propelled by steam or sails, which are floated or towed by tug-boats or horses, and used exclusively for carrying coal, oil, minerals, or agricultural products to market, shall be required hereafter, in lieu of enrolment fees or tonnage tax, to pay an annual special tax, for each and every such boat of a capacity exceeding twenty-five tons, and not exceeding one hundred tons, five dollars; and when exceeding one hundred tons, as aforesaid, shall be required to pay ten dollars; and said tax shall be assessed and collected as other special taxes provided for in this act.

May add the tax to the rates of fare.

Proviso. Exemption.

Certain boats, barges, and flats to pay an annual special tax, in lieu of enrolment fees or tonnage tax.

75. That * * * * * * the receipts of vessels paying tonnage duty shall not be subject to the tax provided in section one hundred and three of "An act to provide internal revenue to support the government, to pay interest on the public debt, and for other purposes," approved June thirtieth, eighteen hundred and sixty-four, nor by any act amendatory thereof.

* * * * * *

Amendatory tariff act, March 3, 1863, §4.

Receipts of vessels paying tonnage duty exempt from tax.

76. That any person, firm, company, or corporation carrying on or doing an express business, shall be subject to and pay a duty of three per centum on the gross amount of all the receipts of such express business.

30 June, 1864, § 104.

A tax of three per centum upon gross receipts of express business.

77. That there shall be levied, collected, and paid a duty of one and a half of one per centum upon the gross receipts of premiums or assessments for insurance from loss or damage by fire or by the perils of the sea, made by every insurance company, whether inland or marine, or fire insurance company, and by every association or individual engaged in the business of insurance against loss or damage by fire or by the perils of the sea; and by every person, firm, company, or corporation who shall issue tickets or contracts of insurance against injury to persons while travelling by land or water; and a like duty shall be paid by the agent of any foreign insurance company having an office or doing business within the United States; and that in the account or return to be rendered, they shall state the amount insured, renewed, or continued, the gross amount of premiums received and assessments collected, and the duties by law accruing thereon.

30 June, 1864, § 105.
3 March, 1865, § 1.

Tax of 1½ per centum upon the gross receipts of premiums by inland, fire, and marine insurance companies.

To include tickets and contracts of insurance against injury to persons travelling.

Foreign companies to pay tax of 1½ per cent.

Returns to state the amount insured, &c., and gross amount of premiums and the duties thereon.

78. That any person, firm, company, or corporation owning or possessing or having the care or management of any telegraphic line by which telegraphic despatches or messages are received or trans-

30 June, 1864, § 107.
13 July, 1866, § 9.

Tax of three per centum on gross

receipts of telegraph companies.

mitted, shall be subject to and pay a tax of three per centum on the gross amount of all receipts of such person, firm, company, or corporation.

30 June, 1864, § 108.

Tax of two per centum upon the gross receipts of theatres, circuses, and other exhibitions and shows.

79. That any person, firm, or corporation, or the manager or agent thereof, owning, conducting, or having the care or management of any theatre, opera, circus, museum, or other public exhibition of dramatic or operatic representations, plays, performances, musical entertainments, feats of horsemanship, acrobatic sports, or other shows which are opened to the public for pay, but not including occasional concerts, school exhibitions, lectures, or exhibitions of works of art, shall be subject to and pay a duty of two per centum on the gross amount of all receipts derived by such person, firm, company, or corporation from such representations, plays, performances, exhibitions, shows, or musical entertainments.

30 June, 1864, § 109.
3 March, 1865, § 1.

Managers of railroads, canals, steamboats, ships, barges, canal-boats, or other vessels, ferries, toll-roads, bridges, insurance companies, telegraphs, theatres, operas, circuses, shows, to make returns within twenty days after the end of each month to the assistant assessor, &c.

Returns to state the gross receipts for the month, and to be verified by oath.

Form of return to be prescribed by Commissioner.

Duties to be paid to collector of the district.

In case of neglect or refusal to make returns for ten days, the assessor or assistant assessor to estimate receipts and taxes, and add ten per cent.

Books of owners or managers to be inspected by assessor or assistant assessor upon demand.

When payment is neglected or refused, a penalty of ten per cent. imposed.

A penalty of $1,000 for any attempt knowingly to evade the payment of duties.

Vide ante § 74.

Lien and distraint as in other cases.

80. That any person, firm, company, or corporation owning or possessing or having the care or management of any railroad, canal, steamboat, ship, barge, canal-boat, or other vessel, or any ferry, toll road, or bridge, as enumerated and described in section one hundred and three of this act; or carrying on or doing an express business; or engaged in the business of insurance, as hereinbefore described; or owning or having the care and management of any telegraph line, or owning, possessing, leasing, or having the control or management of any circus, theatre, opera, or museum, shall, within twenty days after the end of each and every month, make a list or return in duplicate to the assistant assessor of the district, stating the gross amount of their receipts, respectively, for the month next preceding, which return shall be verified by the oath or affirmation of such owner, possessor, manager, agent, or other proper officer, in the manner and form to be prescribed from time to time by the Commissioner of Internal Revenue; and shall also pay to the collector the full amount of duties which have accrued on such receipts for the month aforesaid. And in case of neglect or refusal to make said lists or return for the space of ten days after such return should have been made as aforesaid, the assessor or assistant assessor shall proceed to estimate the amount received and the duties payable thereon, and shall add thereto ten per centum as hereinbefore provided in other cases of delinquency to make return for purposes of assessment; and for the purpose of making such assessment, or of ascertaining the correctness of any such return, the books of any such person, firm, company, or corporation shall be subject to the inspection of the assessor or assistant assessor on his demand or request therefor. And in case of neglect or refusal to pay the duties, with the addition aforesaid, when the same have been ascertained, for the space of ten days after the same shall have become payable, the owner, possessor, or person having the management as aforesaid, shall pay, in addition, ten per centum on the amount of such duties and addition; and for any attempt knowingly to evade the payment of such duties, the said owner, possessor, or person having the care or management as aforesaid, shall be liable to pay a penalty of one thousand dollars for every such attempt, to be recovered as provided in this act for the recovery of penalties. And all provisions of this act in relation to liens and collections by distraint, not incompatible herewith, shall apply to this section and the objects therein embraced.

30 June, 1864, § 106.

Passports subject to a tax of $5.

May be paid to any collector.

81. That for every passport issued from the office of the Secretary of State there shall be paid the sum of five dollars; which amount may be paid to any collector appointed under this act, and his re-

ceipt therefor shall be forwarded with the application for such passport to the office of the Secretary of State, or any agent appointed by him, to be transmitted to the Commissioner of Internal Revenue, there to be charged to the account of such collector. And the collectors shall account for all moneys received for passports in the manner hereinbefore provided, and a like amount shall be paid for every passport issued by any minister or consul of the United States, who shall account therefor to the treasury.

Receipts and application to be forwarded to Secretary of State, who is to transmit the receipt to the Commissioner of Internal Revenue.

Moneys to be charged to collectors.

The same sum to be paid to ministers and consuls, who are to account therefor to the treasury.

82. That every individual partnership, firm, and association, being proprietors, managers, or agents of lotteries, and all lottery ticket dealers, shall pay a tax of five per centum on the gross amount of the receipts from the said business; and all persons making such sales shall, within ten days after the first day of each and every month, make and render a list or return in duplicate to the assistant assessor of the gross amount of such sales, made as aforesaid, with the amount of duty which has accrued or should accrue thereon; which list shall have annexed thereto a declaration, under oath or affirmation, in such form and signed by such officer, agent, or clerk, as may be prescribed by the Commissioner of Internal Revenue, that the same is true and correct, and the said proprietors, managers, and agents shall, on or before the twentieth day of each and every month, as aforesaid, pay the collector or deputy collector of the proper district the amount of the duty or tax as aforesaid. And in default of making such lists or returns, the said proprietors, managers, and agents, and all other persons making such sales, shall be subject to and pay a penalty of one thousand dollars, besides the additions, penalties, and forfeitures in other cases provided; and the said proprietors, managers, and agents shall, in default of paying the said duty or tax at the time herein required, be subject to and pay a penalty of one thousand dollars, or be imprisoned not exceeding one year. In all cases of delinquency in making said list, return, or payment, the assessments and collections shall be made in the manner prescribed in the provisions of this act in relation to manufactures, articles, and products: *Provided*, That the managers of any sanitary fair, or of any charitable, benevolent, or religious association, may apply to the collector of the district and present to him proof that the proceeds of any contemplated lottery, raffle, or gift enterprise will be applied to the relief of sick and wounded soldiers, or to some other charitable use, and thereupon the Commissioner shall grant a permit to hold such lottery, raffle, or gift enterprise, and the said sanitary fair, or charitable or benevolent association, shall be exempt from all charge, whether from tax or license, in respect of such lottery, raffle, or gift enterprise: *Provided further*, That nothing in this section contained shall be construed to legalize any lottery.

30 June, 1864, § 111. 13 July, 1866, § 9.

Tax of five per centum upon the gross receipts of lotteries.

Returns to be made monthly and in duplicate to the assistant assessor with the amount of duty.

To be verified by oath or affirmat'n.

Form of return to be prescribed by Commissioner.

Payment to be made to collector on or before the 20th day of each month.

Penalty of $1,000 in case of default to make lists in addition to ordinary penalties.

Penalty of $1,000 in case of non-payment, and imprisonment not exceeding one year.

In case of delinquency the assessment and collections to be made as provided in sections 84 and 85.

Commissioner may grant free permits to managers of certain fairs whose proceeds are to be applied to the relief of sick and wounded soldiers or other charitable purpose.

Lotteries not legalized.

83. That each lottery ticket or certificate supplementary thereto shall be legibly stamped at the time of sale with the name of the vendor and the date of such sale, under a penalty of fifty dollars, to be paid by the vendor of each lottery ticket or certificate supplementary thereto sold without being first stamped as aforesaid.

30 June, 1864, § 112.

Lottery tickets to be stamped with name of vendor and date of sale.

Penalty of $50 for neglect.

84. That, in addition to all other penalties and forfeitures now imposed by law for the evasion of license fees or other taxes upon the lottery business, any person who shall hereafter sell or dispose of any lottery ticket or certificate supplementary thereto, or any device in the nature thereof, without having first duly obtained a

30 June, 1864, § 113.

Sales without license subject the seller to a penalty of $500, additional to other penalties.

Purchasers of tickets from unlicensed lottery ticket vendors may recover twice the amount paid at any time within three years with costs.

license, as hereinbefore mentioned, shall incur a penalty of five hundred dollars for each and every such offence; and any person who shall purchase, obtain, or receive any lottery ticket or any policy of numbers, tokens, certificate, wager, or device, representing or intended to represent a lottery ticket or fractional part thereof, from any person not having a license to deal in lottery tickets, as provided by law, may recover from such person of whom the same was purchased, obtained, or received, at any time within three years thereafter, before any court of competent jurisdiction, a sum equal to twice the amount paid for the same, with just and legal costs.

3 March, 1865, § 13. 27 July, 1866.

Lottery dealers neglecting to take license to be assessed with penalty of $1,000.

85. That all persons and every person who shall engage or be concerned in the business of a lottery dealer without paying the special tax therefor, under such rules and regulations as shall be prescribed by the Secretary of the Treasury, shall forfeit and pay a penalty of one thousand dollars, to be assessed by the assessor of the proper district and collected as assessed taxes are collected, subject, nevertheless, to the provisions of law relating to erroneous assessments, and shall, on conviction by any court of competent jurisdiction, suffer imprisonment for a period not exceeding a year, at the discretion of the court. And it shall be the duty of all managers and proprietors, and their agents, to keep, or cause to be kept, just and true books of account, wherein all their transactions shall be plainly and legibly set forth, which books of account shall at all reasonable times and hours be subject to the inspection of the assessor, assistant assessor, revenue agent, and inspector of the proper district; and any manager, proprietor, agent, or vendor under this act, who shall refuse or prohibit such inspection of his or their books, as aforesaid, shall pay a penalty of one thousand dollars, or suffer imprisonment for a term not exceeding one year, for every such offence.

Manager to keep books.

30 June, 1864, § 114. 13 July, 1866, § 9.

Tax of three per cent. upon advertisements in newspapers, magazines &c.

86. That there shall be levied, collected, and paid by any person or persons, firm, or company publishing any newspaper, magazine, review, or other literary, scientific, or news publication issued periodically or otherwise, or publishing any guide, almanac, catalogue, directory, or any other paper or book, on the gross receipts for all advertisements, or all matters for the insertion of which in said newspaper or other publication, as aforesaid, or in extras, supplements, sheets, or fly-leaves accompanying the same, pay is required or received, a duty of three per centum; and the person or persons, firm, or company owning, possessing, or having the care or management of any and every such newspaper or other publication, as aforesaid, shall make a list or return on the first day of January, April, July, and October of each year, containing the gross amount of receipts as aforesaid, and the amount of duties which have accrued thereon, and render the same in duplicate to the assistant assessor of the district where such newspaper, magazine, review, or other literary or news publication is or may be published; which list or return shall have annexed a declaration, under oath or affirmation, to be made according to the manner and form which may be from time to time prescribed by the Commissioner of Internal Revenue, of the owner, possessor, or person having the care or management of such newspaper, magazine, review, or other publication, as aforesaid, that the same is true and correct; and shall also, quarterly, within ten days after the time of making said list or return, pay to the collector or deputy collector of the district the full amount of said duties. And in case of neglect or

Owners and managers to make returns quarterly, giving the gross receipts and duties.

Return to be made to the assistant assessor, and in duplicate.

To be verified by oath or affirmation.

Form to be prescribed by Commissioner.

Payment to be made to collector or deputy within ten days.

refusal to comply with any of the provisions contained in this section, or to make and render said list or return, for the space of ten days after the time when said list or return ought to have been made, as aforesaid, the assistant assessors of the respective districts shall proceed to estimate the duties as heretofore provided in other cases of delinquency; and in case of neglect or refusal to pay the duties, as aforesaid, for the space of ten days after said duties become due and payable, and have been demanded, said owner, possessor, or person or persons having the care or management of said newspapers or publications, as aforesaid, shall pay, in addition thereto, a penalty of ten per centum on the amount due. And in case of fraud or evasion, whereby the revenue is attempted to be defrauded, or the duty withheld, said owners, possessors, or person or persons having the care or management of said newspapers or other publications, as aforesaid, shall forfeit and pay a penalty of one thousand dollars for each offence, or for any sum fraudulently unaccounted for. And all provisions in this act in relation to returns, additions, penalties, forfeitures, liens, assessments, and collection, not incompatible herewith, shall apply to this section and the objects herein embraced: *Provided*, That in all cases where the rate or price of advertising is fixed by any law of the United States, State, or Territory, it shall be lawful for the company, person or persons publishing said advertisements, to add the duty or tax imposed by this act to the price of said advertisements, any law to the contrary notwithstanding; and that the receipts for advertisements to the amount of six hundred dollars annually, by any person or persons, firm, or company publishing any newspaper, magazine, review, or other literary, scientific or news publication, issued periodically, shall be exempt from duty: *And provided further*, That all newspapers whose average circulation does not exceed two thousand copies shall be exempted from all taxes for advertisements.

Assistant assessor to estimate duties in case of neglect or refusal for ten days.

Penalty of ten per cent. in case of neglect or refusal to pay the duties for ten days.

In case of attempt to defraud the revenue, a penalty of $1,000 for each offence.

General provisions in regard to returns, additions, penalties, &c., applicable to this section.

When prices of advertising are fixed by law, proprietors may add the tax thereto.

Receipts to the amount of $600 annually exempt.

Newspapers whose average circulation does not exceed 2,000 copies exempt from tax.

87. That whenever by this act any license, duty, or tax of any description has been imposed on any person or corporate body, or property of any person, or incorporated or unincorporated company, having more than one place of business, it shall be lawful for the Commissioner of Internal Revenue to prescribe and determine in what district such tax shall be assessed and collected, and to what officer thereof the official notices required in that behalf shall be given, and of whom payment of such tax shall be demanded: *Provided*, That all taxes on manufactures, manufacturing companies, and manufacturing corporations shall be assessed and the tax collected in the district within which the place of manufacture is located, unless otherwise provided.

30 June, 1864, § 115.

Persons, &c., taxable in more than one district.

Commissioner to decide.

Proviso as to manufactures.

V.—MANUFACTURES, MINERALS, AND PRODUCTS.

1. IN GENERAL.—*a*. EXEMPTIONS.

88. That manual labor schools and colleges shall not be required to pay a manufacturer's or special tax while the proceeds of the labor of such institutions are applied exclusively to the support and maintenance of such institutions.

13 July, 1866, § 18.

Manual labor schools and colleges exempt.

89. That every person, firm, or corporation, who shall have made any contract prior to the passage of this act, and without other provision therein for the payment of duties imposed by law enacted subsequent thereto, upon articles to be delivered under such contract, is hereby authorized and empowered to add to the price thereof so much money as will be equivalent to the duty so subsequently imposed on said articles, and not previously paid by the vendee, and shall be entitled by virtue hereof to be paid and to sue

30 June, 1864, § 97.

Manufacturers, delivering goods under contract made prior to this act, are allowed to add to the price of such goods so much as will be equivalent to the duty subsequently imposed.

Proviso, when the United States is the purchaser.

for and recover the same accordingly: *Provided,* That where the United States is the purchaser under such prior contract, the certificate of the proper officer of the department by which the contract was made, showing, according to regulations to be prescribed by the Secretary of the Treasury, the articles so purchased by the United States, and liable to such subsequent duty, shall be taken and received, so far as the same is applicable, in discharge of such subsequent duties on articles so contracted to be delivered to the United States and actually delivered according to such contract.

3 March, 1865, § 17.

Goods may be purchased by government free of tax.

90. That the privilege of purchasing supplies of goods imported from foreign countries for the use of the United States, duty free, which now does or hereafter shall exist by provision of law, shall be extended, under such regulations as the Secretary of the Treasury may prescribe, to all articles of domestic production which are subject to tax by the provisions of this act.

13 July, 1866, § 10.

Articles and products exempt.

91. That from and after the passage of this act the articles and products hereinafter enumerated shall be exempt from internal tax:

Alum; aluminum; aluminous cake, patent alum, sulphate of alumina, and cobalt;
Aniline and aniline colors;
Animal charcoal, or carbon;
Anvils;
Articles manufactured in institutions for the blind, and in institutions for the deaf and dumb, which are sold to aid in their support, or the support of the pupils;
Barrels and casks, other than those used for the reception of fluids; packing-boxes made of wood; and boxes of wood or paper for friction matches, cigar lights, and wax tapers;
Beeswax, crude or unrefined;
Bi-chromate and prussiate of potash;
Bleaching powders;
Blue vitriol;
Borax, and boracic acid;
Brass not more advanced than rods or sheets;
Brick, fire-brick, draining tiles, cement, drain and sewer pipes, earthen and stone water-pipes, retorts and tiles made of clay;
Bristles;
Brooms made from corn, brush, or palm-leaf;
Building stone of all kinds, including slate, marble, freestone, and soapstone, and rock, and ground gypsum;
Bunting and flags of the United States, and banners made of bunting of domestic manufacture;
Burrstones, millstones, and grindstones, rough or wrought;
Candle wicking;
Chronometers;
Coffins and burial cases;
Copperas;
Copper, lead, and tin, in ingots, pigs, or bars;
Copper and yellow sheathing metal, not more advanced than rods or sheets;
Crates, and grain or farm baskets made of splints;
Crucibles of all kinds;
Crutches and artificial limbs, eyes, and teeth;
Deer-skins, smoked, or not oil-dressed;
Feather beds, mattresses, palliasses, bolsters, and pillows;

Articles and products exempt.

Fertilizers of all kinds;
Flasks and patterns used by founders;
Flax and the manufactures thereof;
Flavoring extracts solely for cooking purposes;
German silver in bars or sheets;
Gold leaf and gold foil;
Hemp and jute prepared for textile or felting purposes;
Hulls of ships and other vessels;
Illuminating gas manufactured by educational institutions for their own use exclusively;
India-rubber springs used exclusively for railroad cars;
Iron bridges, and castings for iron bridges;
Iron drain and sewer pipes;
Keys, actions, and strings for musical instruments;
Litharge and orange mineral;
Machines driven by horse-power and used exclusively for cutting firewood, staves, and shingle bolts; and hand-saws;
Magnesium, calcined magnesia, and carbonate of magnesia;
Malleable iron castings, unfinished;
Manganese;
Masts, spars, ship and vessel blocks, and tree-nail wedges and deck plugs, cordage, ropes, and cables made of vegetable fibre;
Medicinal and mineral waters, of all kinds, sold in bottles or from fountains, and mead;
Mounting and machinery of telescopes for astronomical purposes;
Mills and machinery for the manufacture of sugar, sirup, and molasses from sorghum, imphee, beets and corn;
Mineral coal of all kinds, and peat;
Monuments of stone of all kinds, not exceeding in value the sum of one hundred dollars: *Provided*, That monuments exceeding the value aforesaid, erected by public or private contributions to commemorate the service of Union soldiers who have fallen in battle, shall be exempt from taxation;
Mouldings for looking-glasses and picture frames;
Muriatic, nitric, and acetic acids;
Nickel, quicksilver, and sodium;
Nitrate of lead;
Oakum;
Original paintings, statues, and groups of statuary and casts made thereof by the artist from the original designs;
Oxide of zinc;
Paints, painters' and paper stainers' colors;
Printing paper of all descriptions; and tarred paper for roofing and other purposes; books, maps, charts, and all printed matter, and book-binding; paraffine; paraffine oil, not exceeding in specific gravity thirty-six degrees Baumé's hydrometer, a residuum of distillation or the products thereof; lubricating oil made from crude petroleum, coal, or shale, not exceeding in specific gravity thirty-six degrees Baumé's hydrometer: *Provided*, That such oil shall be subject to the same inspection as illuminating oil; crude petroleum, and crude oil the product of the first and single distillation of coal, shale, asphaltum, peat, or other bituminous substances;
Photographs or any other sun picture, being copies of engravings or works of art, when the same are sold by the producer at wholesale at a price not exceeding fifteen cents each, or are used for the illustration of books;

4

Articles and products exempt.

Pickles when sold by the gallon and not contained in glass packages;

Pig-iron; muck bar; blooms, slabs, and loops;

Ploughs, cultivators, harrows, straw and hay cutters, planters, seed-drills, horse-rakes, hand-rakes, cotton gins, grain cradles, and winnowing-mills;

Pot and pearl ashes;

Productions of stereotypers, lithographers, engravers, and electrotypers;

Putty;

Quinine, morphine, and other vegetable alkaloids, and phosphorus;

Railroad iron, and railroad iron re-rolled;

Railroad chairs and fish plates; railroad, boat, and ship spikes; axe polls; iron axles; shoes for horses, mules, and oxen; rivets, horseshoe nails, nuts, washers, and bolts; vices, iron chains, and anchors; when such articles are made of wrought iron which has previously paid the tax or duty assessed thereon;

Reapers, mowers, threshing machines, and separators; corn-shellers and wooden ware; cotton and hay presses;

Repairs of articles of all kinds;

Residuums, the product of mineral, vegetable, or animal substances drawn from stills after distillation;

Roman and water cements, and lime;

Roofing slate, slabs, and tiles;

Saleratus, sal soda, caustic soda, crude soda, alumino-silicate of soda; aluminate of soda; bi-carbonate of soda; and silicate of soda;

Sails, tents, awnings, and bags made by sewing from fabrics or other articles upon which a duty or tax has been paid; and bags made of paper;

Saltpetre;

Salts of tin;

Silex used in the manufacture of glass;

Soap, valued at not above three cents per pound;

Spelter;

Spindles and castings of all descriptions made specially for locks, safes, looms, spinning machines, steam engines, hot-air and hot-water furnaces, and sewing machines, and not sold or used for any other purposes, and upon which a tax is assessed and paid on the article of which the casting is a part;

Spokes, hubs, bows, and felloes; poles, shafts, arms, and wheels not ironed or finished for carriages or wagons; wooden handles for ploughs, and for other agricultural, household, and mechanical tools and implements; and pail and tub ears and handles; and wooden tanks, and cisterns for crude mineral oil;

Starch;

Steel, made from iron advanced beyond muck bar, blooms, slabs, or loops in ingots, bars, rails made and fitted for railroads, sheet, plate, coil, or wire, hoop-skirt wire covered or uncovered; car-wheels, thimble skeins and pipe boxes, and springs, tire and axles made of steel used exclusively for vehicles, cars or locomotives; and clock springs, faces and hands;

Stoves, composed in part of cast iron and in part of sheet iron, or of soapstone, fire-brick, or freestone, with or without cast iron or sheet iron: *Provided*, That the cast and sheet iron shall have paid the tax or duty previously assessed thereon;

Sugar, molasses, or sirup made from beets, corn, sugar maple, or from sorghum, or imphee; Articles and products exempt.

Sulphate of barytes;

Sulphur, flowers of sulphur, and sulphur flour;

Tar and crude turpentine;

Tin cans used for preserved meats, fish, shell-fish, fruits, vegetables, jams, jellies, paints, oils, and spices;

Umbrellas and parasols, and sticks and frames for the same;

Value of bullion used in the manufacture of wares, watches, and watch-cases, and bullion prepared for the use of platers and watchmakers;

Vegetable, animal, and fish oils of all descriptions, not otherwise provided for, including red oil, oleic acid, and admixtures of the same with paraffine oil, not exceeding in specific gravity thirty-six degrees Baumé's hydrometer;

Verdigris;

Vinegar;

White and red lead;

Whiting; Paris white;

Window glass of all kinds;

Wine made of grapes, currants or other fruits, and rhubarb;

Wire made from wire less than number twenty wire gauge, upon which a tax has been assessed and paid as wire, and no manufactured wire shall pay a greater tax than that imposed on number twenty wire gauge;

Yarn and warp for weaving, braiding or manufacturing purposes exclusively;

Yeast powders and baking powders;

Zinc, in ingots or sheets:

Provided further, That the exemptions aforesaid shall, in all cases, be confined exclusively to said articles in the state and condition specified in the foregoing enumeration, and shall not extend to articles in any other form, nor to manufactures from said articles. Proviso.

92. That 30 June, 1864, § 96. 3 March, 1865, § 1.

Newspapers; Articles and products exempt.

Boards, shingles, laths, and other lumber;

Staves, hoops, shooks, headings, and timber partially wrought and unfinished for chairs, tubs, pails, hubs, spokes, felloes, snaths, lasts, shovel and fork handles;

Matchwood, umbrella stretchers;

Alcohol made or manufactured of spirits or materials upon which the duties imposed by law shall have been paid;

Bone dust, plaster or gypsum;

Malt, burning fluid, printers' ink;

Flax prepared for textile or felting purposes until actually woven;

Marble and slate or other building stones in block, rough and unwrought;

Charcoal, coke, all flour and meal made from grain, bread and breadstuffs;

Butter, cheese, concentrated milk, cider, and cider vinegar, and sugar or molasses made from other articles than the sugar-cane;

Paraffine, whale and fish oil;

Value of the bullion used in the manufacture of silver ware;

Silver bullion rolled or prepared for platers' use exclusively, and cut tapes and small wares used in the manufacture of hoops skirts, shall be, and hereby are, exempt from duty.

Manufactures exempt when the increased value does not exceed five per centum.

And also all goods, wares, and merchandise, and articles made or manufactured from materials which have been subject to and upon which internal duties have been actually paid, or materials imported upon which duties have been paid or upon which no duties have been imposed by law, where the increased value of such goods, wares, or merchandise, and articles so made or manufactured, shall not exceed the amount of five per centum ad valorem, shall be, and hereby are, exempt from duty.

30 June, 1864, § 93.
13 July, 1866, § 9.

Manufactures where the product shall not exceed the rate of $600 per annum under certain circumstances exempt, except refined petroleum, refined coal oil, cotton, gold and silver, spirituous and malt liquors, manufactured tobacco, and snuff and cigars.

Tax when the rate exceeds $600, but does not exceed $1,000 per annum.

Tax in all other cases.

Tax to be assessed on articles, &c., when removed for consumption or use.

Naphtha and other similar bituminous substances, when used on the premises for fuel or cleaning, exempt.

93. That all goods, wares, and merchandise, or articles manufactured, made, or produced (except refined petroleum, refined coal oil, cotton, gold and silver, spirituous and malt liquors, manufactured tobacco, snuff, and cigars) by any person or firm, where the product shall not exceed the rate of one thousand dollars per annum, and shall be made or produced by the labor of such person or firm, or by his or their family, shall be, and are hereby, exempt from tax; where the product shall exceed such rate, and not exceed the rate of three thousand dollars, the tax shall be levied, assessed, and collected only upon the excess above the rate of one thousand dollars per annum; and in all other cases the whole annual product, including any business or transaction where one party has been furnished with materials, or any part thereof, and employed by another party to manufacture, make, or finish the goods, wares and merchandise, or articles, paying or promising to pay therefor, and to whom the same are returned when so made and finished, shall be assessed and the tax paid thereon by the producer or manufacturer: *Provided*, That whenever a producer or manufacturer shall use or consume, or shall remove for consumption or use, any articles, goods, wares or merchandise, which, if removed for sale, would be liable to taxation, he shall be assessed for the tax upon the articles, goods, wares, or merchandise so used, or so removed for consumption or use; but naphtha, the product of the distillation of petroleum, and other similar bituminous substances, when used or consumed on the premises for fuel or cleaning, shall be exempt from tax.

b. ARTICLES TAXED AND RATES OF TAXATION.

30 June, 1864, § 94.
3 March, 1865, § 1.
13 July, 1866, § 9.

Duties on manufactures.

94. That upon the articles, goods, wares, and merchandise hereinafter mentioned, except where otherwise provided, which shall be produced and sold, or be manufactured or made and sold, or be consumed or used by the manufacturer or producer thereof, or removed for consumption, or use, or for delivery to others than agents of the manufacturer or producer within the United States or Territories thereof, there shall be assessed, collected, and paid the following taxes, to be paid by the producer or manufacturer thereof, that is to say:

Candles.

On candles, of whatever material made, a tax of five per centum ad valorem.

Gas.

Rate of duty regulated by the average monthly product.

On gas, illuminating, made of coal wholly or in part, or any other material, when the product shall not be above two hundred thousand cubic feet per month, a tax of ten cents per one thousand cubic feet; when the product shall be above two and not exceeding five hundred thousand cubic feet per month, a tax of fifteen cents per one thousand cubic feet; when the product shall be above five hundred thousand and not exceeding five millions of cubic feet per month, a tax of twenty cents per one thousand cubic feet; when the product shall be above five millions, a tax of twenty-five cents per one thousand cubic feet.

And the general average of the monthly product for the year preceding the return required by law shall determine the rate of tax herein imposed. And where any gas-works have not been in operation for the next year preceding the return as aforesaid, then the rate shall be determined by the estimated average of the monthly product: *Provided*, That the product required to be returned by law by any gas company shall be understood to be, in addition to the gas consumed by said company or other party, the product charged in the bills actually rendered by the gas company during the month preceding the return; and until the thirtieth day of April, eighteen hundred and sixty-seven, all gas companies whose price is fixed by law are authorized to add the tax herein imposed to the price per thousand feet on gas sold; and all such companies which have heretofore contracted to furnish gas to municipal corporations are, in like manner and for the same period, authorized to add such tax to such contract price: *Provided further*, That all gas furnished for lighting street lamps or for other purposes, and not measured, and all gas made for and used by any hotel, inn, tavern, and private dwelling-house, shall be subject to tax whatever the amount of product, and may be estimated; and if the returns in any case shall be understated or underestimated, it shall be the duty of the assistant assessor of the district to increase the same as he shall deem just and proper: *And provided further*, That gas companies located within the corporate limits of any city or town, whether in the same district or otherwise, or so located as to compete with each other, shall pay the rate of tax imposed by law upon the company having the largest production: *And provided further*, That coal tar and ammoniacal liquor produced in the manufacture of illuminating gas, and the products of the re-distillation of coal tar, and the products of the manufacture of ammoniacal liquor thus produced, shall be exempt from tax.

Where gas-works have not been in operation the preceding year.

The product to be returned to be the same as that charged in the bills actually rendered.

Companies may charge tax to consumers.

For lighting streets, &c.

Assistant assessor may increase the amount when underestimated.

Rate of tax where gas-companies may compete with each other.

Coal tar and ammoniacal liquor produced in the manufacture of gas, &c., exempt.

On illuminating, lubricating, or other mineral oils, marking not less than thirty-six nor more than fifty-nine degrees Baumé's hydrometer, the product of the distillation, re-distillation, or refining of crude petroleum, twenty cents per gallon; and all such oils between the specific gravity, by Baumé's test, of thirty-six and fifty-nine degrees, inclusive, shall be deemed refined illuminating oil; and any person or persons who, for the purpose of sale or consumption, shall mix any of the heavier paraffine oils with such illuminating oils, or with naphtha, or either one with the other, shall be deemed manufacturers of illuminating oil, and taxed as such; and said oil thus mixed, either with or without further distillation, shall be subject to a tax of twenty cents per gallon if, after said mixing or distillation, the product marks, by Baumé's hydrometer, between said points of thirty-six and fifty-nine degrees, inclusive.

Oils.

Who shall be deemed manufacturers of.

On illuminating, lubricating, or other mineral oils, marking not less than thirty-six nor more than fifty-nine degrees Baumé's hydrometer, the exclusive product of the refining of crude oil produced by a single distillation of coal, shale, asphaltum, peat, or other bituminous substances, not otherwise provided for, ten cents per gallon.

Oils.

On oil, naphtha, benzine, benzole, or gasoline, marking more than fifty-nine degrees Baumé's hydrometer, the product of the distillation, re-distillation, or refining of crude petroleum, or of

Coal oil, naphtha, benzine, and benzole.

Distillers of coal oil subject to the provisions of law applicable to distillers of spirits so far as deemed necessary by the Commissioner. Proviso.

crude oil produced by a single distillation of coal, shale, peat, asphaltum, or other bituminous substances, a tax of ten cents per gallon: *Provided,* That distillers and refiners of illuminating, lubricating, or other mineral oil, naphtha, benzine, benzole, or gasoline, shall be subject to all the provisions of law applicable to distillers of spirits, with regard to special taxes, bonds, returns, assessments, removing to and withdrawing from warehouses, liens, penalties, forfeitures, drawbacks, and all other provisions designed for the purpose of ascertaining the quantity distilled, and securing the payment of taxes, so far as the same may, in the judgment of the Commissioner of Internal Revenue, and under regulations prescribed by him, be deemed necessary for that purpose: *And provided further,* That distillers and refiners of coal or mineral oil, whose product shall not exceed twenty-five barrels per day, on a monthly average, shall not be required to make returns oftener than once in thirty days.

Spirits of turpentine.

On spirits of turpentine, ten cents per gallon.

Ground coffee. Ground spices. Mustard. Proviso.

On coffee, roasted or ground, on all ground spices and dry mustard, and upon all articles intended for use as substitutes for or as adulterations of coffee, spices, or mustard, and upon all compounds and mixtures prepared for sale, or intended for use and sale as coffee, spices, or mustard, or as substitutes therefor, one cent per pound: *Provided,* That the exemption of one thousand dollars in annual value of product manufactured shall not apply to any of the above-specified articles mentioned in this paragraph.

Molasses produced from sugar cane.

On molasses produced from the sugar-cane, and not from sorghum or imphee, a tax of three cents per gallon.

Sirup of molasses or sugar cane juice when removed from the plantation, &c.

On sirup of molasses or sugar-cane juice, when removed from the plantation, concentrated molasses or melado, and cistern bottoms, of sugar produced from the sugar-cane and not made from sorghum or imphee, a tax of three-fourths of one cent per pound.

Sugars not above number 12.

On sugars not above number twelve Dutch standard in color, produced from the sugar-cane and not from sorghum or imphee, other than those produced by the refiner, a tax of one cent per pound.

Sugars above number 12 and not above number 18.

On sugars above number twelve and not above number eighteen Dutch standard in color, produced directly from the sugar-cane and not from sorghum or imphee, a tax of one and a half cent per pound.

Sugars above number 18.

On sugars above number eighteen Dutch standard in color, produced directly from the sugar-cane and not from sorghum or imphee, a tax of two cents per pound.

Duty on gross amount of sales of sugar refiners. Who are sugar refiners.

On the gross amount of the sales of sugar refiners, including all the products of their manufactories or refineries, a tax of two and one-half of one per centum ad valorem: *Provided,* That every person shall be regarded as a sugar refiner, and pay the taxes required by law, whose business it is to advance the quality and value of sugar upon which a tax or duty has been paid, by melting and recrystallization, or by liquoring, claying, or other washing process, or by any other chemical or mechanical means, or who shall by boiling or other process advance the quality or value of molasses, concentrated molasses, or melado, upon which a tax or duty has been paid.

Sugar candy and confectionery.

On sugar candy and all confectionery made wholly or in part of sugar, valued at not exceeding twenty cents per pound, including the tax, a tax of two cents per pound; exceeding twenty and not exceeding forty cents per pound, including the tax, a tax of four cents per pound; when exceeding forty cents per pound, including the tax, or sold by the box, package, or otherwise than by the pound, a tax of ten per centum ad valorem.

Chocolate.

On chocolate and cocoa prepared, a tax of one and a half cent per pound.

Gun cotton.

On gun cotton, a tax of five per centum ad valorem.

Gunpowder.

On gunpowder, and all explosive substances used for mining, blasting, artillery, or sporting purposes, not otherwise provided for, when valued at thirty-eight cents per pound or less, including the tax, a tax of five per centum ad valorem; and when valued at above thirty-eight cents per pound, including the tax, a tax of ten cents per pound.

Varnish or Japan.

On varnish or japan, made wholly or in part of gum copal, or other gums or substances, a tax of five per centum ad valorem.

Glue and gelatine.

On glue and gelatine of all descriptions, in the solid state, a tax of one cent per pound.

Cement and glue.

On glue and cement, made wholly or in part of glue, sold in the liquid state, a tax of forty cents per gallon.

Pins.

On pins, solid head or other, a tax of five per centum ad valorem.

Photographs, ambrotypes, &c.

On photographs, ambrotypes, daguerreotypes, or other pictures taken by the action of light, and not hereinafter exempted from tax, a tax of five per centum ad valorem.

Wood screws.

On screws, commonly called wood screws, a tax of ten per centum ad valorem.

Clocks, timepieces, and clock movements.

On clocks and timepieces, and on clock movements, when sold without being cased, a tax of five per centum ad valorem.

Soap.

On all soaps valued at above three cents per pound, not perfumed, and on salt-water soap made of cocoa-nut oil, a tax of five mills per pound.

Fancy soap.

On all perfumed soaps, a tax of three cents per pound.

Uncompounded chemicals.

On all uncompounded chemical productions not otherwise provided for, a tax of five per centum ad valorem.

Essential oils.

On essential oils of all descriptions, a tax of five per centum ad valorem.

Furniture sold unfinished.

On all furniture, or other articles made of wood, sold in the rough or unfinished, not otherwise provided for, a tax of five per centum ad valorem: *Provided*, That all furniture, or other articles made of wood, previously assessed, and a tax paid thereon, shall be assessed a tax of five per centum ad valorem upon the increased value only thereof when sold in a finished condition.

Proviso relative to finished furniture sold under certain circumstances.

Salt.

On salt, a tax of three cents per one hundred pounds.

Scales, pumps, garden engines, and hydraulic rams.

On scales, pumps, garden engines, and hydraulic rams, a tax of three per centum ad valorem.

Tin ware.

On tin ware of all descriptions, not otherwise provided for, a tax of five per centum ad valorem.

Iron not advanced beyond bars, &c.

On all iron, not otherwise provided for, advanced beyond muck-bar, blooms, slabs, or loops, and not advanced beyond bars, and band, hoop, and sheet iron not thinner than number eighteen wire-gauge, and plate iron not less than one-eighth of an inch in thickness, a tax of three dollars per ton: *Provided*, That a ton shall, for all the purposes of this act, be deemed and taken to be two thousand pounds.

Proviso.

Ton two thousand pounds.

Band, hoop, and sheet iron; cut nails and spikes not put up and sold in papers.

On band, hoop, and sheet iron, thinner than number eighteen wire-gauge, plate iron less than one-eighth of an inch in thickness, and cut nails and spikes, not including nails, tacks, brads, or finishing nails, usually put up and sold in papers, whether in papers or otherwise, a tax of five dollars per ton: *Provided*, That rods, bands, hoops, sheets, plates, spikes, and nails, not including such as are usually put up in papers as before mentioned, manufactured from iron upon which the tax of three dollars has been levied and paid, shall be subject only to a tax of two dollars per ton in addition thereto, anything in this act to the contrary notwithstanding.

Proviso.

Steel made directly from muck-bar, blooms, &c.

On steel made directly from muck-bar, blooms, slabs, or loops, a tax of three dollars per ton.

Stoves and hollow ware.

On stoves, and hollow ware in all conditions, whether rough, tinned, or enamelled, and castings of iron, not otherwise provided for, a tax of three dollars per ton.

Tubes made of wrought iron.

On tubes made of wrought iron, a tax of five dollars per ton.

Steam engines.

On steam, locomotive, and marine engines, including the boilers, and on railroad cars, a tax of five per centum ad valorem: *Provided*, That when the boilers, tubes, wheels, tire[s], axles, bells, shafts, cranks, wrists, or head-lights of such engines or cars shall have been once assessed, and a tax previously paid thereon, the amount so paid shall be deducted from the taxes on the finished engine or cars.

Boilers, water tanks, &c.

On boilers of all kinds, water tanks, sugar tanks, oil stills, sewing machines, lathes, tools, planes, planing machines, shafting, and gearing, a tax of five per centum ad valorem.

Iron railings, gates, &c.

On railings, gates, fences, furniture, and statuary made of iron, a tax of five per centum ad valorem.

Copper and brass tubes, nails or rivets, sheet lead and lead pipes and shot.

On copper and brass tubes, nails, or rivets, sheet lead, and lead pipes and shot, a tax of five per centum ad valorem.

Goat, &c., skins, in rough.

On goat, calf, kid, sheep, horse, hog, and dog skins, tanned or dressed in the rough, a tax of five per centum ad valorem.

Goat, &c., skins, finished.

Proviso.

On goat, calf, kid, sheep, horse, hog, and dog skins, curried or finished, a tax of five per centum ad valorem: *Provided*, That all goat, calf, kid, sheep, horse, hog, and dog skins upon which duties or taxes have been actually paid, shall be assessed on the increased value only when curried or finished.

Patent, enamelled, and japanned leather.

On patent, enamelled, and japanned leather and skins of every description, a tax of five per centum ad valorem: *Provided*, That when a tax or duty has been paid on the leather in the rough, the tax shall be assessed and paid only on the increased value.

Oil-dressed leather, &c.

On oil-dressed leather, a tax of five per centum ad valorem.

Leather in the rough.

On leather of all descriptions, tanned or partially tanned, in the rough, a tax of five per centum ad valorem.

Leather curried or finished.

Proviso.

On leather of all descriptions, curried or finished, a tax of five per centum ad valorem: *Provided*, That all leather in the rough upon which duties or taxes have been actually paid, shall be assessed on the increased value only when curried or finished.

Wine from grapes, currants, rhubarb, &c.

On all liquors known or denominated as wine, not made from grapes, currants, rhubarb, or berries, produced by being rectified or mixed with other spirits, or into which any matter whatever may be infused to be sold as wine, or by any other name, and not otherwise provided for in this act, a tax of fifty cents per gallon: *Provided*, That the return, assessment, collection, and the time of collection of the taxes on such wines shall be subject to the regulations of the Commissioner of Internal Revenue. And any person who shall willingly and knowingly sell or offer for sale any such wine made after the passage of this act, upon which the tax herein imposed has not been paid, or which has been fraudulently evaded, shall, upon conviction thereof, be subject to a fine of five

Proviso.

Penalty.

hundred dollars or to imprisonment not exceeding two years, at the discretion of the court.

Cloth.

On cloth and all textile or knitted or felted articles or fabrics of cotton, wool, or other materials, before the same has been dyed, printed, or bleached, and on all cloth painted, enamelled, shirred, tarred, varnished, or oiled, a tax of five per centum ad valorem.

Thread and twine.

On thread and twine, a tax of five per centum ad valorem.

Clothing manufactured or produced for sale by weaving, &c. Silk hats, bonnets and hoop skirts. Parts of clothing; trimmings. Clothing made from India-rubber, gutta-percha, fur, &c. Proviso.

On articles of clothing manufactured or produced for sale by weaving, knitting, or felting; on silk hats, bonnets, and hoop-skirts; on articles manufactured or produced for sale as constituent parts of clothing, or for trimming or ornamenting the same, and on articles of wearing apparel manufactured or produced for sale from India-rubber, gutta-percha, or from fur, or fur skins dressed with the fur on, a tax of five per centum ad valorem: *Provided*, That on all articles made of fur, the value of which shall not exceed twenty dollars, a tax of two per centum only shall be paid.

Boots, shoes, and shoe strings. Proviso.

On boots, shoes, and shoe-strings, a tax of two per centum ad valorem, to be paid by every person making, manufacturing, or producing for sale boots or shoes, or furnishing the materials or any part thereof, and employing others to make, manufacture, or produce them: *Provided*, That any boot or shoemaker making boots or shoes to order as custom work only, and not for general sale, and whose work, exclusive of the materials, does not exceed annually in value one thousand dollars, shall be exempt from this tax.

Clothing not otherwise assessed and taxed. Proviso. Tailors, &c., making custom work only, and whose work does not exceed annually $1,000, exempt. Articles of dress made or trimmed by milliners or dressmakers for the wear of women and children exempt. Proviso. Artificial flowers.

On clothing, gloves, mittens, moccasins, caps, felt hats, and other articles of dress for the wear of men, women, and children, not otherwise assessed and taxed, a tax of two per centum ad valorem, to be paid by every person making, manufacturing, or producing for sale clothing, gloves, mittens, moccasins, caps, felt hats, and other articles of dress, or furnishing the materials or any part thereof, and employing others to make, manufacture, or produce them: *Provided*, That any tailor, or any maker of gloves, mittens, moccasins, caps, felt hats, or other articles of dress to order as custom work only, and not for general sale, and whose work, exclusive of the materials, does not exceed annually in value one thousand dollars, shall be exempt from this tax; and articles of dress made or trimmed by milliners or dress-makers for the wear of women and children shall also be exempt from this tax: *Provided*, That the branching into sprays, branches, or wreaths of artificial flowers, on which an impost or internal tax has already been paid, shall not be considered a manufacture within the meaning of this act.

Paper not otherwise provided for.

On paper not otherwise herein provided for, a tax of three per centum ad valorem.

Manufactures of cotton, wool, &c. Proviso. Tax assessed only on increased value of cloths, &c., on which a tax has been paid before same were dyed. Proviso in regard to thread, yarn, &c.

On all manufactures not otherwise provided for, of cotton, wool, silk, worsted, hemp, jute, India-rubber, gutta-percha, wood, glass, pottery ware, leather, paper, iron, steel, lead, tin, copper, zinc, brass, gold, silver, horn, ivory, bone, bristles, wholly or in part, or of other materials, a tax of five per centum ad valorem: *Provided*, That on all cloths or articles dyed, printed, or bleached, on which a tax or duty shall have been paid before the same were so dyed, printed, or bleached, the said tax of five per centum shall be assessed only upon the increased value thereof: *And provided further*, That any cloth or fabrics or articles as aforesaid, when made of thread, yarn, or warps, imported, or upon which an internal tax shall have been assessed and paid, shall be assessed and pay a tax on the increased value only thereof; and when made wholly by the same manufacturer, shall be subject to a tax only of five per centum ad valorem: *And provided further*, That brown earthen and common or gray stoneware shall be subject to a tax of two and one-half per centum ad valorem, and no more.

Proviso in regard to earthenware.

Diamonds, &c.

Proviso in regard to imported diamonds.

On all diamonds, emeralds, precious stones and imitations thereof, and all other jewelry, a tax of five per centum ad valorem: *Provided*, That when diamonds, emeralds, precious stones, or imitations thereof, imported from foreign countries, and upon which import duties have been paid, shall be set or reset in gold or any other material, the tax shall be assessed and paid only upon the value of the settings.

Bullion.

Shall be stamped under regulations.

What sales, &c., of, are unlawful.

Penalty.

Gold or silver not to be wrought until stamped.

Nor to be exported.

Penalty.

Proviso.

On bullion in lump, ingot, bar, or otherwise, a tax of one-half of one per centum ad valorem, to be paid by the assayer of the same, who shall stamp the product of the assay as the Commissioner of Internal Revenue, under the direction of the Secretary of the Treasury, may prescribe by general regulations. And all sales, transfers, exchanges, transportation, and exportation of gold or silver assayed at any mint of the United States, or by any private assayer, unless stamped as prescribed by general regulations, as aforesaid, are hereby declared unlawful; and every person or corporation who shall sell, transfer, transport, exchange, export, or deal in the same, shall be subject to a penalty of one thousand dollars for each offence, and to a fine not exceeding that sum, and to imprisonment for a term not exceeding two years nor less than six months. No jeweller, worker or artificer in gold or silver shall use either of those metals except it shall have first been stamped as aforesaid, as required by this act. No person or corporation shall export or cause to be exported from the United States any gold or silver in its natural state, not coined, assayed, or stamped, as aforesaid; and for every violation of this paragraph every offender shall be subject to the penalties herein provided: *Provided*, That nothing herein contained shall apply to the reworking of old gold or silver in lump, ingot, or bar, as aforesaid.

Snuff.

On snuff, manufactured of tobacco or any substitute for tobacco, ground, dry, or damp, pickled, scented, or otherwise, of all descriptions, when prepared for use, a tax of forty cents per pound.

Manufactured tobacco not otherwise provided for.

On cavendish, plug, twist, and all other kinds of manufactured tobacco, not herein otherwise provided for, a tax of forty cents per pound.

Tobacco twisted by hand, &c.

On tobacco twisted by hand, or reduced from leaf into a condition to be consumed without the use of any machine or instrument, and without being pressed, sweetened, or otherwise prepared, and on fine-cut shorts, a tax of thirty cents per pound.

Fine cut chewing tobacco.

On fine-cut chewing tobacco, whether manufactured with the stems in or not, or however sold, whether loose, in bulk, or in rolls, packages, papers, wrappers, or boxes, a tax of forty cents per pound.

Smoking tobacco, sweetened, &c.

On smoking tobacco, sweetened, stemmed, or butted, a tax of forty cents per pound.

Not sweetened. Stems.

On smoking tobacco of all kinds, not sweetened, nor stemmed, nor butted, including that made of stems, or in part of stems, and imitations thereof, a tax of fifteen cents per pound.

Cigarettes, cheroots and short-sixes, market value not over $8 per thousand.

On cigarettes, or small cigars, made of tobacco enclosed in a wrapper, or binder, and not over three and a half inches in length, and on cigars made with twisted heads, and on cheroots, and on cigars known as short-sixes, the market value of which is not over eight dollars per thousand, a tax of two dollars per thousand.

On all cheroots, cigarettes, and cigars, the market value of which is over eight dollars and not over twelve dollars per thousand, a tax of four dollars per thousand.

Over $8 and not over $12 per thousand.

On all cheroots, cigarettes, and cigars, the market value of which is over twelve dollars per thousand, a tax of four dollars per thousand, and, in addition thereto, twenty per centum ad valorem on the market value thereof. And the Commissioner of Internal Revenue, with the approval of the Secretary of the Treasury, may prescribe such regulations for the inspection and valuation of cigars, cheroots, and cigarettes, and the collection of the tax thereon, as shall, in his judgment, be most effective for the prevention of inequalities and frauds in the payment of such tax. And, in addition to other regulations, it shall be the duty of the inspector or assessor who appraises any cigars, cigarettes, or cheroots to examine the manufacturer thereof or his agent under oath, which oath shall be administered by the inspecting and appraising officer, and reduced to writing, and signed by such manufacturer or his agent, with a view to ascertaining whether such manufacturer has any interest, direct or indirect, in any sale that has been made, or any resale to be made of said cigars, cigarettes, or cheroots, by the concealment of which he seeks to obtain a false, fraudulent, or deceptive appraisement.

Over $12 per thousand.

Regulations to be prescribed for the inspection and valuation, and the collection of the tax.

Manufacturer to be examined under oath.

95. That on all wines, liquors, or compounds known or denominated as wine, made in imitation of sparkling wine or champagne, and put up in bottles in imitation of any imported wine, or with the pretence of being imported wine, or wine of foreign growth or manufacture, there shall be levied and paid a tax of six dollars per dozen bottles, each bottle containing more than one pint, and not more than one quart, or three dollars per dozen bottles, each bottle containing not more than one pint; said tax to be paid by the manufacturer, owner, or person having possession thereof; and the returns, assessment, collection, and time of collection of the tax on such imitation wines shall be subject to the regulations of the Commissioner of Internal Revenue. And any person who shall wilfully and knowingly sell or offer for sale any such wine made after this act takes effect, upon which the tax herein imposed has not been paid, or which has been fraudulently evaded, shall, upon conviction thereof, be subject to a penalty of one thousand dollars, or to imprisonment not exceeding one year, at the discretion of the court.

13 July, 1866, § 36.

Imitation wines, $6 per dozen quarts.

$3 per dozen pints.

Manufacturer, owner, or possessor to pay the same.

Assessment and collection thereof.

Penalty.

c. RETURNS AND COLLECTION OF TAXES.

96. That whenever any manufactured articles, goods, wares, or merchandise, on which an excise or impost duty has been paid, and which are not specially provided for, are increased in value by being polished, painted, varnished, waxed, oiled, gilded, electrotyped, galvanized, plated, framed, ground, pressed, colored, dyed, trimmed, ornamented, or otherwise more completely finished or fitted for use or sale, without changing the original character or purposes for which the same are intended to be used, there shall be levied, collected, and paid a tax of five per centum ad valorem upon the amount of such increased value, to be ascertained by deducting from the value of the finished article when sold, or removed for sale, delivery, or consumption, the cost or value of the original article to the person, firm, or company, liable to the duty imposed upon the increased value thereof. The increasing of values in the manner aforesaid shall be deemed manufacturing, and any person, firm, company, or corporation engaged therein shall be liable to all the provisions of law for the collection of internal duties relating

30 June, 1864, § 95.

Tax on increased value in certain cases.

Increased value, how ascertained.

Increasing of values deemed manufacturing.

to manufactures as to licenses, returns, payment of taxes, liens, fines, penalties, and forfeitures.

30 June, 1864, § 82.

Definition of person or persons liable to tax under this act.

97. That every individual, partnership, firm, association, or corporation, (and any word or words in this act indicating or referring to person or persons shall be taken to mean and include partnerships, firms, associations, or corporations, when not otherwise designated or manifestly incompatible with the intent thereof,) shall comply with the following requirements, that is to say:

Manufacturer to furnish a sworn statement before commencing business as to place, articles manufactured, proposed market, &c.

First. Before commencing, or, if already commenced, before continuing, any manufacture liable to be assessed under the provisions of this act, and which shall not be differently provided for elsewhere, every person shall furnish, without previous demand therefor, to the assistant assessor a statement, subscribed and sworn to, or affirmed, setting forth the place where the manufacture is to be carried on, and the principal place of business for sales, the name of the manufactured article, the proposed market for the same, whether foreign or domestic, and generally the kind and quality manufactured or proposed to be manufactured.

To make monthly return of products and sales in manner prescribed by Commissioner.

Second. He shall within ten days after the first day of each and every month, or on or before a day prescribed by the Commissioner of Internal Revenue, make return under oath or affirmation of the products and sales or delivery of such manufacture in form and detail as may be required, from time to time, by the Commissioner of Internal Revenue.

Returns made under oath.

Third. All such returns, statements, descriptions, memoranda, oaths, and affirmations, shall be in form, scope, and detail as may be prescribed, from time to time, by the Commissioner of Internal Revenue.

30 June, 1864, § 87.
3 March, 1865, § 1.
13 July, 1866, § 9.

Manufacturer of tobacco, snuff, or cigars required to make additional statement.

98. That any person, firm, company, or corporation who may now be engaged in the manufacture of tobacco, snuff, or cigars, or who shall hereafter commence or engage in such manufacture, before commencing, or, if already commenced, before continuing, such manufacture for which they may be liable to be assessed under the provisions of law, shall, in addition to a compliance with all other provisions of law, furnish to the assessor or assistant assessor a statement, subscribed under oath or affirmation, accurately setting forth the place, and, if in a city, the street and number of the street where the manufacturing is, or is to be, carried on, the name and description of the manufactured article, and, if the same shall be manufactured for or to be sold and delivered to any other person or party, the name and residence and business or occupation of the person or party for whom the said article is to be manufactured or to whom it is to be delivered, and generally the kind and quality manufactured or proposed to be manufactured;

And shall give a bond.

and shall give a bond to the United States, with one or more sureties to be approved by the collector of the district, in the sum of three thousand dollars for each cutting machine kept for use, in the sum of one thousand dollars for each screw-press kept for use in making plug or pressed tobacco, in the sum of five thousand dollars for each hydraulic press kept for use, in the sum of one thousand dollars for each snuff mull kept for use, and in the sum of one hundred dollars for each person employed by said person, firm, company, or corporation in making cigars, conditioned that he will comply with all the requirements of law in regard to the manufacture of tobacco, snuff, or cigars; that he will not employ others to manufacture cigars who have not obtained the requisite permit for making cigars; that he will not engage in any attempt, by himself or by collusion with others, to defraud the government of any tax on any manufacture of tobacco, snuff, or cigars; that he will render truly and correctly all the returns, statements, and inventories prescribed for manufacturers of tobacco, snuff, and cigars; that whenever he shall add to the number of cutting machines, presses, snuff mulls, or cigar-makers, used or employed by him, he will immediately give notice thereof to the collector who holds the bond, that he will pay to the collector of the district all the taxes which may or should be assessed and due on any tobacco, snuff, or cigars so manufactured, and that he will not knowingly sell, purchase, or receive for sale any such tobacco, snuff, or cigars which have not been inspected, branded, or stamped as required by law, or upon which the tax has not been paid if it has accrued or become payable. And the said bond may be renewed or changed from time to time, in regard to the sureties or amount thereof, according to the discretion of the collector, under the instructions of the Commissioner of Internal Revenue. And every person, firm, company, or corporation aforesaid shall exhibit, whenever demanded by any officer of internal revenue, a certificate from the collector, who is hereby authorized and directed to issue the same, setting forth the kind and number of machines, presses, snuff mulls, and number of cigar-makers for which the bond has been given. And any person, firm, or corporation manufacturing tobacco, snuff, or cigars of any description without first furnishing the bond in the cases herein required, shall be subject to a fine of three hundred dollars, and in addition thereto, upon conviction thereof, shall be liable to imprisonment for a term not exceeding one year, at the discretion of the court.

Conditions.

Bond may be renewed.

Shall exhibit certificate from collector.

Penalty for non-compliance with this section.

99. That it shall be the duty of the assistant assessor of each district to keep a record, in a book or books to be provided for the purpose, to be open to the inspection of any person upon reasonable request, of the name of any and every person, firm, company, or corporation who may be engaged in the manufacture of tobacco, snuff, or cigars in his district, together with the place where such manufacture is carried on and the place of residence of the person or persons engaged therein; and the assistant assessor shall enter in said record, under the name of each manufacturer, an abstract of his monthly returns; and each assessor shall keep a similar record for the entire district.

30 June, 1864, § 88.
13 July, 1866, § 9.

Assistant assessor to keep a book containing names of all persons in his district having permits.

100. That any person, firm, company, or corporation, manufacturing or producing goods, wares, and merchandise, sold or removed for consumption or use, upon which taxes are imposed by law, shall, in their return of the value and quantity, render an account of the full amount of actual sales made by the manufacturer, producer, or agent thereof, and shall state whether any part, and if so, what part, of said goods, wares, and merchandise, has been consumed or used by the owner, owners, or agent, or used for the production of another manufacture or product, together with the market value of the same at the time of such use or consumption; whether such goods, wares, and merchandise were shipped for a foreign port or consigned to auction or commission merchants, other than agents, for sale; and shall make a return according to the value at the place of shipment, when shipped for a foreign port, or according to the value at the place of manufacture or production, when removed for use or consumption, or consigned to others than agents of the manufacturer or producer. The value and quantity of the goods, wares, and merchandise required to be stated as

30 June, 1864, § 86.
3 March, 1865, § 1.
13 July, 1866, § 9.

Manufacturers shall render an account of the full amount of actual sales.

Quantity consumed.

Quantity used for another manufacture.

Return to be made according to the value at place of shipment or place of production.

aforesaid shall be estimated by the actual sales made by the manufacturer or by his agent. And where such goods, wares, and merchandise have been removed for consumption or for delivery to others, or placed on shipboard, or are no longer within the custody or control of the manufacturer or his agent, not being in his factory, store, or warehouse, the value shall be estimated at the average of the market value of the like goods, wares, and merchandise at the time when the same became liable to tax.

Value to be estimated how. In certain cases.

30 June, 1864, § 90. 3 March, 1865, § 1. 13 July, 1866, § 9.

Manufacturer required to make an inventory of the quantity owned by him on the first day of January in each year.

101. That any person, firm, company, or corporation, now or hereafter engaged in the manufacture of tobacco, snuff, or cigars, of any description whatsoever, shall be, and hereby is, required to make out and deliver to the assistant assessor of the assessment district a true statement or inventory of the quantity of each of the different kinds of tobacco, snuff-flour, snuff, cigars, tinfoil, licorice, and stems, held or owned by him or them on the first day of January of each year, or at the time of commencing business under this act, setting forth what portion of said goods was manufactured or produced by him or them, and what was purchased from others, whether chewing, smoking, fine-cut, shorts, pressed, plug, snuff-flour or prepared snuff, or cigars, which statement or inventory shall be verified by the oath or affirmation of such person or persons, and be in manner and form as prescribed by the Commissioner of Internal Revenue; and every such person, company, or corporation shall keep in book form an accurate account of all the articles aforesaid thereafter purchased by him or them, the quantity of tobacco, snuff, snuff-flour, or cigars, of whatever description, manufactured, sold, consumed, or removed for consumption or sale, or removed from the place of manufacture; and he or they shall, on or before the tenth day of each month, furnish to the assistant assessor of the district a true and accurate abstract of all such purchases and sales, or removals, which abstract shall be verified by oath or affirmation; and in case of refusal or neglect to deliver the inventory, or keep the account, or furnish the abstract aforesaid, he or they shall forfeit the sum of five hundred dollars, to be recovered with costs of suit. And it shall be the duty of any manufacturer or vender of tinfoil, or other material used in manufacturing tobacco, snuff, or cigars, on demand of any officer of internal revenue, to render to such officer a correct statement, verified by oath or affirmation, of the quantity and amount of tinfoil or other materials sold or delivered to any person or persons named in such demand; and in case of refusal or neglect to render such statement, or of cause to believe such statement to be incorrect or fraudulent, the assessor of the district may cause an examination of persons, books, and papers to be made in the same manner as provided in the fourteenth section of this act. And all the provisions of law relating to manufacturers generally, so far as applicable and not inconsistent herewith, shall be held to apply to the manufacture of tobacco, snuff, and cigars: *Provided*, That the tax imposed upon the manufacturer of tobacco, snuff, and cigars, shall be held to accrue upon the sale or removal from the place of manufacture, unless removed to a bonded warehouse: *Provided further*, That manufactured tobacco, snuff, or cigars, whether of domestic manufacture or imported, may be transferred, without payment of the tax, to a bonded warehouse established in conformity with law and treasury regulations, under such rules and regulations and upon the execution of such transportation bonds or other security as may

Account to be kept in a book in manner as prescribed by the Commissioner.

A copy of entries to be furnished the assistant assessor.

Penalty for neglect.

Tinfoil used in covering tobacco.

Examination as in section 14, June 30, 1864.

General provisions of law applicable to tobacco, &c.

Tax to accrue on removal from place of manufacture, &c.

Transfer may be made to a bonded warehouse without payment of the duty.

be prescribed by the Commissioner of Internal Revenue, subject to the approval of the Secretary of the Treasury, said bonds or other security to be taken by the collector of the district from which such removal is made; and may be transported from such a warehouse to any other bonded warehouse established as aforesaid, and may be withdrawn from bonded warehouse for consumption on payment of the tax, or removed for export to a foreign country without payment of tax, in conformity with the provisions of law relating to the removal of distilled spirits, all the rules, regulations, and conditions of which, so far as applicable, shall apply to tobacco, snuff, or cigars in bonded warehouse. And no drawback shall in any case be allowed upon any manufactured tobacco, snuff, or cigars.

Regulations for the removal of distilled spirits to be observed in regard to the removal of tobacco, so far as applicable.

No drawback to be allowed.

102. That all lists or returns required to be made monthly, by any person, firm, company, corporation, or party whatsoever, liable to tax, shall be made on or before the tenth day of each and every month, and the tax assessed or due thereon shall be certified or returned by the assessor to the collector on or before the last day of each and every month. And all lists or returns required to be made quarterly, and all other lists or returns for which no provision is otherwise made, shall be made on or before the tenth day of each and every month in which said list or return is required to be made, or succeeding the time when the tax may be due and liable to be assessed, and the tax thereon shall be certified or returned as herein provided for monthly lists or returns. And the tax shall be due and payable on or before the last day of each and every month. And in case said tax is not paid on or before the last day of each and every month the collector shall add ten per centum thereto: *Provided*, That notice of the time when said tax shall become due and payable shall be given in such manner as shall be prescribed by the Commissioner of Internal Revenue; and if said tax shall not be paid on or before the last day of the month as aforesaid, it shall be the duty of said collector to demand payment thereof, with ten per centum additional thereto in the manner prescribed by law; and if said tax and ten per centum additional are not paid within ten days from and after such demand thereof, it shall be lawful for the collector or his deputy to make distraint therefor, as provided by law, and so much of section eighty-three of the act of June thirtieth, eighteen hundred and sixty-four, as amended by the act of March third, eighteen hundred and sixty-five, as relates to the time of payment and collection of tax, is hereby repealed; and in all cases of neglect to make such lists or returns, or in case of false and fraudulent returns, the provisions of existing law, as amended by this act, shall be applicable thereto.

13 July, 1866, § 11.

When monthly returns to be made

When tax to be certified to collector.

Quarterly returns likewise.

When payable.

If not paid ten per cent. to be added.

But notice to be given.

Demand to be made.

Distraint.

Part of sec. 83, act June 30, 1864, repealed.

In case of neglect.

103. That in case of the manufacture and sale or production and sale, consumption or delivery, of any goods, wares, merchandise, or articles as hereinafter mentioned, without compliance on the part of the party manufacturing or producing the same with all the requirements and regulations prescribed by law in relation thereto, the assistant assessor may, upon such information as he may have, assume and estimate the amount and value of such manufactures or products, and upon such assumed amount assess the duties, and add thereto fifty per centum; and said duties shall be collected in like manner as in case the provisions of this act in relation thereto had been complied with, and to such articles all the foregoing provisions for liens, fines, penalties, and forfeitures shall in like manner apply.

30 June, 1864, § 85.

The assistant assessor to assume and estimate duties in certain cases.

30 June, 1864, § 91. 3 March, 1865, § 1. 13 July, 1866, § 9.

Tobacco, snuff, and cigars to be inspected.

Package to be marked or stamp'd

Fees of inspector.

Penalties for fraudulent use of inspection marks.

104. That all manufactured tobacco, snuff, or cigars shall, before the same is used or removed for consumption, be inspected by an inspector appointed under the provisions of law, who shall mark or affix a stamp upon the box or other package containing such tobacco, snuff, or cigars in a manner to be prescribed by the Commissioner of Internal Revenue, denoting the kind, quantity, or number contained in each package, with the date of inspection and the name of the inspector, and the collection district. The fees of such inspector shall in all cases be paid by the owner of the manufactured tobacco, snuff, or cigars so inspected. And any person who shall affix upon any box or other package containing such tobacco, snuff, or cigars any mark or stamp which shall be false or fraudulent in any of the particulars before recited in this section, or shall, with intent to defraud the United States, or to cause the same to be defrauded, change in any manner such stamp or mark, or such box or package so marked or stamped, shall be liable to a fine of not less than fifty dollars, or to imprisonment not exceeding two years, for every such offence. And all cigars manufactured after the passage of this act shall be packed in boxes or paper packages. And any manufactured tobacco, snuff, and cigars, whether of domestic manufacture or imported, which shall be sold or pass out of the hands of the manufacturer or importer, except into a bonded warehouse, without the inspection marks or stamps affixed, unless otherwise provided, shall be forfeited, and may be seized wherever found, and shall be sold, and the proceeds of such sale shall be distributed between the United States and the informer, if there be any, as provided by law. The Commissioner of Internal Revenue shall keep an account of all stamps delivered to the several inspectors; and said inspectors shall also keep an account of all stamps by them used or placed upon boxes containing cigars, and of all tobacco, snuff, and cigars inspected, and the name of the person, firm, or company for whom the same were so inspected, and shall return to the assessor of the district a separate and distinct account of the same, and also return to the said Commissioner, on demand, all stamps not otherwise accounted for, and shall give a bond for a faithful performance of all the duties to which he may be assigned, and to return or account for all stamps which may be placed in his hands.

All cigars to be packed in boxes.

If sold without inspection, to be forfeited.

Account to be kept of stamps.

Inspector to give bond.

30 June, 1864, § 92. March 3, 1865, § 1. July 13, 1866, § 9.

Penalty when any one other than the manufacturer parts with the possession of tobacco, snuff, or cigars, on which duties imposed by law have not been paid.

Penalty for receiving tobacco, snuff, or cigars under certain circumstances.

Penalty for receiving tobacco, snuff, or cigars from a manufacturer who has not paid the special tax.

Manufacturer to procure permit.

105. That if any person other than the manufacturer shall sell, or consign, or remove for sale, or part with the possession of any manufactured tobacco, snuff, or cigars upon which the taxes imposed by law have not been paid, with the knowledge thereof, such person shall be liable to a penalty of one hundred dollars for each offence. And any person who shall purchase or receive for sale any such tobacco, snuff, or cigars, which has not been inspected, branded, or stamped as required by law, or upon which the tax has not been paid, if it has accrued or become payable, with knowledge thereof, shall be liable to a penalty of fifty dollars for each and every offence. And any person who shall purchase or receive for sale any such tobacco, snuff, or cigars from any manufacturer who has not paid the special tax, shall be liable for each and every offence to a penalty of one hundred dollars, and, in addition thereto, a forfeiture of all the articles, as aforesaid, so purchased or received, or the full value thereof. And every person, before making any cigars after the passage of this act, shall apply for and procure from the assistant assessor of the district in which he resides a permit authorizing such persons to carry on the

trade of cigar-making, for which permit he shall pay said assistant assessor the sum of twenty-five cents. And every person employed or working at the business of cigar-making in any other district than that in which he or she is a resident shall, before making any cigars in such other district, present said permit to the assistant assessor of the district where so employed or working, and procure the indorsement of said assistant assessor thereon, authorizing said business in said district, for which indorsement the assistant assessor shall be entitled to receive from the applicant the sum of ten cents. And it shall be the duty of every assistant assessor, upon application of any person residing in his district, to furnish a permit, or to indorse upon the permit of the applicant, if resident in another district, authority to pursue the trade of cigar-making within the proper district of such assistant assessor; and said assistant assessor shall keep a record of all permits granted or indorsed by him, showing the date of each permit, the name, residence, and place of employment of the party named therein, the name and district of the officer who originally granted the same, or who may have made any subsequent indorsements thereon, and the name or names of the party or parties by whom the person named in such permit is employed, or, if working for himself, stating such fact; and every person making cigars shall keep an accurate account in a book of all the cigars made by him, for whom, and their kind or quality; and, if made for any other person, shall state in said account the name of the person for whom the same were made, and his place of business, and shall, on the first Monday of every month, deliver to the assistant assessor of the district a copy of such account, verified by oath or affirmation that the same is true and correct. And if any person shall make any cigars without procuring such permit, or the proper indorsements thereon, or neglect to keep such account in book-form, he shall be punished by a fine of five dollars for each day he shall so offend, or by imprisonment for such time as the court may order for each day's offence, not exceeding thirty days in the whole, upon any one conviction. And if any person making cigars shall fail to make the return herein required, or shall make a false return, he shall be punished by a fine not exceeding one hundred dollars, or by imprisonment not exceeding thirty days. And any person may apply to the assistant assessor or inspector of the district to have any cigars of his own manufacture counted; and on receiving a certificate of the number, for which such fee as may be prescribed by the Commissioner of Internal Revenue shall be paid by the owner thereof, may sell and deliver such cigars to any purchaser, in the presence of said assistant assessor or inspector, in bulk or unpacked, without payment of the tax. A copy of the certificate shall be retained by the assistant assessor, or by the inspector, who shall return the same to the assessor of the district. The purchaser shall pack such cigars in boxes or paper packages, and have the same inspected and marked or stamped according to the provisions of law, and shall make a return of the same, as inspected, to the assistant assessor of the district, wherein the same were manufactured, and, unless removed to a bonded warehouse, shall pay the taxes on such cigars within fifteen days after purchasing them, to the collector of the district wherein they were manufactured, and before the same have been removed from the store or building of such purchaser, or from his possession; and if such purchaser shall neglect for more than fifteen days to pack and have such cigars

Fee for issuing.

Manufacturer in district other than place of residence to procure indorsement of permit.

Fee.

Assessor to furnish and indorse permits.

To keep a record thereof.

Manufacturer to keep an account.

To make a monthly return.

Penalty for making cigars without permit, &c

For making false return.

Manufacturer may have cigars counted, &c.

Fee.

May sell and deliver.

Copy of certificate to be retained and returned.

Purchaser shall pack, &c.

Shall return and pay tax.

Penalties for neglect.

duly inspected, and to pay the taxes thereon according to law, he shall be fined not exceeding five hundred dollars, and be imprisoned not exceeding six months, at the discretion of the court, and the cigars may be seized by the collector and shall be forfeited to the United States. And if any person, firm, company, or corporation shall employ or procure any person to make any cigars, who has not the permit or the indorsement thereon required by this act, he shall be punished by a fine of ten dollars for each day he shall so employ such person, or by imprisonment not exceeding ten days. And if any person shall be found making cigars without such permit, or the indorsement thereon, the collector of the district may seize any cigars, or tobacco for making cigars, which may be found in possession of such person, and the same shall be forfeited to the United States and sold; and the proceeds of such sale shall be distributed between the United States and the informer, if there be any, as provided by law.

Penalty for employing persons without permit.

For making without permit.

Proceeds to be distributed.

30 June, 1864, § 83. 3 March, 1865, § 1. 13 July, 1866, § 11.

Manufacturer paying the duty may have lien on goods.

106. * * * * And in all cases of goods manufactured or produced in whole or in part upon commission, or where the material is furnished by one party and manufactured by another, if the manufacturer shall be required to pay under this act the tax hereby imposed, such person or persons so paying the same shall be entitled to collect the amount thereof of the owner or owners, and shall have a lien for the amount thus paid upon the produced or manufactured goods.

30 June, 1864, § 89. 13 July, 1866, § 9.

Where the material is furnished by one party and manufactured by another.

Penalty in case of fraud or collusion.

107. That in all cases where tobacco, snuff, or cigars, of any description, are manufactured, in whole or in part, upon commission or shares, or where the material from which any such articles are made, or are to be made, is furnished by one party and manufactured by another, or where the material is furnished or sold by one party with an understanding or contract with another that the manufactured article is to be received in payment therefor or any part thereof, the tax imposed by law thereon may be assessed upon the party for whom the same was made, or to whom the same was delivered as aforesaid, or upon the person or party who made the same, as the assessor shall deem best for the collection of the revenue. And in case of fraud on the part of either of said parties in respect to said manufacture, or of any collusion on their part with intent to defraud the revenue, such material and manufactured articles shall be liable to forfeiture; and such articles shall be liable to be assessed the highest rates of tax imposed by law upon any article of like kind.

30 June, 1864, § 84. 3 March, 1865, § 1.

Proceedings for neglect or refusal to pay duties.

Forfeiture.

Seizure.

Proceedings.

108. That for neglect or refusal to pay the duties provided by law on manufactured articles, or articles produced as aforesaid, the goods, wares, and merchandise manufactured or produced and unsold by or not passed out of the possession of such manufacturer or producer shall be forfeited to the United States, and may be sold or disposed of for the benefit of the same, in manner as shall be prescribed by the Commissioner of Internal Revenue, under the direction of the Secretary of the Treasury. In such case the collector or deputy collector may take possession of said articles, and may maintain such possession in the premises and buildings where they may have been manufactured, or deposited, or may be. He shall summon, giving notice of not less than two nor more than ten days, the parties in possession of said goods, enjoining them to appear before the assessor or assistant assessor, at a day and hour in such summons fixed, then and there to show cause, if any there be, why, for such neglect or refusal, such arti-

cles should not be declared forfeited to the United States. The manufacturers or producers thereof shall be deemed to be the parties interested, if the articles shall be, at the time of taking such possession, upon the premises where manufactured or produced; if they shall at such time have been removed from the place of manufacture or production, the parties interested shall be deemed to be the persons or parties in whose custody or possession the articles shall be found. Such summons shall be served upon such parties in person, or by leaving a copy thereof at the place of abode or business of the party to whom the same may be directed. In case no such party or place can be found, which fact shall be determined by the collector's return on the summons, such notice, in the nature of a summons, shall be given by advertisement for the term of three weeks in one newspaper in the county nearest to the place of such sale. If at or before such hearing such duties shall not have been paid, and the assessor or assistant assessor shall adjudge the summons and notice, service and return of the same to be sufficient, the said articles shall be by him declared forfeit, and shall be sold, disposed of, or turned over by the collector to the use of any department of the government as may be directed by the Secretary of the Treasury, who may require of any officer of the government into whose possession the same may be turned over the proper voucher therefor; and the proceeds of sale of said articles, if any there be after deducting the duties and additions thereon, together with the fees, costs, and expenses of all proceedings incident to the seizure and sale, to be determined by said Commissioner, shall be refunded and paid to the owner, or, if he cannot be found, to the manufacturer or producer in whose custody the articles were when seized, as the said Commissioner may deem just, by draft on the same or some other collector; or if the said articles are turned over without sale to the use of any department of the government, the excess of the value of said articles, after deducting the amount of the duties, additions, fees, costs, and expenses accrued thereon when turned over as aforesaid, shall be refunded and paid by the said department to the owner, or, if he cannot be found, to the manufacturer or producer in whose custody or possession the said articles were when seized as aforesaid. The Commissioner of Internal Revenue, with the approval of the Secretary of the Treasury, may review any such case of forfeiture and do justice in the premises. If the forfeiture shall have been wrongly declared, and sale made, the Secretary is hereby authorized, in case the specific articles cannot be restored to the party aggrieved in as good order and condition as when seized, to make up to such party in money his loss and damage from the contingent fund of his department. Immediate notice of any seizure of manufactured articles or products shall be given to the Commissioner of Internal Revenue by the collector or deputy collector, who shall also make return of his proceedings to the said Commissioner after he shall have sold or otherwise disposed of the articles or products so forfeited; and the assessor or assistant assessor shall also make return of his proceedings relating to such forfeiture to the said Commissioner. And any violation of, or refusal to comply with, the provisions of the eighty-second section of this act, shall be good cause for seizure and forfeiture, substantially in manner as detailed in this section; but before forfeiture shall be declared by virtue of the provisions of this section, the amount of duties which may be

Parties interested.

Summons, how served.

Declaration of forfeiture and disposal of property.

Proceeds, after deducting duties and all expenses, to be paid to the owner.

Or to the manufacturer or producer.

Under certain circumstances, the Commiss'ner, with the approval of the Secretary, may review proceedings.

Immediate returns of seizures to be made to Commissioner.

Violation of 82d section 30 June, 1864, good cause for seizure. Vide § 97 ante.

The amount of duties to be ascertained before forfeiture.

due from the person whose manufactures or products are seized, shall first be ascertained in the manner prescribed in the eighty-fifth section of this act; and such violation or refusal to comply shall further make any party so violating or refusing to comply liable to a fine or penalty of five hundred dollars, to be recovered in manner and form as provided in this act. Articles which the collector may adjudge perishable may be sold or disposed of before declaration of forfeiture. Said sales shall be made at public auction, and notice thereof shall be given as the said Commissioner shall prescribe.

Penalty.

Perishable articles, how disposed of.

2. COTTON.

13 July, 1866, § 1; vide 30 June, 1864, § 94.

Tax three cents per pound.

Four per cent. tare allowed.

Tax to be a lien.

No drawback when exported raw or unmanufactured.

No tax on imported.

109. That on and after the first day of August, eighteen hundred and sixty-six, in lieu of the taxes on unmanufactured cotton, as provided in "An act to provide internal revenue to support the government, to pay interest on the public debt, and for other purposes," approved June thirtieth, eighteen hundred and sixty-four, as amended by the act of March third, eighteen hundred and sixty-five, there shall be paid by the producer, owner, or holder, upon all cotton produced within the United States, and upon which no tax has been levied, paid, or collected, a tax of three cents per pound, as hereinafter provided; and the weight of such cotton shall be ascertained by deducting four per centum for tare from the gross weight of each bale or package; and such tax shall be and remain a lien thereon, in the possession of any person whomsoever, from the time when this law takes effect, or such cotton is produced, as aforesaid, until the same shall have been paid; and no drawback shall, in any case, be allowed on raw or unmanufactured cotton of any tax paid thereon when exported in the raw or unmanufactured condition. But no tax shall be imposed upon any cotton imported from other countries, and on which an import duty shall have been paid.

13 July, 1866, § 2; vide June 30, 1864, § 177.

Tax to be levied on producer, owner, or holder.

To be paid in the district in which produced and before removal.

Evidence of payment of tax to be marked on package or bale.

Collector to give permit.

To keep record.

And make return.

110. That the aforesaid tax upon cotton shall be levied by the assessor on the producer, owner, or holder thereof. And said tax shall be paid to the collector of internal revenue within and for the collection district in which said cotton shall have been produced, and before the same shall have been removed therefrom, except where otherwise provided in this act; and every collector to whom any tax upon cotton shall be paid shall mark the bales or other packages upon which the tax shall have been paid in such manner as may clearly indicate the payment thereof, and shall give to the owner or other person having charge of such cotton a permit for the removal of the same, stating therein the amount and payment of the tax, the time and place of payment, and the weight and marks upon the bales and packages, so that the same may be fully identified; and it shall be the duty of every such collector to keep clear and sufficient records of all such cotton inspected or marked, and of all marks and identifications thereof, and of all permits for the removal of the same, and of all his transactions relating thereto, and he shall make full returns thereof, monthly, to the Commissioner of Internal Revenue.

13 July, 1866, § 3.

Places where cotton may be marked to be designated.

Cotton to be marked in any place if certain expenses are paid.

111. That the Commissioner of Internal Revenue is hereby authorized to designate one or more places in each collection district where an assessor or an assistant assessor and a collector or deputy collector shall be located, and where cotton may be brought for the purpose of being weighed and appropriately marked: *Provided*, That it shall be the duty of the assessor or assistant assessor and

the collector or deputy collector to assess and cause to be properly marked the cotton, wherever it may be in said district, provided their necessary travelling expenses to and from said designated place, for that purpose, be paid by the owners thereof.

112. That all cotton having been weighed and marked as herein provided, and for which permits shall have been duly obtained of the assessor, may be removed from the district in which it has been produced to any one other district, without prepayment of the tax due thereon, upon the execution of such transportation bonds or other security and in accordance with such regulations as shall be prescribed by the Commissioner of Internal Revenue, subject to the approval of the Secretary of the Treasury. The said cotton so removed shall be delivered to the collector of internal revenue or his deputy forthwith upon its arrival at its point of destination, and shall remain subject to his control until the taxes thereon, and any necessary charges of custody thereof, shall have been paid, but nothing herein contained shall authorize any delay of the payment of said taxes for more than ninety days from the date of the permits; and when cotton shall have been weighed and marked for which a permit shall have been granted without prepayment of the tax, it shall be the duty of the assessor granting such permit to give immediate notice of such permit to the collector of internal revenue for the district to which said cotton is to be transported, and he shall also transmit therewith a statement of the taxes due thereon, and of the bonds or other securities for the payment thereof, and he shall make full returns and statements of the same to the Commissioner of Internal Revenue.

13 July, 1866, § 4.

When and how cotton may be removed without prepayment of tax

Payment not to be delayed more than 90 days.

Assessor to give notice of permit and transmit statements to collector.

To make returns to Commissioner.

113. That it shall be unlawful from and after the first day of September, eighteen hundred and sixty-six, for the owner, master, supercargo, agent, or other person having charge of any vessel, or for any railroad company, or other transportation company, or for any common carrier, or other person, to convey, or attempt to convey, or transport any cotton—the growth or produce of the United States—from any point in the district in which it shall have been produced, unless each bale or package thereof shall have attached to or accompanying it the proper marks or evidence of the payment of the revenue tax and a permit of the collector for such removal, or the permit of the assessor, as hereinbefore provided, under regulations of the Commissioner of Internal Revenue, subject to the approval of the Secretary of the Treasury, or to convey or transport any cotton from any State in which cotton is produced to any port or place in the United States, without a certificate from the collector of internal revenue of the district from which it was brought, and such other evidence as the Commissioner of Internal Revenue, subject to the approval of the Secretary of the Treasury, may prescribe, that the tax has been paid thereon, or the permit of the assessor as hereinbefore provided, and such certificate and evidence as aforesaid shall be furnished to the collector of the district to which it is transported, and his permit obtained before landing, discharging, or delivering such cotton at the place to which it is transported as aforesaid. And any person or persons who shall violate the provisions of this act in this respect, or who shall convey or attempt to convey from any State in which cotton is produced to any port or place without the United States any cotton upon which the tax has not been paid, shall be liable to a penalty of one hundred dollars for each bale of cotton so conveyed or transported, or

13 July, 1866, § 5.

Transportation unlawful without payment shown or permit.

Before landing permit to be obtained, &c.

Penalty for violation of this section.

attempted to be conveyed or transported, or to imprisonment for not more than one year, or both; and all vessels and vehicles employed in such conveyance or transportation shall be liable to seizure and forfeiture, by proceedings in any court of the United States having competent jurisdiction. And all cotton so shipped or attempted to be shipped or transported without payment of the tax, or the execution of such transportation bonds or other security, as provided in this act, shall be forfeited to the United States, and the proceeds thereof distributed according to the statute in like cases provided.

Forfeiture.

13 July, 1866, § 7.

Manufacturer in producing district to make monthly returns.

114. That it shall be the duty of every person, firm, or corporation, manufacturing cotton for any purpose whatever, in any district where cotton is produced, to return to the assessor or assistant assessor of the district in which such manufacture is carried on, a true statement in writing, signed by him, and verified by his oath or affirmation, on or before the tenth day of each month; and the first statement so rendered shall be on or before the tenth day of August, eighteen hundred and sixty-six, and shall state the quantity of cotton which such manufacturer had on hand and unmanufactured, or in process of manufacture, on the first day of said month; and each subsequent statement shall show the whole quantity in pounds, gross weight, of cotton purchased or obtained, and the whole quantity consumed by him in any business or process of manufacture during the last preceding calendar month, and the quantity and character of the goods manufactured therefrom; and every such manufacturer or consumer shall keep a book, in which he shall enter the quantity, in pounds, of cotton which he has on hand on the first day of August, eighteen hundred and sixty-six, and each quantity or lot purchased or obtained by him thereafter; the time when and the party or parties from whom the same was obtained; the quantity of said cotton, if any, which is the growth of the collection district where the same is manufactured; the quantity, if any, which has not been weighed and marked by any officer herein authorized to weigh and mark the same; the quantity, if any, upon which the tax had not been paid, so far as can be ascertained, before the manufacture thereof; and also the quantities used or disposed of by him from time to time in any process of manufacture or otherwise, and the quantity and character of the product thereof, which book shall, at all times during business hours, be open to the inspection of the assessor, assistant assessors, collector or deputy collectors of the district, inspectors, or of revenue agents; and such manufacturer shall pay monthly to the collector, within the time prescribed by law, the tax herein specified, subject to no deductions, on all cotton so consumed by him in any manufacture, and on which no excise tax has previously been paid; and every such manufacturer or person whose duty it is so to do, who shall neglect or refuse to make such returns to the assessor, or to keep such book, or who shall make false or fraudulent returns, or make false entries in such book, or procure the same to be so done, in addition to the payment of the tax to be assessed thereon, shall forfeit to the United States all cotton and all products of cotton in his possession, and shall be liable to a penalty of not less than one thousand nor more than five thousand dollars, to be recovered with costs of suit, or to imprisonment not exceeding two years, in the discretion of the court; and any person or persons who shall make any false oath or affirmation in relation to any matter or thing herein required

Particulars.

Manufacturer or consumer to enter in a book certain particulars.

Book open to inspection.

Tax to be paid monthly.

Penalties for violation.

Perjury.

shall be guilty of perjury, and shall be subject to the punishment prescribed by existing statutes for that offence: *Provided*, That nothing herein contained shall be construed in any manner to affect the liability of any person for any tax imposed by law on the goods manufactured from such cotton.

Manufacturer's liability not affected.

115. That the provisions of the act of June thirty, eighteen hundred and sixty-four, as amended by the act of March third, eighteen hundred and sixty-five, relating to the assessment of taxes and enforcing the collection of the same, and all proceedings and remedies relating thereto, shall apply to the assessment and collection of the tax, fines, and penalties imposed by, and not inconsistent with, the provisions of the preceding sections of this act; and the Commissioner of Internal Revenue, subject to the approval of the Secretary of the Treasury, shall make all necessary rules and regulations for ascertaining the weight of all cotton to be assessed, and for appropriately marking the same, and generally for carrying into effect the foregoing provisions. And the Secretary of the Treasury is authorized to appoint all necessary inspectors, weighers, and markers of cotton, whose compensation shall be determined by the Commissioner of Internal Revenue, and paid in the same manner as inspectors of tobacco are paid.

13 July, 1866, § 8.

Other laws to this tax.

Commissioner to make regulations.

Appointment of inspectors, &c.

Compensation.

116. That all cotton sold by or on account of the government of the United States shall be free and exempt from duty at the time of and after the sale thereof, and the same shall be marked free, and the purchaser furnished with such a bill of sale as shall clearly and accurately describe the same, which shall be deemed and taken to be a permit authorizing the sale or removal thereof.

30 June, 1864, § 177.
13 July, 1866, § 2.
Vide ante, § 109.

Cotton sold on account of the United States exempt.

3. DISTILLED SPIRITS.

117. That there shall be levied, collected, and paid on all distilled spirits, upon which no tax has been paid according to law, a tax of two dollars on each and every proof gallon, to be paid by the distiller, owner, or any person having possession thereof; and the tax shall be a lien on the spirits distilled, on the distillery used for distilling the same, with the stills, vessels, fixtures, and tools therein, and on the interest of said distiller in the lot or tract of land whereon the said distillery is situated, from the time said spirits are distilled, until the said tax shall be paid: *Provided*, That the tax on all spirits shall be collected at no lower rate than the basis of first-proof, and shall be increased in proportion for any greater strength than the strength of first-proof.

13 July, 1866, § 32.

Tax on distilled spirits.

Tax a lien on the spirits, distillery, &c.

Proviso.
Tax collected at no lower rate than the basis of first-proof.

118. That proof spirit shall be held and taken to be that alcoholic liquor which contains one-half its volume of alcohol of a specific gravity of seven thousand nine hundred and thirty-nine (.7939) ten thousandths at sixty degrees Fahrenheit; and the Secretary of the Treasury is hereby authorized to adopt, procure, and prescribe for use, such hydrometers, weighing and gauging instruments, meters or other means for ascertaining the strength and quantity of spirits subject to tax, and to prescribe such rules and regulations as he may deem necessary to insure a uniform and correct system of inspection, weighing, and gauging of spirits subject to tax throughout the United States. And in all sales of spirits hereafter made, where not otherwise specially agreed, a gallon shall be taken to be a gallon of first-proof, according to the foregoing standard set forth and declared for the inspection and gauging of spirits throughout the United States.

13 July, 1866, § 33.

Proof spirit, definition of.

Secretary of the Treasury authorized to adopt hydrometers for ascertaining the strength, &c., and to prescribe rules and regulations.

Gallon shall be taken to be a gallon of first-proof.

13 July, 1866, § 21.

Distiller, definition of.

119. That every person, firm, or corporation who distils or manufactures spirits or alcohol by continuous distillation from grain, who brews or makes mash, wort, or wash, for distillation or the production of spirits, shall be deemed a distiller, under this act. And the making or keeping by any person of grain, mash, wash, or beer, prepared or fit for distillation, together with the possession by such person of a still or other apparatus capable of use for distilling, upon the same premises, shall be deemed and taken as presumptive evidence that such person is a distiller within the meaning of this act.

13 July, 1866, § 22.

Rectifier, definition of.

120. That every person, firm, or corporation who rectifies, purifies, or refines distilled spirits or wines by any process, or who, by mixing distilled spirits or wine with any materials, manufactures any spurious, imitation, or compound liquors for sale, under the name of whiskey, brandy, gin, rum, wine, "spirits," or "wine bitters," or any other name, shall be regarded as a rectifier under this act.

13 July, 1866, § 23.

Penalty for distilling or rectifying without having paid the special tax.

Liquors, stills, &c., forfeited to the United States.

121. That if any person shall carry on the business of a distiller or rectifier without having paid the special tax, as required by law, he shall for every such offence be liable to a fine of not less than double the tax imposed upon the spirits distilled, or double the special tax due for the spirits rectified by such person or found upon the premises hereinafter mentioned, and to imprisonment for a term not exceeding two years; and all spirituous liquors so distilled or rectified, or owned by such person, or found as hereinafter mentioned, and all materials for making or preparing the same, and all vessels containing the same, and all stills or other apparatus capable of being used for distilling, owned by such person or found upon any premises where such business shall be carried on in violation of this section, shall be forfeited to the United States, and may be seized by the collector or deputy collector of the district within which such offence is committed.

13 July, 1866, § 24.

Notice shall be given of names and place of residence of persons by whom and place where the business is to be carried on.

Bond to be given by distiller.

122. That every person engaged in, or intending to be engaged in, the business of a distiller or rectifier, shall give notice in writing, subscribed by him, to the assessor of the district within which such business is to be carried on, stating the name or style under which, the name or names, and the place or places of residence of the person or persons by whom, and the place where said business is to be carried on, and whether of distilling or rectifying. In case of a distiller, the notice shall also state the kind of stills, boilers, and other implements to be used, the capacity of each, the name or names of the owner or owners of the premises on which the distillery is or is to be situated, and if such premises are leased, the terms of the lease. In case of any change in the location, form, capacity, ownership, agency, or superintendence of such distillery, stills, boilers, or other implements, like notice shall be given as aforesaid, within twenty-four hours, of such change. Such person shall also give bond, in form to be prescribed by the Commissioner of Internal Revenue, with sureties approved by the collector of the district, who may approve the same if he shall be satisfied, by affidavits made on said bond, of the sufficiency of said sureties, conditioned that he will comply with all the requirements of the law in relation to distilled spirits. The penal sum of such bond shall not be more than double the amount of the tax on the spirits that can be distilled by such still or stills or other implements during a period of fifteen days. Said collector may refuse to approve

said bond when, in his judgment, the location of the distillery is such as would enable the distiller to defraud the revenue; and in case of such refusal, the distiller may appeal to the Commissioner of Internal Revenue, whose decision in the matter shall be final. A new bond may be required in case of the death, insolvency, or removal of either of the sureties, or in any other contingency, at the discretion of the collector. Any person failing or refusing to give the notice or bond hereinbefore required, or giving a false or fraudulent notice, shall be liable to the fine and forfeitures provided in the last preceding section.

When approval may be refused.

Penalty for failing to give notice or bond.

123. That no person shall use any still, boiler, or other vessel, for the purpose of distilling in any building or on any premises where beer, lager beer, ale, porter, or other fermented liquors, vinegar, or ether, are manufactured or produced, or where sugars or sirups are refined, or where liquors of any description are retailed, or any other business is carried on, or in any dwelling-house; and every person who shall use such still, boiler, or other vessel, for the purpose of distilling, as aforesaid, in any building or other premises where the above specified articles are manufactured, produced, or other business is carried on, or in any dwelling-house, or who shall procure the same to be done, shall forfeit such stills, boilers, or other vessels so used, and all the spirits distilled, and pay a fine of one thousand dollars, or be imprisoned for not more than one year, in the discretion of the court; and any person who shall manufacture any still, boiler, or other vessel, to be used for the purpose of distilling, shall, before the same is removed from the place of manufacture, notify the collector where such still, boiler, or other vessel is to be used or sent, and by whom it is to be used, and of its capacity, and the time when the same is to be sent or set up; and no such still, boiler, or other vessel, shall be set up without the permit in writing of the collector for that purpose; and any person who shall set up such still, boiler, or other vessel, without first obtaining a permit from the collector of the district in which such still, boiler, or other vessel is intended to be used, or who shall fail to give such notice, shall pay in either case the sum of five hundred dollars, and shall forfeit the distilling apparatus thus removed or set up in violation of law: *Provided*, That saleratus may be made or manufactured in any building or on any premises where spirits are distilled: *Provided further*, That any boiler used in generating steam or heating water to be used in such distillery may be located in any other building or on any other premises to be connected with such still or boiling tubs, by suitable pipes or other apparatus, or the steam from such boiler in the distillery may be conveyed to other premises to be used for manufacturing or other purposes.

13 July, 1866, § 25.

Forbids certain places of distilling.

Notice to be given to collector by manufacturer of still, boiler, &c.

Where same is to be used, &c.

Permit of collector to be obtained for setting up still.

Penalty for failure.

Proviso. Saleratus.

Proviso.

Boiler may be located in any other building.

124. That every person making or distilling spirits, or owning any still, boiler, or other vessel used for the purpose of distilling spirits, or having such still, boiler, or other vessel so used under his superintendence, either as agent or owner, or using any such still, boiler, or other vessel, shall, from day to day, make, or cause to be made, true and exact entry in a book, to be kept in such form as the Commissioner of Internal Revenue may prescribe, of the number of pounds or gallons of materials used for the purpose of producing spirits, the number of gallons of spirits distilled, the number of gallons placed in warehouse, and the proof thereof, and the number of gallons sold, with the proof thereof,

13 July, 1866, § 31.

Requires true and exact entries to be made.

and the name and place of business or residence of the person to whom sold; and shall also on the first, eleventh, and twenty-first days of each month, or within five days thereafter, render to the assessor or assistant assessor an account in duplicate, taken from his books in the particulars hereinbefore recited, and verified by oath, of all the facts occurring after the last day of account preceding. The entries to be made in the books of the distiller as aforesaid shall, upon the several days when the returns are made, as provided, be verified by oath or affirmation of the person or persons by whom such entries shall have been made, in the presence of the assessor or assistant assessor, or other proper officer, who shall append thereto his certificate of the execution of the same. The owner, agent, or superintendent of any distillery shall, in case the original entries required to be made in his books by this act shall not have been made by himself, subjoin to the certificate of the person by whom they were made the following oath or affirmation: "I do certify that to the best of my knowledge and belief the foregoing entries are just and true, and that I have taken all the means in my power to make them so." Said book shall always be open for the inspection of any assessor, assistant assessor, collector, deputy collector, revenue agents, or inspectors, and any premises where distilling shall be carried on shall be open to said officers, or either of them, at all times. Any person who shall violate the provisions of this section shall for every such offence be liable to a fine of five hundred dollars. Any person who shall render an account under the provisions of this section which shall be false or fraudulent shall be liable to a fine of not less than five hundred dollars, or to imprisonment not less than six months.

Penalty for violating provisions of this section.

13 July, 1866, § 34.

Required to erect cisterns.

125. That the owner, agent, or superintendent of any distillery established as hereinbefore provided, shall erect, in a room or building to be provided and used for that purpose, and for no other, two or more receiving cisterns, each to be at least of sufficient capacity to hold all the spirits distilled during the day of twenty-four hours, into one of which shall be conveyed each day all the spirits manufactured in said distillery during that day; and such cisterns shall be so constructed as to leave an open space of at least three feet between the tops thereof and the floor or roof above, and of not less than eighteen inches between the bottoms thereof and the floor below, and shall be separated in such a manner as will enable the inspector to pass around the same, and shall be connected with the outlet of the stills, boilers, or other vessels used for distilling, by suitable pipes or other apparatus so constructed as always to be exposed to the view of the inspector; such cisterns and the room in which they are contained shall be in charge of and under the lock and seal of the inspector; and on the third day after the spirits are conveyed into such cisterns the same shall be drawn off into casks or other packages, under the supervision of the inspector, and shall be immediately inspected, gauged, proved, and the casks or packages marked as herein provided, and be removed directly to the bonded warehouse before mentioned: *Provided*, That the spirits may be drawn off from said cisterns at any time previous to the third day, if so desired by the owner, agent, or superintendent of such distillery; and all locks and seals required by law shall be provided by the Secretary of the Treasury, at the expense of the owner of the distillery or warehouse, and the keys shall

Description of.

Proviso.

Locks and seals provided by Secretary Treasury.

always be in the custody of the inspector or assistant inspector, or the officer having charge of the distillery or warehouse.

126. That the owner or owners of any distillery shall provide at his or their own expense a warehouse suitable for the storage of bonded spirits, of [his or] their own manufacture only; or he or they may provide a secure room in a suitable building, to be used as such warehouse, but no dwelling-house shall be used for such purpose; and no door, window, or other opening shall be made or permitted in the walls thereof, leading to any other room or building used for any other purpose, or into the distillery; and after a bond has been given, as hereinafter provided, such warehouse or room, when approved by the Secretary of the Treasury, on report of the district collector, is hereby declared to be a bonded warehouse of the United States, and shall be used only for the storing of spirits manufactured by the owner, agent, or superintendent of such distillery, and shall be under the custody of the inspector as hereinafter provided; and shall be kept locked up by the proper officer in charge, at all times, except when he shall be present; and the tax on the spirits stored in such warehouse shall be paid before removal from such warehouse, unless removed in pursuance of law. And the owner or owners of such warehouse shall execute a general bond to the United States with two or more sureties, to be approved by the collector; and such bond shall be for not less than the amount of taxes on the spirits to be covered thereby, and in such form, and containing such conditions, as shall be approved by the Secretary of the Treasury, and shall be changed or renewed from time to time in regard to the amount and sureties thereof, as the collector, with the approval of the Secretary of the Treasury, may require.

13 July, 1866, § 27.
Required to provide warehouse for storage.
To be bonded warehouse when approved.
Owners of to execute bond.

127. That the owner or owners of any distillery or oil refinery may provide, at his or their own expense, a warehouse, in conformity with such regulations as the Secretary of the Treasury may prescribe; and such warehouse, when approved by the collector, is hereby declared a bonded warehouse of the United States, and shall be used only for storing distilled spirits, or refined coal oil, or naphtha, and to be under the custody of the collector or his deputy. And the duty on the spirits, coal oil, or naphtha stored in such warehouse shall be paid before it is removed from such warehouse, unless removed in pursuance of law.

30 June, 1864, § 60.
Distillers and refiners of coal oil may erect warehouse.
Declared bonded warehouse.
Duty to be paid before removal from warehouse.

128. That general bonded warehouses, for the storage of spirits or other merchandise allowed by law to be placed in bond to secure the payment of the internal revenue tax thereon, or the exportation thereof, may be established under such rules and regulations and upon the execution of such bonds as the Secretary of the Treasury may prescribe, and shall be in the immediate custody of storekeepers who shall be appointed for that purpose, whose compensation shall be paid monthly to the collector of the district by the owners or proprietors of such warehouse, and shall not exceed the rates which may be allowed to storekeepers of bonded warehouses established under the laws and regulations relating to customs: *Provided*, That any article manufactured in a bonded warehouse established under the one hundred and sixty-eighth section of the internal revenue act of June thirtieth, eighteen hundred and sixty-four, and located in any of the Atlantic States, may be removed therefrom for transportation to a customs bonded warehouse at any port on the Pacific coast of

13 July, 1866, § 28.
General bonded warehouses.
To be in charge of storekeeper.
Removal therefrom.

the United States, for the purpose only of being exported therefrom, under such rules and regulations and upon the execution of such bonds or other security as the Secretary of the Treasury may prescribe.

13 July, 1866, § 29.

Inspector appointed for every distillery.

129. That there shall be appointed by the Secretary of the Treasury an inspector for every distillery established according to law, who shall take an oath faithfully to perform his duties; and who shall take an account of all the meal and vegetable productions or other substances to be used for the purpose of producing spirits, when put into the mash tub or otherwise used;

Duties of.

and shall inspect, gauge and prove all the spirits distilled, under such rules and regulations as may be prescribed by the Commissioner of Internal Revenue; and shall take charge of the bonded warehouse established for the distillery in conformity to law; and such warehouse shall be in the joint custody of such inspector and the owner thereof, his agent or superintendent; and when any spirits shall be placed in such warehouse, an entry therefor, in such form as shall be prescribed by regulations, shall immediately be made and signed by the owner of said spirits, and shall have indorsed thereon a certificate of the inspector that the spirits mentioned have been duly inspected and received in said warehouse, and such entry and certificate shall be filed with the collector of the district;

Compensation of.

and said inspector shall not engage in any other business while employed as an inspector, and shall be paid five dollars per day for the time during which he is engaged; and the amount of compensation thus paid for inspection shall be assessed by the assessor upon the distiller, and returned to the collector monthly for collection; and, in addition to the above compensation, such inspector shall receive such fee as may be prescribed by the Commissioner of Internal Revenue for each and every proof gallon of distilled spirits inspected by him and removed to the bonded warehouse, which shall be paid by the distiller or owner of the spirits; but no compensation shall be allowed to such inspector for more than one inspection of such spirits.

Assistant inspector to be appointed in certain cases.

And in case the duties of such inspector shall be greater at any time than he can perform, upon the joint application of the inspector and owner of such distillery, the Secretary of the Treasury may appoint an assistant inspector; and upon the refusal of the distiller to join in such application, the collector shall decide as to such necessity; and such assistant inspector shall qualify in the same manner and be subject to the same penalties as the inspector, and he shall be paid in the same manner as the inspector, at a rate not exceeding the sum of three dollars per day while so employed; and in case of disagreement as to the necessity of retaining the services of such assistant, between the owner of the distillery and the inspector, the collector shall decide as to such necessity, and his decision in the matter shall be final. And in case of absence by sickness, or from any other cause, of such inspector or assistant, the collector may designate a person to take temporary charge of such distillery and warehouse, who shall during such absence perform the duties, receive the same rate of pay, and be paid in the same manner, as said inspector or assistant for the time he may be so employed:

Penalty for distilling, &c., without obtaining permission.

Provided, That the owner, agent, or superintendent of any distillery who shall use, cause or permit to be used, any materials for the purpose of producing spirits, or shall distil or remove any spirits in the absence of the acting inspector or assistant, without permission granted by the collector of the district, shall forfeit and pay double the amount of taxes on the spirits so produced, distilled, or removed, and, in addition thereto, be liable to a fine of one thousand dollars, to be recovered in the manner provided for other penalties: *Provided further*, That any person who shall ship, transport or remove any spirituous or fermented liquors or wines, under any other than the proper name or brand known to the trade as designating the kind and quality of the contents of the casks or packages containing the same, or who shall cause the same to be done, shall forfeit the same, and shall, on conviction thereof, be subject to and pay a fine of five hundred dollars.

Penalty for shipping or removing without proper brand.

130. That there shall be appointed by the Secretary of the Treasury, in every collection district where the same may be necessary, one or more general inspectors of spirits, who shall be entitled to receive such fee as may be prescribed by the Commissioner of Internal Revenue for each and every proof gallon gauged and proved by him, to be paid by the owner of the spirits; and any owner, agent, or superintendent of any distillery or bonded warehouse who shall refuse to admit an inspector upon such premises, so far as it may be necessary for the performance of his duties, or who shall obstruct an inspector in the performance of his duties, shall forfeit and pay the sum of five hundred dollars, to be recovered in the manner provided for recovery of other penalties imposed by this act.

13 July, 1866, § 30.

General inspectors.

131. That all spirits distilled shall, before the same are removed to the bonded warehouse, be inspected, gauged, and proved by the inspector appointed for that purpose, after the same has been drawn into casks or packages, each of not less capacity than twenty gallons, wine measure, and said inspector shall mark by cutting, branding, or otherwise, upon the cask or package containing such spirits, in a manner to be prescribed by the Commissioner of Internal Revenue, the quantity and proof of the contents of such cask or package, with the date of inspection, the collection district, the name of the inspector and the name of the distiller, and also the number of each cask in progressive order, such progressive number, for every distiller, to begin with number one with the first cask or package inspected after this act takes effect, and subsequently with number one with the first cask inspected on or after the first day of January, in each year, and no two or more casks warehoused in the same year by the same distiller shall be marked with the same number, and the officer in charge of the warehouse shall refuse to allow any cask of spirits to be taken out therefrom which has not marked thereon all the several particulars aforesaid, and in the manner required by law. And the inspector or other revenue officer in charge of any distillery shall make a prompt return of all spirits inspected by him in accordance with the provisions of law, and the name of the distiller, to the collector, and a duplicate thereof to the assessor of the district; and any person who shall fraudulently evade or attempt fraudulently to evade the payment of the tax upon any spirits distilled as aforesaid, by changing any marks upon any such cask or package, or in any other manner whatever, or who shall fraudulently put into such cask or package spirits of greater strength than that inspected and certified to by the inspector, shall pay double the amount of tax on each proof gallon of the quantity of such spirits,

13 July, 1866, § 38.

Inspection, gauging, and branding.

Inspector to make return to collector and assessor.

Penalty for evasion.

Inspector subject to penalty in certain cases.

to be assessed and collected as in case of other taxes, and forfeit and pay as a penalty the additional sum of five hundred dollars for each cask or package so altered or changed, to be recovered as provided by law; and any inspector, assistant inspector, or officer temporarily in charge of any distillery, who shall conspire with the proprietor of any distillery or with any other person or persons to defraud the United States of the revenue or tax arising from distilled spirits or any part thereof, or who shall, with intent to defraud the United States of such revenue or tax, make any false or fraudulent entry, certificate, or return, or place any false or fraudulent mark upon any cask or package, shall, on conviction thereof, pay a fine of not less than one thousand nor more than five thousand dollars, and be imprisoned for not less than two nor more than five years; and any person who shall fraudulently use any cask or package bearing inspection marks, for the purpose of selling any other spirits than that so inspected, or for selling spirits of a quantity or quality different from that so inspected, shall be imprisoned for a term of six months, or shall pay a fine of one hundred dollars for each cask or package so used, in the discretion of the court; and any person who shall knowingly purchase or sell, with inspection marks thereon, any cask or package, after the same has been used for distilled spirits, or who shall fraudulently omit to erase or obliterate the inspection marks upon any such package or cask at the time of emptying the same, shall forfeit and pay the sum of two hundred dollars for every cask so purchased or used, or on which the marks are not so obliterated. And any person who shall, with fraudulent intent, use any inspector's brands or plates upon any cask or package containing or purporting to contain distilled spirits, or who shall knowingly make or use any counterfeit or spurious brand or plate upon any cask or package of distilled spirits, as aforesaid, shall be deemed guilty of a felony, and, on conviction thereof, shall pay a fine of one thousand dollars and be imprisoned for not less than two nor more than five years, and such cask or package, with its contents, shall be forfeited to the United States. And any inspector who shall permit any person not employed by him to use any of his brands or plates, or who shall negligently or wilfully leave such brands or plates where they can be used by any other person than those who may be in his employ, shall pay a fine not exceeding one thousand dollars, in the discretion of the court. And any inspector who shall employ any owner, agent, or superintendent of any distillery or warehouse under his supervision, or who shall employ any person in the service of such owner, agent, or superintendent, to use his plates or brands, or to discharge any of the duties imposed by law upon such inspector, shall, for each offence so committed, be subject to the fine last mentioned.

Penalty for fraudulently using, purchasing, or selling any cask, &c., bearing inspection marks.

Fraudulent use of inspector's brands or plates.

13 July, 1866, § 37.

Premises, &c., to be inspected.

132. That every owner, agent, or superintendent of any distillery shall, at all times when required, supply all assistance, lights, ladders, tools, staging, or other things necessary for inspecting the premises, stock, tools, and apparatus, belonging to such person, and shall open all doors, and open for examination all boxes, packages, and all casks, barrels, and other vessels not under the control of the inspector, when required so to do by any duly authorized officer, under a penalty of two hundred dollars for any refusal or neglect so to do.

133. That any spirits or other merchandise may be removed from bonded warehouse, for the purpose of being exported, upon the order of the superintendent of exports for the port whence the spirits are to be exported; and such order shall state the port to which such spirits are to be shipped, and the name of the vessel, and also the number of proof gallons, and the marks of the packages or casks; and such spirits or other merchandise shall be branded "U. S. bonded warehouse, for export," and shall be put on board of the vessel in or by which they are to be exported, by an officer under direction of the superintendent of exports, and placed under the supervision of an officer of the customs, after a bond with good and sufficient sureties shall have been given in such form and containing such conditions as the Commissioner of Internal Revenue, subject to the approval of the Secretary of the Treasury, may prescribe. And such bond shall be cancelled upon the presentation of the proper certificate that said spirits have been landed at the port named in said bond, or at any other port without the jurisdiction of the United States, or upon satisfactory proof that after shipment the spirits have been lost. And at any port where there shall be no superintendent of exports, all the duties and services required of superintendents of exports and drawback shall devolve upon and be performed by the collector of internal revenue designated to have charge of exportation.

13 July, 1866, § 41.
Removal from bonded warehouse for exportation.
Vide post, "Drawback," §217
Bond to be executed.
Cancellation of bond.

134. That any person who shall remove any distilled spirits from the place where the same are distilled, otherwise than into a bonded warehouse as provided by law, shall be liable to a fine of double the amount of the tax imposed thereon, or to imprisonment for not less than three months. All distilled spirits so removed, and all distilled spirits found elsewhere than in a bonded warehouse, not having been removed from such warehouse according to law, and the tax imposed by law on the same not having been paid, shall be forfeited to the United States, or may, immediately upon discovery, be seized, and, after assessment of the tax thereon, may be sold by the collector for the tax and expenses of seizure and sale. And proceedings upon such seizure shall be according to existing provisions of law in relation to distraint, and in conformity with any regulations which shall be made by the Commissioner of Internal Revenue. And the burden of proof shall be upon the claimant of said spirits to show that the requirements of law in regard to the same have been complied with. And any person who shall aid or abet in the removal of distilled spirits from any distillery otherwise than to a bonded warehouse as provided by law, or shall aid in the concealment of such spirits so removed, shall be liable, on conviction thereof, to a fine of not less than two hundred nor more than one thousand dollars, or to imprisonment for not less than three nor more than twelve months. And any person who shall remove, or shall aid or abet in the removal of any distilled spirits from any bonded warehouse, other than is allowed by law, shall be liable to a fine of not more than one thousand dollars, or to imprisonment for not less than three nor more than twelve months.

13 July, 1866, § 45.
Penalty for removing, except as provided by law.

135. That any distilled spirits which have been inspected, gauged, proved, and marked by the inspector, according to the provisions of law, may be removed without the payment of tax from the bonded warehouse owned by the distiller, under such rules and regulations, and upon the execution of such transporta-

13 July, 1866, § 40.
May be removed without payment of tax from bonded warehouse owned by distiller, under prescribed regulations.

tion bonds or other security, as the Commissioner of Internal Revenue, subject to the approval of the Secretary of the Treasury, may prescribe, and may be transported to any general bonded warehouse used for the storage of distilled spirits, established under the internal revenue laws and regulations, after having been branded as follows: "U. S. bonded warehouse, ——— district, ———: for transportation to ——— district, ———," (inserting in each case the number of the district and name of the State;) and immediately after the arrival of such distilled spirits at the district of the collector to which it has been transferred, it shall again be inspected and placed in a bonded warehouse; and the tax shall be paid on the difference between the number of proof gallons as stated in the bond given at the place of shipment and the number received at the warehouse, less the allowance for leakage as established by the regulations of the Commissioner of Internal Revenue; and except for actual destruction by unavoidable accident, by the elements, or by the public enemy, no other allowance for loss shall be made; and any distilled spirits entered in a general bonded warehouse shall be subject to such rules and regulations as the Commissioner of Internal Revenue may prescribe, and be chargeable with the same costs and expenses, in all respects, to which imported goods deposited in public store or bonded warehouse may be subject, and shall be in charge of a storekeeper, to be appointed by the Secretary of the Treasury, who, with the owner and proprietor of the warehouse, shall have the joint custody of all the distilled spirits so stored in said warehouse, which shall be at the risk of the owner of the said spirits; and all labor on the same shall be performed by the owner or proprietor of the warehouse, under the supervision of the officer in charge of the same, and at the expense of said owner or proprietor. And the same fees shall be paid for the execution of all papers, instruments, and documents relating to the exportation of any spirits or other merchandise, as are charged to exporters for like services in the custom-house; and all expense and services required in the removal, transfer, and shipment of the same for export shall be paid by the owner thereof: *Provided,* That any distilled spirits may be withdrawn from a bonded warehouse, after having been inspected and gauged by the proper officer, and after the payment to the collector of internal revenue for the district in which the warehouse is situated of the tax imposed by law; and when so delivered, shall be branded "U. S. bonded warehouse, tax paid;" or may be removed from said warehouse without the payment of the tax for the purpose of being exported, or for the purpose of being rectified, or re-distilled, canned, or put into other packages, after the quantity and proof of the spirits to be removed have been ascertained and inspected as required by law, under such rules and regulations and the execution of such bonds or other security as the Commissioner of Internal Revenue, subject to the approval of the Secretary of the Treasury, may prescribe; but such removal of bonded spirits for the purpose of being rectified, re-distilled, or put into other packages, shall be allowed but once on the same spirits; and all spirits so removed for re distillation, rectification, or change of package, shall be returned to the same warehouse, and shall again be inspected; and the tax shall be paid to the said collector on any deficiency or reduction beyond

Tax to be paid on difference, &c.

Enterd in a general bonded warehouse subject to rules, and chargeable with costs, &c., same as imported goods.

Proviso, withdrawal from warehouse.

three per cent. And upon spirits removed under bond for the purpose of being re-distilled or rectified, or change of package as aforesaid, and upon which an allowance shall have been made, as herein provided, the duty upon such allowance shall be paid, together with the taxes imposed by law upon such spirits, in case such spirits shall be withdrawn for consumption or sale, or for transportation without being exported. And no drawback shall be allowed on any distilled spirits on which the tax has been paid; but nothing in this section shall be so construed as to prevent the manufacture in bond for exportation, without the payment of taxes, of medicines, preparations, compositions, perfumery, cosmetics, cordials, and other liquors manufactured wholly or in part of domestic spirits, as provided by law.

Taxes to be paid when removed for redistillation.

Drawback not allowed where tax has been paid.

136. That all distilled spirits, and all distilled or refined coal oil, distillate, benzine or benzole, and naphtha, upon which an excise duty is imposed by law, may, after being inspected, gauged, proved, and marked by the inspector according to the provisions of this act, be removed, without payment of the duty, under such rules and regulations, and upon the execution of such transportation bonds or other security as the Secretary of the Treasury may prescribe. The said spirits, oil, or naphtha so removed shall be transferred directly from the distillery or refinery to a bonded warehouse, established in conformity with law and treasury regulations, and may be transported from such warehouse to any one other bonded warehouse used for the storage of distilled spirits, coal oil, or naphtha. And after the arrival of such distilled spirits, coal oil, or naphtha at the bonded warehouse within the district of the assessor to which it has been transferred, it shall be again inspected, and the duty shall be assessed and paid on any deficiency or reduction of the number of proof gallons beyond such allowance for leakage as may be established by the regulations of the Commissioner of Internal Revenue, received at the warehouse, from the number of proof gallons as stated in the bond given at the place of shipment. And any distilled spirits, coal oil, or naphtha in the public warehouses shall be subject to the same rules and regulations, and be chargeable with the same costs and expenses in all respects, to which imported goods deposited in public store or bonded warehouse may be subject; and shall be in charge of a proper officer, to be designated by the Secretary of the Treasury, who, with the owner and proprietor of the warehouse, shall have the joint custody of all the distilled spirits, oil, or naphtha so stored in said warehouse, which shall be at the risk of the owner of the said spirits, oil, or naphtha. And all labor on the same shall be performed by the owner or proprietor of the warehouse, under the supervision of the officer in charge of the same, and at the expense of said owner or proprietor of the warehouse; and the same fees shall be paid for exports as are charged to exporters for like services in the custom-house. And no drawback shall in any case be allowed on any distilled spirits, coal oil, or naphtha, upon which an excise duty shall have been paid, either before or after it shall have been placed in a bonded warehouse: *Provided,* That any distilled spirits, coal oil, or naphtha may be withdrawn from the bonded warehouse after payment, to the collector of internal revenue for the district in which the warehouse is situated, of the duty imposed by law, or may be removed without payment of the duty

30 June, 1864, § 61.
3 March, 1865, § 1.

Distilled spirits, coal oil, and naphtha, may be removed without payment of duty under bond, &c.

Transfer from one to another bonded warehouse

Reinspection and payment of duty required on any deficiency beyond the allowance for leakage.

Cost and expenses chargeable same as on imported goods deposited in bonded warehouse.

Spirits, oil, or naphtha in the custody of officer while in a bonded warehouse, and at the risk of the owner.

Owner to pay expenses of labor upon goods in bonded warehouse

No drawback to be allowed.

Distilled spirits, coal oil, or naphtha, may be withdrawn from bonded warehouse under certain circumstances.

for the purpose of being exported, or for the purpose of being redistilled or canned for export, after the quantity and proof of the spirits, oil, or naphtha to be removed has been ascertained and inspected according to the provisions of law, under such rules and regulations and the execution of such bond or other security as the Secretary of the Treasury may prescribe. And any spirits, oil, or naphtha so removed for distillation shall be returned to the warehouse and shall be again inspected, and the duty shall be paid to the said collector on any deficiency of reduction beyond the allowance for loss by redistillation established by the Commissioner of Internal Revenue, in the number of proof gallons received at the warehouse for the purpose of being exported, as aforesaid. And nothing in this section shall be construed to prevent the manufacture for exportation, without payment of duty, of medicines, preparations, compositions, perfumery, cosmetics, cordials, and other liquors manufactured wholly or in part of domestic spirits, as provided for in this act.

Spirits, &c., removed for distillation to be returned to the warehouse and again inspected.

Medicines, &c., may be manufactured for exportation without payment of duty.

13 July, 1866, § 42.

Penalty for executing or signing any false or fraudulent bond, permit, &c.

137. That any person or persons who shall execute or sign any false or fraudulent bond, permit, entry, or other document, required by law or regulations; or who shall fraudulently procure the same to be executed; or who shall connive at the execution thereof, by which the payment of any internal revenue tax or duty shall be evaded, or attempted to be evaded, or which shall be executed, or purport to be executed, for the purpose of placing in, or withdrawing from, any bonded warehouse any spirits or other merchandise for any purpose whatever, or which shall in any way be used or attempted to be used in fraud of the internal revenue laws and regulations, on conviction thereof, shall forfeit all property in such spirits or other merchandise to which such instrument relates, or purports to relate, and shall be imprisoned for a term not less than one nor more than five years, at the discretion of the court.

13 July, 1866, § 35.

Penalty.

False weights or measures.

138. That any person who shall knowingly and fraudulently use any false weights or measures in ascertaining, weighing, or measuring the quantities of grain, meal, or vegetable materials, molasses, beer, or other substances to be used for distillation, or who shall fraudulently make false record of the same, or who shall destroy or tamper with any locks or seal which may be placed on any cistern, rooms, or buildings, by the duly authorized officers of the revenue, shall on conviction thereof be imprisoned for the term of two years, and pay a fine not exceeding one thousand dollars, in the discretion of the court; and any person who shall use any molasses, beer, or other substances, whether fermented on the premises or elsewhere, for the purpose of producing spirits, before an account of the same shall have been registered in the proper record book provided for this purpose, shall forfeit and pay the sum of one thousand dollars for each and every offence so committed.

13 July, 1866, § 39.

Penalty for adding ingredients.

139. That any person or persons who shall add, or cause to be added, any ingredients to any spirits before the tax imposed by law shall have been paid thereon, for the purpose of creating a fictitious proof, shall, upon conviction, be subject to a fine of one thousand dollars for each cask or package so adulterated, and be imprisoned for not less than one nor more than two years, in the discretion of the court, and such cask or package, with its contents, shall be forfeited to the United States.

140. That every rectifier or wholesale dealer in distilled spirits shall enter, daily, in a book or books kept for the purpose, under such rules and regulations as the Commissioner of Internal Revenue may prescribe, the number of proof gallons of spirits purchased or received, of whom purchased and received, and the number of proof gallons sold or delivered; and every rectifier or wholesale dealer who shall neglect or refuse to keep such record shall forfeit all spirits in his possession, together with the apparatus, tools, and implements used, and be subject to a fine of five hundred dollars, or imprisonment for not less than six months nor more than one year, in the discretion of the court. And every rectifier shall mark with a stencil-plate on each package of five gallons or more of distilled or rectified spirits sold by him, his name and place of business.

13 July, 1866, § 26. Entries to be made in a book of number of gallons received, &c.

Penalty for failure.

141. That all boilers, stills, or other vessels, tools, and implements, used in distilling or rectifying, and forfeited under any of the provisions of this act, and all condemned material, together with any engine or other machinery connected therewith, and all empty barrels, and all grain or other material suitable for distillation, shall, under the direction of the court in which the forfeiture is recovered, be sold at public auction, and the proceeds thereof, after deducting the expenses of sale, shall be disposed of according to law. And all spirits or spirituous liquors which may be forfeited under the provisions of this act, unless herein otherwise provided, shall be disposed of by the Commissioner of Internal Revenue as the Secretary of the Treasury may direct. And the Commissioner of Internal Revenue is hereby authorized, with the approval of the Secretary of the Treasury, to exempt distillers of brandy from apples, peaches, or grapes exclusively, from such of the provisions of this act relating to the manufacture of spirits as in his judgment may seem expedient. And any word or words in any and all parts of this act, and of all acts to which this act is additional, indicating or referring to person or persons, shall be taken to include partnerships, firms, associations, bodies corporate or politic, or any other party whatsoever, when not otherwise designated, or manifestly incompatible with the intent thereof.

13 July, 1866, § 44. Forfeited boilers, stills, &c., to be sold at public auction.

Forfeited liquors to be disposed of by Commissioner.

Certain distillers may be exempt.

Words person or persons to include partnerships, &c.

142. That any person owning any distilled spirits intended for sale, manufactured prior to the time when this act takes effect, exceeding fifty gallons altogether, shall notify in writing the collector of the district wherein such spirits may be stored, held, or owned, within sixty days thereafter, to gauge and prove the same; and upon the receipt of said notice the collector shall cause said spirits to be gauged and proved, and the casks or packages containing the same to be marked by the inspector in the following manner:

13 July, 1866, § 43. Owner of certain spirits to notify collector to gauge the same.

Said spirits to be gauged and marked.

> Manufactured prior to
> ————, 186–.
> ————, Inspector,
> —— District.
> Inspected ——, 186–.

And no spirits so manufactured, held, or owned, shall be gauged, proved, or marked in any cistern or other stationary vessel, but shall be gauged, proved, and marked only in barrels, casks, or

Not to be gauged, &c., in cisterns, &c.

In leach-tubs to be estimated.

packages in which the same shall have been placed; and the quantity held in leach-tubs shall be estimated by the inspector, and when drawn off into packages, shall be gauged and marked as herein provided. Upon the receipt of the return the collector shall immediately forward to the Commissioner of Internal Revenue a copy thereof; and any person holding or owning such spirits, and refusing or neglecting to notify the collector, as in this section provided, shall forfeit the same and pay the sum of five hundred dollars, to be collected in the manner provided by law for the collection of other penalties. No distilled spirits on which the tax has been paid shall be stored or allowed to remain on any distillery premises, under the penalty of a forfeiture of all spirits so found. And all spirits, after being removed from the original package in which they were inspected and gauged into other packages for purposes of rectification, redistillation or change of proof, shall again be inspected and gauged and properly branded; and the absence of an inspector's brand shall be taken and held as sufficient cause or evidence upon which any spirits so found may be forfeited. And any person who shall change the character of any spirits, either by rectification, mixing, or otherwise, after they have been duly inspected and marked, as hereinbefore provided, and place the same in other packages for consumption or sale without first stamping or branding upon such package, in such manner as the Commissioner of Internal Revenue may prescribe, the word "Rectified," shall forfeit such spirits, and the same may be seized by the collector or deputy collector of the district where such spirits may be found, or by such other collector or deputy collector as may be specially authorized by the Commissioner of Internal Revenue for that purpose. And any person who shall so brand any package containing spirits, knowing the taxes thereon have not been paid, shall forfeit such spirits, and be deemed guilty of a misdemeanor, and upon conviction shall be imprisoned for not more than two years, at the discretion of the court.

Collector to forward copy of return to Commissioner.

Penalty for neglect or refusal to notify collector.

Spirits found on distillery premises after payment of tax to be forfeited.

When removed from original package to be reinspected, &c.

Absence of brand thereon cause for forfeiture.

Penalty for changing the character of spirits after inspection, without properly branding.

By whom the same may be seized.

Penalty for fraudulently branding, &c.

4. FERMENTED LIQUORS.

13 July, 1866, §48.

Tax on beer, lager beer, ale, porter, and other similar fermented liquors.

143. That there shall be paid on all beer, lager beer, ale, porter, and other similar fermented liquors, by whatever name such liquors may be called, a tax of one dollar for every barrel containing not more than thirty-one gallons; and at a like rate for any other quantity or for any fractional part of a barrel which shall be brewed or manufactured and sold, or removed for consumption or sale, within the United States; which tax shall be paid by the owner, agent or superintendent of the brewery or premises in which such fermented liquors shall be made, in the manner and at the time hereinafter specified: *Provided*, That fractional parts of a barrel shall be halves, quarters, sixths, and eighths; and any fractional part of a barrel containing less than one-eighth shall be accounted one-eighth; more than one-eighth and not more than one-sixth, shall be accounted one-sixth; more than one-sixth and not more than one-quarter, shall be accounted one-quarter; more than one-quarter and not more than one-half, shall be accounted one-half; more than one-half and not more than one barrel, shall be accounted one barrel; and more than one barrel and not more than sixty-three gallons, shall be accounted two barrels, or a hogshead.

Mode of reckoning fractional parts

144. That every brewer shall, before commencing or continuing business after this act takes effect, file with the assistant assessor of the assessment district in which he shall design to carry on his business, a notice in writing, stating therein the name of the person, company, corporation, or firm, and the names of the members of any such company or firm, together with the place or places of residence of such person or persons, and a description of the premises on which the brewery is situated, and of his or their title thereto, and the name or names of the owner or owners thereof; and also the whole quantity of malt liquors annually made and sold or removed from the brewery for two years next preceding the date of filing such notice.

13 July, 1866, § 46.

Brewer required to file notice before commencing business.

Contents of notice.

145. That every brewer shall execute a bond to the United States, to be approved by the collector of the district, in a sum equal to twice the amount of tax which, in the opinion of the assessor, said brewer will be liable to pay during any one month, which bond shall be renewed on the first day of May in each year, and shall be conditioned that he will pay, or cause to be paid, as herein provided, the tax required by law on all beer, lager beer, ale, porter, and other fermented liquors aforesaid made by him, or for him, before the same is sold or removed for consumption or sale, except as hereinafter provided; and that he will keep, or cause to be kept, a book in the manner and for the purposes hereinafter specified, which shall be open to inspection by the proper officers as by law required, and that he will in all respects faithfully comply, without fraud or evasion, with all requirements of law relating to the manufacture and sale of any malt liquors before mentioned: *Provided*, That no brewer shall be required to pay a special tax as a wholesale dealer, by reason of selling at wholesale, at a place other than his brewery, malt liquors manufactured by him.

13 July, 1866, § 47.

Brewer required to execute bond, which shall be renewed on the first day of May in each year.

Proviso regarding special tax.

146. That every person owning or occupying any brewery or premises used, or intended to be used, for the purpose of brewing or making such fermented liquors, or who shall have such premises under his control or superintendence as agent for the owner or occupant, or shall have in his possession or custody any brewing materials, utensils, or apparatus, used or intended to be used on said premises in the manufacture of beer, lager beer, ale, porter, or other similar fermented liquors, either as owner, agent, or superintendent, shall, from day to day, enter or cause to be entered, in a book to be kept by him for that purpose, the kind of such fermented liquors, the description of packages, and number of barrels and fractional parts of barrels of fermented liquors made, and also the quantity sold or removed for consumption or sale, and shall also, from day to day, enter or cause to be entered, in a separate book to be kept by him for that purpose, on [an] account of all material by him purchased for the purpose of producing such fermented liquors, including grain and malt; and shall render to said assessor or assistant assessor, on or before the tenth day of each month, a true statement in writing, taken from his books, of the whole quantity or number of barrels and fractional parts of barrels of fermented liquors brewed and sold, or removed for consumption or sale, during the preceding month; and shall verify, or cause to be verified, the said statement, and the facts therein set forth, by oath or affirmation to be taken before the assessor or assistant assessor of the district, according to the form required by law, and

13 July, 1866, § 49.

Persons owning or occupying any brewery, &c., shall keep a book where he shall enter the quantity, &c., of fermented liquors made; also, the quantity sold or removed for consumption or sale; said book to be at all times open to the assistant assessor.

shall immediately forward to the collector of the district a duplicate of said statement, duly certified by the assessor or assistant assessor. And said books shall be open at all times for the inspection of any assessor or assistant assessor, collector, deputy collector, inspector, or revenue agent, who may take memorandums and transcripts therefrom.

13 July, 1866, § 50.

Entries to be verified by oath on or before the tenth day of each month.

147. That the entries made in such books shall, on or before the tenth day of each month, be verified by the oath or affirmation of the person or persons by whom such entries shall have been made, which oath or affirmation shall be written in the book at the end of such entries, and be certified by the officer administering the same, and shall be in form as follows: "I do swear (or affirm) that the foregoing entries were made by me, and that they state truly, according to the best of my knowledge and belief, the whole quantity of fermented liquors brewed, the quantity sold, and the quantity removed from the brewery owned by ———, in the county of ———. And further, that I have no knowledge of any matter or thing, required by law to be stated in said entries, which has been omitted therefrom." And the owner, agent, or superintendent aforesaid, shall also, in case the original entries made in his books shall not have been made by himself, subjoin thereto the following oath or affirmation, to be taken in manner as aforesaid: "I do swear (or affirm) that, to the best of my knowledge and belief, the foregoing entries fully set forth all the matters therein required by law, and that the same are just and true, and that I have taken all the means in my power to make them so."

Form of oath.

13 July, 1866, § 52.

Stamps to be furnished denoting the amount of tax, which shall be sold by collectors to brewers only.

148. That the Commissioner of Internal Revenue shall cause to be prepared, for the payment of the tax aforesaid, suitable stamps denoting the amount of tax required to be paid on the hogshead, barrels, and halves, quarters, sixths, and eighths of a barrel of such fermented liquors, and shall furnish the same to the collectors of internal revenue, who shall each be required to keep on hand, at all times, a supply equal in amount to two months' sales thereof, if there shall be any brewery or brewery warehouse in his district, and the same shall be sold by such collectors only to the brewers of their districts, respectively; and such collectors shall keep an account of the number and values of the stamps sold by them to each of such brewers, respectively; and the Commissioner of Internal Revenue shall allow upon all sales of such stamps to any brewer, and by him used in his business, a deduction of seven and one-half per centum. And the amount paid into the treasury by any collector on account of the sale of such stamps to brewers shall be included in estimating the commissions of such collector and of the assessor of the same district.

Account of such stamps to be kept by collector.

Deduction allowed on sale of.

Included in estimating commissions.

13 July, 1866, § 53.

Stamps required to be affixed to the spigot-hole or tap of every hogshead, barrel, &c.

149. That every brewer shall obtain, from the collector of the district in which his brewery or brewery warehouse may be situated, and not otherwise, unless said collector shall fail to furnish the same upon application to him, the proper stamp or stamps, and shall affix upon the spigot-hole or tap (of which there shall be but one) of each and every hogshead, barrel, keg, or other receptacle, in which any fermented liquor shall be contained, when sold or removed from such brewery or warehouse, a stamp denoting the amount of the tax required upon such fermented liquor, in such a way that the said stamp or stamps will be destroyed upon the withdrawal of the liquor from such hogshead, barrel, keg, or other vessel, or upon the introduction of a faucet or other instru-

ment for that purpose; and shall also, at the time of affixing such stamp or stamps as aforesaid, cancel the same by writing or imprinting thereon the name of the person, firm, or corporation by whom such liquor may have been made, or the initial letters thereof, and the date when cancelled. Every brewer who shall refuse or neglect to affix and cancel the stamp or stamps required by law in the manner aforesaid, or who shall affix a false or fraudulent stamp thereto, or knowingly permit the same to be done, shall be liable to pay a penalty of one hundred dollars for each barrel or package on which such omission or fraud occurs, and shall be liable to imprisonment for not more than one year.

Cancellation of same.

Penalty for neglect or refusal.

13 July, 1866, § 55.

Every hogshead to be marked in manner prescribed before sale or removal.

150. That every brewer shall mark or cause to be marked, in such manner as shall be prescribed by the Commissioner of Internal Revenue, upon every hogshead, barrel, keg, or other vessel containing the fermented liquor made by him, before it is sold or removed from the brewery, or brewery warehouse, or other place of manufacture, the name of the person, firm, or corporation by whom such liquor was manufactured, and the place where the same shall have been made; and any person, other than the owner thereof, or his agent, who shall intentionally remove or deface such mark therefrom, shall be liable to a penalty of fifty dollars for each cask from which the mark is so removed or defaced.

Penalty for intentionally removing or defacing marks.

13 July, 1866, § 51.

Penalty for any violation, evasion, neglect, or refusal.

151. That the owner, agent, or superintendent of any brewery, vessels, or utensils used in making fermented liquors, who shall evade or attempt to evade the payment of the tax thereon, or fraudulently neglect or refuse to make true and exact entry and report of the same in the manner required by law, or to do or cause to be done any of the things by law required to be done by him as aforesaid, or who shall intentionally make false entry in said book or in said statement, or knowingly allow or procure the same to be done, shall forfeit, for every such offence, all the liquors made by him or for him, and all the vessels, utensils, and apparatus used in making the same, and be liable to a penalty of not less than five hundred nor more than one thousand dollars, to be recovered with costs of suit, and shall be deemed guilty of a misdemeanor, and shall be imprisoned for a term not exceeding one year. And any brewer who shall neglect to keep the books, or refuse to furnish the account and duplicate thereof as provided by law, or who shall refuse to permit the proper officer to examine the books in the manner provided, shall, for every such refusal or neglect, forfeit and pay the sum of three hundred dollars.

13 July, 1866, § 54.

Penalty for removing without proper stamp being affixed.

152. That any brewer, carman, agent for transportation, or other person, who shall sell, remove, receive, or purchase, or in any way aid in the sale, removal, receipt, or purchase of any fermented liquor contained in any hogshead, barrel, keg, or other vessel from any brewery or brewery warehouse, upon which the stamp required by law shall not have been affixed, or on which a false or fraudulent stamp is affixed, with knowledge that it is such, or on which a stamp once cancelled is used a second time; and any retail dealer or other person, who shall withdraw or aid in the withdrawal of any fermented liquor from any hogshead, barrel, keg, or other vessel containing the same, without destroying or defacing the stamp affixed upon the same, or shall withdraw or aid in the withdrawal of any fermented liquor from any hogshead, barrel, keg, or other vessel, upon which the proper stamp shall not have been affixed, or on which a false or fraudulent stamp is affixed,

shall be liable to a fine of one hundred dollars, and to imprisonment not more than one year. Every person who shall make, sell, or use any false or counterfeit stamp or die for printing or making stamps which shall be in imitation of or purport to be a lawful stamp or die of the kind before mentioned, or who shall procure the same to be done, shall be imprisoned for not less than one nor more than five years: *Provided*, That every brewer, who sells fermented liquor at retail at the brewery or other place where the same is made, shall affix and cancel the proper stamp or stamps upon the hogsheads, barrels, kegs, or other vessels in which the same is contained, and shall keep an account of the quantity so sold by him, and of the number and size of the hogsheads, barrels, kegs, or other vessels in which the same may have been contained, and shall make a report thereof, verified by oath, monthly to the assessor, and forward a duplicate of the same to the collector of the district: *And provided further*, That brewers may remove malt liquors of their own manufacture from their breweries or other places of manufacture to a warehouse or other place of storage occupied by them within the same district in quantities of not less than six barrels in one vessel without affixing the proper stamp or stamps, but shall affix the same upon such liquor when sold or removed from such warehouse or other place of storage. But when the manufacturer of any ale or porter manufactures the same in one collection district, and owns, occupies, or hires a depot or warehouse for the storage and sale of such ale or porter in another collection district, he may, without affixing the stamps on the casks at the brewery, as herein provided for, remove or transport, or cause to be removed or transported, said ale or porter, in quantities not less than one hundred barrels at a time, under a permit from the collector of the district wherein said ale or porter is manufactured, to said depot or warehouse, but to no other place, under such rules and regulations as the Commissioner of Internal Revenue may prescribe, and thereafter the manufacturer of the ale or porter so removed shall stamp the same when it leaves such depot or warehouse, in the same manner and under the same penalties and liabilities as when stamped at the brewery as herein provided; and the collector of the district in which such depot or warehouse is situated shall furnish the manufacturer with the stamps for stamping the same, as if the said ale or porter had been manufactured in his district: *And provided further*, That where fermented liquor has become sour or damaged, so as to be incapable of use as such, brewers may sell the same for manufacturing purposes, and may remove the same to places where it may be used for such purposes, in casks, or other vessels, unlike those ordinarily used for fermented liquors, containing respectively not less than one barrel each, and having the nature of their contents marked upon them, without affixing thereon the stamp or stamps required.

Penalty for making, selling, or using any false stamp or die for printing or making stamps.

Stamps required on hogsheads, &c., where liquor is sold at retail.

Account to be kept of quantity sold, and report made of same to assessor monthly.

Brewers may remove malt liquors of their own manufacture to a place of storage within the same district, in quantities of not less than six barrels, without affixing stamps. Same shall be affixed when liquor is sold or removed from such place of storage.

Where the manufacturer of beer, &c., manufactures the same in one district and has a depot for storage and sale of the same in another collection district.

Liquor soured or damaged.

13 July, 1866, § 56.

Penalty for removing or defacing stamps.

153. That every person, other than the purchaser or owner of any fermented liquor, or person acting on his behalf, or as his agent, who shall intentionally remove or deface the stamp affixed upon the hogshead, barrel, keg, or other vessel, in which the same may be contained, shall be liable to a fine of fifty dollars for each such vessel from which the stamp is so removed or defaced, and to render compensation to such purchaser or owner for all damages sustained by him therefrom.

154. That every person who shall withdraw any fermented liquor from any hogshead, barrel, keg, or other vessel upon which the proper stamp or stamps shall not have been affixed, for the purpose of bottling the same, or who shall carry on, or attempt to carry on, the business of bottling fermented liquor in any brewery or other place in which fermented liquor is made, or upon any premises having communication with such brewery or any warehouse, shall be liable to a fine of five hundred dollars, and the property used in such bottling or business shall be liable to forfeiture. 13 July, 1866, § 58. Penalty for withdrawing liquor for the purpose of bottling, where proper stamps have not been affixed.

155. That the ownership or possession by any person of any fermented liquor after its sale or removal from brewery or warehouse, or other place where it was made, upon which the tax required shall not have been paid, shall render the same liable to seizure wherever found, and to forfeiture; and that the want of the proper stamp or stamps upon any hogshead, barrel, keg, or other vessel in which fermented liquor may be contained after its sale or removal from the brewery where the same was made, or warehouse as aforesaid, shall be notice to all persons that the tax has not been paid thereon, and shall be prima facie evidence of the non-payment thereof. 13 July, 1866, § 57. Liquor liable to seizure and forfeiture after sale or removal if tax has not been paid. What is notice that tax has not been paid.

156. That so much of this act as changes the existing law relating to distilled spirits and fermented liquors shall take effect from and after the first day of September, eighteen hundred and sixty-six. 13 July, 1866, § 61. 3 Mar., 1865, § 1. When changes relating to distilled spirits and fermented liquors take effect.

VI.—PROPERTY AND INCOME.

1. PROPERTY.—SCHEDULE A.

157. That there shall be levied, annually, on every carriage, gold watch, and billiard table, and on all gold or silver plate, the tax or sums of money set down in figures against the same, respectively, or otherwise specified and set forth in schedule A, hereto annexed, to be paid by the person or persons owning, possessing, or keeping the same on the first day in May, in each year, and the same shall be and remain a lien thereon until paid. 30 June, 1864, § 100. 13 July, 1866, § 9. Annual tax on carriages, &c.

SCHEDULE A.

Carriage, phæton, carryall, rockaway, or other like carriage, and any coach, hackney coach, omnibus, or four-wheeled carriage, the body of which rests upon springs of any description, which may be kept for use, for hire, or for passengers, and which shall not be used exclusively in husbandry or for the transportation of merchandise, valued at exceeding three hundred dollars and not above five hundred dollars each, including harness used therewith, six dollars...	$6 00	Carriages, &c.
Carriages of like description, valued above five hundred dollars, each, ten dollars........	10 00	
On gold watches, composed wholly or in part of gold or gilt, kept for use, valued at one hundred dollars or less, each, one dollar.......	1 00	Gold watches.
On gold watches, composed wholly or in part of gold or gilt, kept for use, valued at above one hundred dollars, each, two dollars.......	2 00	
Billiard tables, kept for use, each, ten dollars..........	10 00	Billiard tables. Vide § —, ante.
Provided, That billiard tables kept for hire, and upon which a special tax has been imposed, shall not be required to pay the tax on billiard tables kept for use, as aforesaid, anything herein contained to the contrary notwithstanding.		
On plate, of gold, kept for use, per ounce troy, fifty cents..........	50	Plate of gold.
On plate, of silver, kept for use, per ounce troy, five cents..........	05	Plate of silver.
Provided, That silver spoons or plate of silver used by one family to an amount not exceeding forty ounces troy belonging to any one person, plate belonging to religious societies, and souvenirs and keepsakes actually given and received as such and not kept for use; also, all premiums awarded as a token of merit by any agricultural society, corporation, or association of persons, for any purpose whatever, shall be exempt from tax.		Proviso.

30 June, 1864, § 116
3 March, 1865, § 1.

2. INCOME.

Income tax to be assessed annually upon every person in the U. States, and upon every citizen thereof residing abroad.
Enumeration of sources of income taxable.
Tax of 5 per cent. over $600 and not over $5,000.
Tax of 10 per cent. on excess of $5,000.

158. That there shall be levied, collected, and paid annually, upon the annual gains, profits, and income of every person residing in the United States, or of any citizen of the United States residing abroad, whether derived from any kind of property, rents, interests, dividends, or salaries, or from any profession, trade, employment, or vocation, carried on in the United States or elsewhere, or from any other source whatever, a duty of five per centum on the excess over six hundred dollars and not exceeding five thousand dollars, and a duty of ten per centum on the excess over five thousand dollars.

13 July, 1866, § 9.

Like tax on other income in the United States.
Tax withheld by banks, &c., to be deducted from tax upon whole income.

And a like tax shall be levied, collected, and paid annually, upon the gains, profits, and income of every business, trade, or profession carried on in the United States by persons residing without the United States not citizens thereof. And in ascertaining the income of any person liable to an income tax, the amount of income received from institutions whose officers, as required by law, withhold a per centum of the dividends made by such institutions and pay the same to the Commissioner of Internal Revenue, or other officer authorized to receive the same, shall be included; and the amount so withheld shall be deducted from the tax which otherwise would be assessed upon such person. And the duty herein provided for shall be assessed, collected, and paid upon the gains, profits, and income for the year ending the thirty-first day of December next preceding the time for levying, collecting, and paying said duty:

Income from notes, bonds, and securities of the United States to be included.
But one deduction of $600 from the income of a single family, unless separate income is derived from separate estate or labor.
Profit and loss on sales of real estate purchased and sold within the year to be included in estimating income.

Provided, That income derived from interest upon notes, bonds, and other securities of the United States, and also all premiums upon gold and coupons, shall be included in estimating incomes under this section: *Provided further*, That only one deduction of six hundred dollars shall be made from the aggregate incomes of all the members of any family, composed of parents and minor children, or husband and wife: *And provided further*, That net profits realized by sales of real estate purchased within the year, for which income is estimated, shall be chargeable as income; and losses on sales of real estate purchased within the year, for which income is estimated, shall be deducted from the income of such year.

30 June, 1864, § 117.
3 March, 1865, § 1.

In estimating income, taxes assessed and paid to be deducted.
Salaries and payments to public officers in excess of $600 to be deducted.
Also, rent paid for homestead.

159. That in estimating the annual gains, profits, and income of any person, all national, State, county, and municipal taxes, paid within the year shall be deducted from the gains, profits, or income of the person who has actually paid the same, whether owner, tenant, or mortgagor; also the salary or pay received for services in the civil, military, naval, or other service of the United States, including senators, representatives, and delegates in Congress, above the rate of six hundred dollars per annum; also the amount paid by any person for the rent of the homestead used or occupied by himself or his family, and the rental value of any homestead used or occupied by any person or by his family, in his own right or in the right of his wife, shall not be included and assessed as part of the income of such person.

Excess of interest receivable over amount of interest paid to be taxed, if it is collectale, whether collected or not.
Income derived from gains by purchase, and sale of property, live

In estimating the annual gains, profits, or income of any person, the interest received or accrued upon all notes, bonds, and mortgages, or other forms of indebtedness bearing interest, whether paid or not, if good and collectable, less the interest paid by or due from said person, shall be included and assessed as part of the income of such person for each year; and also all income or gains derived from the purchase and sale of stocks or other property, real or personal, and of live stock, and the amount of live stock, sugar, wool, butter, cheese, pork, beef, mutton, or other meats, hay and grain, or other vegetable or other productions, being the growth or produce of the estate of such person sold, not including any part thereof unsold or on hand during the year next preceding the thirty-first of December, until the same shall be sold, shall be included and assessed as part of the income of such person for each year, and his share of the gains and profits of all companies, whether incorporated or partnership, shall be included in estimating the annual gains, profits, or income of any person entitled to the same, whether divided or otherwise. In estimating deductions from income, as aforesaid, when any person rents buildings, lands, or other property, or hires labor to cultivate land, or to conduct any other business from which such income is actually derived, or pays interest upon any actual incumbrance thereon, the amount actually paid for such rent, labor, or interest shall be deducted; and also the amount paid out for usual or ordinary repairs, not exceeding the average paid out for such purposes for the preceding five years, shall be deducted, but no deduction shall be made for any amount paid out for new buildings, permanent improvements, or betterments, made to increase the value of any property or estate: *Provided*, That in cases where the salary or other compensation paid to any person in the employment or service of the United States shall not exceed the rate of six hundred dollars per annum, or shall be by fees, or uncertain or irregular in the amount, or in the time during which the same shall have accrued or been earned, such salary or other compensation shall be included in estimating the annual gains, profits, or income of the person to whom the same shall have been paid, in such manner as the Commissioner of Internal Revenue, under the direction of the Secretary of the Treasury, may prescribe.

stock, and agricultural products sold subject to tax.

Excluding articles on hand and not sold during the calendar year aforesaid.

Profits of companies subject to income tax, whether divided or not.

Payments for rents, labor, and interest upon incumbrances on property from which income is derived, to be deducted.

Also payments for repairs, not exceeding the average of last five years.

No deduction for new buildings, permanent improvements, betterments, &c.

The pay of employés of the U. S. who receive less than $600 per year, or who are paid by fees, to be added to other income.

Manner of collection to be prescribed by Commissioner, under direction of Secretary of Treasury.

160. That it shall be the duty of all persons of lawful age to make and render a list or return, in such form and manner as may be prescribed by the Commissioner of Internal Revenue, to the assistant assessor of the district in which they reside, of the amount of their income, gains, and profits, as aforesaid; and all guardians and trustees, whether as executors, administrators, or in any other fiduciary capacity, shall make and render a list or return, as aforesaid, to the assistant assessor of the district in which such guardian or trustee resides, of the amount of income, gains, and profits of any minor or person for whom they act as guardian or trustee; and the assistant assessor shall require every list or return to be verified by the oath or affirmation of the party rendering it, and may increase the amount of any list or return if he has reason to believe that the same is understated; and in case any person, guardian, or trustee shall neglect or refuse to make and render such list or return, or shall render a false or fraudulent list or return, it shall be the duty of the assessor or the assistant assessor to make such list, according to the best information he can obtain, by the examination of such person, and his books and accounts, or any other evidence, and to add twenty-five per centum as a penalty to the amount of the duty due on such list in all cases of wilful neglect or refusal to make and render a list or return; and in all cases of a false or fraudulent list or return having been rendered, to add one hundred per centum, as a penalty, to the amount of duty ascertained to be due, the duty and the additions

30 June, 1864, § 118
3 March, 1865, § 1.

All persons of lawful age to make return of income to the assistant assessor.

Guardians, trustees, &c., required to make return.

Return to be verified by oath.

Assessor may increase amount of return.

In case of neglect or refusal, or of fraudulent return, assessor or assistant assessor to make assessment and add penalty.

thereto as penalty to be assessed and collected in the manner provided for in other cases of wilful neglect or refusal to render a list or return, or of rendering a false and fraudulent return: *Provided*, That any party, in his or her own behalf, or as guardian or trustee, shall be permitted to declare, under oath or affirmation, the form and manner of which shall be prescribed by the Commissioner of Internal Revenue, that he or she, or his or her ward or beneficiary, was not possessed of an income of six hundred dollars, liable to be assessed according to the provisions of this act; or may declare that he or she has been assessed and paid an income duty elsewhere in the same year, under authority of the United States, upon his or her gains and profits, as prescribed by law; and if the assistant assessor shall be satisfied of the truth of the declaration, shall thereupon be exempt from income duty in said district; or if the list or return of any party shall have been increased by the assistant assessor, such party may exhibit his books and accounts, and be permitted to prove and declare, under oath or affirmation, the amount of annual income liable to be assessed; but such oaths and evidence shall not be considered as conclusive of the facts, and no deductions claimed in such cases shall be made or allowed until approved by the assistant assessor. Any person feeling aggrieved by the decision of the assistant assessor in such cases, may appeal to the assessor of the district, and his decision thereon, unless reversed by the Commissioner of Internal Revenue, shall be final, and the form, time, and manner of proceedings shall be subject to rules and regulations to be prescribed by the Commissioner of Internal Revenue.

Party may make declaration under oath.

Declaration not to be conclusive.

Right of appeal to assessor.

His decision final unless reversed by Commissioner.

30 June, 1864, § 119
3 March, 1865, § 1.
13 July, 1866, § 9.

Income tax, when to be levied.

When payable.

Unpaid within ten days after demand, penalty of 10 per cent. to be added.

Except in cases of estates of deceased or insolvent persons.

161. That the taxes on incomes herein imposed shall be levied on the first day of May, and be due and payable on or before the thirtieth day of June, in each year, until and including the year eighteen hundred and seventy, and no longer; and to any sum or sums annually due and unpaid after the thirtieth of June, as aforesaid, and for ten days after notice and demand thereof by the collector, there shall be levied, in addition thereto, the sum of ten per centum on the amount of duties unpaid, as a penalty, except from the estates of deceased or insolvent persons.

30 June, 1864, § 120
3 March, 1865, § 1.
10 March, 1866, § 1.
13 July, 1866, § 9.

Duty of 5 per cent. on dividends of banks, trust companies, savings institutions, and insurance companies.

Same duty on additions to surplus or contingent funds.

Duty to be withheld from all payments on account of such dividends.

Return to be made to assessor within 10 days after dividend is payable.

162. That there shall be levied and collected a tax of five per centum on all dividends in scrip or money thereafter declared due, wherever and whenever the same shall be payable, to stockholders, policy holders, or depositors or parties whatsoever, including non-residents, whether citizens or aliens, as part of the earnings, income, or gains of any bank, trust company, savings institution, and of any fire, marine, life, inland insurance company, either stock or mutual, under whatever name or style known or called, in the United States or Territories, whether specially incorporated or existing under general laws, and on all undistributed sums, or sums made or added during the year to their surplus or contingent funds; and said banks, trust companies, savings institutions, and insurance companies shall pay the said tax, and are hereby authorized to deduct and withhold from all payments made on account of any dividends or sums of money that may be due and payable as aforesaid the said tax of five per centum. And a list or return shall be made and rendered to the assessor or assistant assessor on or before the tenth day of the month following that in which any dividends or sums of money become due or payable as aforesaid; and said list or return shall contain a true and

faithful account of the amount of taxes as aforesaid; and there shall be annexed thereto a declaration of the president, cashier, or treasurer of the bank, trust company, savings institution, or insurance company, under oath or affirmation, in form and manner as may be prescribed by the Commissioner of Internal Revenue, that the same contains a true and faithful account of the taxes as aforesaid. And for any default in the making or rendering of such list or return, with such declaration annexed, the bank, trust company, savings institution, or insurance company making such default shall forfeit as a penalty the sum of one thousand dollars; and in case of any default in making or rendering said list or return, or of any default in the payment of the tax as required, or any part thereof, the assessment and collection of the tax and penalty shall be in accordance with the general provisions of law in other cases of neglect and refusal: *Provided*, That the tax upon the dividends of life insurance companies shall not be deemed due until such dividends are payable; nor shall the portion of premiums returned by mutual life insurance companies to their policy holders, nor the annual or semi-annual interest allowed or paid to the depositors in savings banks or savings institutions, be considered as dividends.

Return to be verified by oath of president, cashier, or treasurer.

Penalty for default in rendering return.

In case of default, assessment and collection to be in accordance with general provisions.

Dividends of life insurance companies not due until payable.

Premiums returned by mutual life insurance companies not dividends.

163. That any bank legally authorized to issue notes as circulation which shall neglect or omit to make dividends or additions to its surplus or contingent fund as often as once in six months, shall make a list or return in duplicate, under oath or affirmation of the president or cashier, to the assessor or assistant assessor of the district in which it is located, on the first day of January and July in each year, or within thirty days thereafter, of the amount of profits which have accrued or been earned and received by said bank during the six months next preceding said first days of January and July; and shall present one of said lists or returns and pay to the collector of the district a duty of five per centum on such profits, and in case of default to make such list or return and payment within the thirty days, as aforesaid, shall be subject to the provisions of the foregoing section of this act: *Provided*, That when any dividend is made which includes any part of the surplus or contingent fund of any bank, trust company, savings institution, insurance or railroad company, which has been assessed and the duty paid thereon, the amount of duty so paid on that portion of the surplus or contingent fund may be deducted from the duty on such dividend.

30 June, 1864, §121

Bank neglecting to make dividend or addition to surplus as often as once in six months to make return on 1st of January and 1st of July.

Duty of 5 per cent. to be paid to the collector.

Duty paid on surplus or contingent fund to be deducted from duty on future dividend.

164. That any railroad, canal, turnpike, canal navigation, or slack-water company, indebted for any money for which bonds or other evidence of indebtedness have been issued, payable in one or more years after date, upon which interest is stipulated to be paid, or coupons representing the interest, or any such company that may have declared any dividend in scrip or money due or payable to its stockholders, including non-residents, whether citizens or aliens, as part of the earnings, profits, income, or gains of such company, and all profits of such company carried to the account of any fund, or used for construction, shall be subject to and pay a tax of five per centum on the amount of all such interest, or coupons, dividends, or profits, whenever and wherever the same shall be payable, and to whatsoever party or person the same may be payable, including non-residents, whether citizens or aliens; and said companies are hereby authorized to deduct and withhold from

30 June, 1864, §122
10 March, 1866, §2.
13 July, 1866, §9.

Duty of 5 per cent. on dividends and interest on bonds of railroad, canal, turnpike, canal navigation, and slack-water companies.

Companies to with'ld duty from all payments.

all payments on account of any interest, or coupons, and dividends, due and payable as aforesaid, the tax of five per centum; and the payment of the amount of said tax so deducted from the interest, or coupons, or dividends, and certified by the president or treasurer of said company, shall discharge said company from that amount of the dividend, or interest, or coupon on the bonds or other evidences of their indebtedness so held by any person or party whatever, except where said companies may have contracted otherwise. And a list or return shall be made and rendered to the assessor or assistant assessor on or before the tenth day of the month following that in which said interest, coupons, or dividends become due and payable, and as often as every six months; and said list or return shall contain a true and faithful account of the amount of tax, and there shall be annexed thereto a declaration of the president or treasurer of the company, under oath or affirmation in form and manner as may be prescribed by the Commissioner of Internal Revenue, that the same contains a true and faithful account of said tax. And for any default in making or rendering such list or return, with the declaration annexed, or of the payment of the tax as aforesaid, the company making such default shall forfeit as a penalty the sum of one thousand dollars; and in case of any default in making or rendering said list or return, or of the payment of the tax or any part thereof, as aforesaid, the assessment and collection of the tax and penalty shall be made according to the provisions of law in other cases of neglect or refusal: *Provided*, That whenever any of the companies mentioned in this section shall be unable to pay the interest on their indebtedness, and shall in fact fail to pay such interest, that in such cases the tax levied by this section shall not be paid to the United States until said company resume the payment of interest on their indebtedness.

Payment to discharge companies from that amount of indebtedness.

Return to be made to assessor on or before the tenth day of the month following that in which dividends were payable, and every six months.

Return to be verified by oath of president or treasurer

Penalty for default in making return.

In case of default in making return, or payment of the duty, assessment, and collection to be according to general provisions.

30 June, 1864, § 123
13 July, 1866, § 9.

Duty of 5 per cent. on salaries in excess of $600.

165. That there shall be levied, collected, and paid on all salaries of officers, or payments for services to persons in the civil, military, naval, or other employment or service of the United States, including senators and representatives and delegates in Congress, when exceeding the rate of six hundred dollars per annum, a tax of five per centum on the excess above the said six hundred dollars, and a tax of ten per centum on the excess over five thousand dollars; and it shall be the duty of all paymasters and all disbursing officers, under the government of the United States, or persons in the employ thereof, when making any payment to any officers or persons as aforesaid, or upon settling and adjusting the accounts of such officers or persons, to deduct and withhold the aforesaid tax, and they shall, at the same time, make a certificate stating the name of the officer or person from whom such deduction was made, and the amount thereof, which shall be transmitted to the office of the Commissioner of Internal Revenue, and entered as part of the internal tax; and the pay-roll, receipts, or account of officers or persons paying such tax, as aforesaid, shall be made to exhibit the fact of such payment. And it shall be the duty of the several Auditors of the Treasury Department, when auditing the accounts of any paymaster or disbursing officer, or any officer withholding his salary from moneys received by him, or when settling or adjusting the accounts of any such officer, to require evidence that the taxes mentioned in this section have been deducted and paid over to the Commissioner of Internal Rev-

Disbursing officers to withhold amount and transmit to Commissioner.

Auditors of the Treasury to require evid'nce that duties have been paid.

enue, or other officer authorized to receive the same: *Provided*, That payments of prize money shall be regarded as income from salaries, and the tax thereon shall be adjusted and collected in like manner: *Provided further*, That this section shall not apply to payments made to mechanics or laborers employed upon public works.

Payments of prize money to be regarded as salaries.

Not to apply to payments to laborers, &c., employed upon public works

166. That consuls of foreign countries in the United States, who are not citizens thereof, shall be, and hereby are, exempt from any income tax imposed by this act which may be derived from their official emoluments, or from property in such countries: *Provided*, That the governments which such consuls may represent shall extend similar exemption to consuls of the United States.

30 June, 1864, § 178

Consuls exempt from income tax in certain cases.

VII.

LEGACIES AND DISTRIBUTIVE SHARES OF PERSONAL PROPERTY.

167. That any person or persons having in charge or trust, as administrators, executors, or trustees, any legacies or distributive shares arising from personal property, where the whole amount of such personal property, as aforesaid, shall exceed the sum of one thousand dollars in actual value, passing, after the passage of this act, from any person possessed of such property, either by will or by the intestate laws of any State or Territory, or any personal property or interest therein, transferred by deed, grant, bargain, sale, or gift, made or intended to take effect in possession or enjoyment after the death of the grantor or bargainor, to any person or persons, or to any body or bodies politic or corporate, in trust or otherwise, shall be, and hereby are, made subject to a duty or tax, to be paid to the United States, as follows, that is to say:

30 June, 1864, § 124.
13 July, 1866, § 9.

Administrators, executors, and trustees to pay tax on legacies, and distributive sh'res, where the whole amount exceeds $1,000.

First. Where the person or persons entitled to any beneficial interest in such property shall be the lineal issue or lineal ancestor, brother or sister, to the person who died possessed of such property, as aforesaid, at the rate of one dollar for each and every hundred dollars of the clear value of such interest in such property.

Lineal issue or lineal ancestor, brother or sister, 1 per cent.

Second. Where the person or persons entitled to any beneficial interest in such property shall be a descendant of a brother or sister of the person who died possessed, as aforesaid, at the rate of two dollars for each and every hundred dollars of the clear value of such interest.

Descendant of brother or sister, 2 per cent.

Third. Where the person or persons entitled to any beneficial interest in such property shall be a brother or sister of the father or mother, or a descendant of a brother or sister of the father or mother, of the person who died posssesed, as aforesaid, at the rate of four dollars for each and every hundred dollars of the clear value of such interest.

Brother or sister of father or mother, or descendant of same, 4 per cent.

Fourth. Where the person or persons entitled to any beneficial interest in such property shall be a brother or sister of the grandfather or grandmother, or a descendant of the brother or sister of the grandfather or grandmother, of the person who died possessed as aforesaid, at the rate of five dollars for each and every hundred dollars of the clear value of such interest.

Brother or sister of grandfather or grandmother, or descendant of same, 5 per cent.

Fifth. Where the person or persons entitled to any beneficial interest in such property shall be in any other degree of collateral consanguinity than is hereinbefore stated, or shall be a stranger in blood to the person who died possessed, as aforesaid, or shall be a

Other degree of consanguinity, or stranger in blood, 6 per cent.

body politic or corporate, at the rate of six dollars for each and every hundred dollars of the clear value of such interest: *Provided*, That all legacies or property passing by will, or by the laws of any State or Territory, to husband or wife of the person who died possessed, as aforesaid, shall be exempt from tax or duty: *Provided further*, That any legacy or share of personal property passing as aforesaid to a minor child of the person who died possessed as aforesaid shall be exempt from taxation under this section, unless such legacy or share shall exceed the sum of one thousand dollars, in which case the excess only above that sum shall be liable to such taxation.

Husband or wife exempt.

Junior child exempt on $1,000.

30 June, 1864, § 125. 3 March, 1865, § 1. 13 July, 1866, § 9.

Tax, when payable.

168. That the tax or duty aforesaid shall be due and payable whenever the party interested in such legacy or distributive share or property or interest aforesaid shall become entitled to the possession or enjoyment thereof, or to the beneficial interest in the profits accruing therefrom, and the same shall be a lien and charge upon the property of every person who may die as aforesaid, for twenty years, or until the same shall, within that period, be fully paid to and discharged by the United States. And every administrator, executor, or trustee, having in charge or trust any legacy or distributive share, as aforesaid, shall give notice thereof in writing to the assessor or assistant assessor of the district where the deceased grantor or bargainor last resided within thirty days after he shall have taken charge of such trust; and every executor, administrator, or trustee, before payment and distribution to the legatees or to any parties entitled to beneficial interest therein, shall pay to the collector or deputy collector of the district of which the deceased person was a resident the amount of the duty or tax assessed upon such legacy or distributive share, and shall also make and render to the assessor or assistant assessor of the said district a schedule, list, or statement, in duplicate, of the amount of such legacy or distributive share, together with the amount of duty which has accrued or shall accrue thereon, verified by his oath or affirmation, to be administered and certified thereon by some magistrate or officer having lawful power to administer such oaths, in such form and manner as shall be prescribed by the Commissioner of Internal Revenue, which schedule, list, or statement shall contain the names of each and every person entitled to any beneficial interest therein, together with the clear value of such interest, the duplicate of which schedule, list, or statement shall be by him immediately delivered, and the tax thereon paid to such collector; and upon such payment and delivery of such schedule, list, or statement, said collector or deputy collector shall grant to such person paying such duty or tax a receipt or receipts for the same in duplicate, which shall be prepared as hereinafter provided. Such receipt or receipts, duly signed and delivered by such collector or deputy collector, shall be sufficient evidence to entitle such executor, administrator, or trustee to be credited and allowed such payment by every tribunal which, by the laws of any State or Territory, is, or may be, empowered to decide upon and settle the accounts of executors and administrators. And in case such executor, administrator, or trustee shall refuse or neglect to pay the aforesaid duty or tax to the collector or deputy collector, as aforesaid, within the time hereinbefore provided, or shall neglect or refuse to deliver to said collector or deputy collector the duplicate of the schedule, list, or statement of such legacies, property,

To be a lien upon the property for 20 years.

13 July, 1866, § 9.

Administrator, &c., to give notice to appear within thirty days after taking charge of trust.

Executor, &c., to pay the tax before the payment of any legacy.

Return to be made to the assessor or assistant.

Return to be under oath.

Receipt of the collector to be sufficient evidence to entitle executor to credit in the settlement of his account.

Proceedings in case of neglect.

or personal estate, under oath, as aforesaid, or shall neglect or refuse to deliver the schedule, list, or statement of such legacies, property, or personal estate, under oath, as aforesaid, or shall deliver to said assessor or assistant assessor a false schedule or statement of such legacies, property, or personal estate, or give the names and relationship of the persons entitled to beneficial interests therein untruly, or shall not truly and correctly set forth and state therein the clear value of such beneficial interest, or where no administration upon such property or personal estate shall have been granted or allowed under existing laws, the assistant assessor shall make out such lists and valuation as in other cases of neglect or refusal, and shall assess the duties thereon. And in case of wilful neglect, refusal, or false statement by such executor, administrator, or trustee, as aforesaid, he shall be liable to a penalty of not exceeding one thousand dollars, to be recovered with costs of suit; and the collector shall commence appropriate proceedings before any court of the United States, in the name of the United States, against such person or persons as may have the actual or constructive custody or possession of such property or personal estate, or any part thereof, and shall subject such property or personal estate, or any portion of the same, to be sold upon the judgment or decree of such court, and from the proceeds of such sale the amount of such tax or duty, together with all costs and expenses of every description to be allowed by such court, shall be first paid, and the balance, if any, deposited according to the order of such court, to be paid under its direction to such person or persons as shall establish title to the same. The deed or deeds, or any proper conveyance of such property or personal estate, or any portion thereof, so sold under such judgment or decree, executed by the officer lawfully charged with carrying the same into effect, shall vest in the purchaser thereof all the title of the delinquent to the property or personal estate sold under and by virtue of such judgment or decree, and shall release every other portion of such property or personal estate from the lien or charge thereon created by this act. And every person or persons who shall have in his possession, charge, or custody any record, file, or paper containing or supposed to contain any information concerning such property or personal estate, as aforesaid, passing from any person who may die, as aforesaid, shall exhibit the same at the request of the assessor or assistant assessor of the district, and to any law officer of the United States, in the performance of his duty under this act, his deputy or agent, who may desire to examine the same. And if any such person, having in his possession, charge, or custody, any such records, files, or papers, shall refuse or neglect to exhibit the same on request, as aforesaid, he shall forfeit and pay the sum of five hundred dollars: *Provided*, In all legal controversies where such deed or title shall be the subject of judicial investigation the recital in said deed shall be prima facie evidence of its truth, and that the requirements of the law had been complied with by the officers of the government. Any tax paid under the provisions of sections one hundred and twenty-four and one hundred and twenty-five shall be deducted from the particular legacy or distributive share on account of which the same is charged.

Assistant assessor to make list and assess the duty.

13 July, 1866, § 9.

Penalty in case of wilful neglect.

Collectors to commence proceedings in United States court.

Property to be sold.

Disposition of proceeds.

Deed of the proper officer to vest title in the purchaser.

Penalty for refusing to exhibit records, files, &c.

Recital in such deed to be *prima facie* evidence of its truth.

13 July, 1866, § 9.

Tax paid under this and the foregoing section to be deducted from the legacy, &c.

VIII.

SUCCESSION TO REAL ESTATE.

30 June, 1864, § 126. "Real estate" defined. "Succession" defined. "Person" defined.

169. That for the purposes of this act the term "real estate" shall include all lands, tenements, and hereditaments, corporeal and incorporeal; that the term "succession" shall denote the devolution of title to any real estate; and that the term "person" shall be held to include persons, body corporate, company, or association.

30 June, 1864, § 127. What shall be deemed a succession. "Successor" and "predecessor."

170. That every past or future disposition of real estate by will, deed, or laws of descent, by reason whereof any person shall become beneficially entitled, in possession or expectancy, to any real estate, or the income thereof, upon the death of any person dying after the passing of this act, shall be deemed to confer, on the person entitled by reason of any such disposition, a "succession;" and the term "successor" shall denote the person so entitled, and the term "predecessor" shall denote the grantor, testator, ancestor, or other person from whom the interest of the successor has been or shall be derived.

30 June, 1864, § 128. Increase of benefit accruing upon the extinction of any estate by death to be deemed a succession.

171. That where any real estate shall, at or after the passing of this act, be subject to any charge, estate, or interest, determinable by the death of any person, or at any period ascertainable only by reference to death, the increase of benefit accruing to any person upon the extinction or determination of such charge, estate, or interest, shall be deemed to be a succession accruing to the person then entitled, beneficially, to the real estate or the income thereof.

30 June, 1864, § 129. Persons taking succession jointly to pay in proportion to their respective interests. Beneficial interests accruing by survivorship to be deemed a new succession.

172. That where any persons, after the passing of this act, shall take any succession jointly, they shall pay the duty chargeable thereon by this act in proportion to their respective interests in the succession; and any beneficial interest in such succession, accruing to any of them by survivorship, shall be deemed to be a new succession, derived from the predecessor from whom the joint title shall have been derived.

30 June, 1864, § 130. Disposition of real estate with reservation of benefit for any term of life to be deemed to confer a succession at the time of the determination of such benefit.

173. That where any disposition of real estate shall be accompanied by the reservation or assurance of, or contract for, any benefit to the grantor, or any other person, for any term of life, or for any period ascertainable only by reference to death, such disposition shall be deemed to confer at the time appointed for the determination of such benefit an increase of beneficial interest in such real estate, as a succession equal in annual value to the yearly amount or yearly value of the benefit so reserved, assured, or contracted for, on the person in whose favor such disposition shall be made.

30 June, 1864, § 131. Where beneficial ownership is reserved by secret trust, &c., for any term of life, such disposition to be deemed a succession.

174. That where any disposition of real estate shall purport to take effect presently, or under such circumstances as not to confer succession, but, by the effect or in consequence of any engagement, secret trust, or arrangement capable of being enforced in a court of law or equity, the beneficial ownership of such real estate shall not, bona fide, pass according to the terms of such disposition, but shall, in fact, be reserved to the grantor or other person for some period ascertainable only by reference to death, the person shall be deemed, for the purposes of this act, to acquire the real estate so passing as a succession derived from the person making the disposition as the predecessor.

175. That if any person shall, by deed of gift or other assurance of title, made without valuable and adequate consideration, and purporting to vest the estate either immediately or in the future, whether or not accompanied by the possession, convey any real estate to any person, such disposition shall be held and taken to confer upon the grantee a succession within the meaning of this act.

30 June, 1864, § 132.

Conveyance, without valuable and adequate consideration, to be deemed to confer a succession.

176. That the interest of any successor in moneys to arise from the sale of real estate under any trust for the sale thereof shall be deemed to be a succession chargeable with duty under this act, and the said duty shall be paid by the trustee, executor, or other person having control of the funds. And every such person having in charge or trust any disposition of real estate or interest therein, subject to tax under this act, shall give notice thereof in writing to the assessor or assistant assessor of the district where the estate is situate, within thirty days from the time when he shall have taken charge of such trust, and prior to any distribution of said real estate, together with a description and value thereof, and the names of the persons interested therein; and for wilful neglect or refusal so to do, shall be liable to a penalty of not exceeding five hundred dollars, to be recovered with costs of suit.

30 June 1864, § 138.
13 July, 1866, § 9.

Interest of successor in moneys to arise from sale of real estate under trust, to be deemed a succession.

Duty to be paid by the trustee or executor.

Trustee, &c., to give notice to assessor within 30 days.

Penalty for neglect.

177. That the interest of any successor in personal property, subject to any trust for the investment thereof in the purchase of real estate to which the successor would be absolutely entitled, shall be chargeable with duty under this act as a succession, and the tax shall be payable by the trustee, executor, or other person having control of the funds.

30 June, 1864, § 139

Interest of successor in personal property under trust to be converted into reality chargeable as a succession.

Duty to be paid by trustee or executor.

178. That there shall be levied and paid to the United States in respect of every such succession as aforesaid, according to the value thereof, the following duties, that is to say:

30 June, 1864, § 133
3 March, 1865, § 1.

Duties on successions.

Where the successor shall be the lineal issue or lineal ancestor of the predecessor, a duty at the rate of one dollar per centum upon such value.

Lineal issue, or lineal ancestor, 1 per cent.

Where the successor shall be a brother or sister, or a descendant of a brother or sister of the predecessor, a duty at the rate of two dollars per centum upon such value.

Brother or sister or descendant of the same, 2 per cent.

Where the successor shall be a brother or sister of the father or mother, or a descendant of a brother or sister of the father or mother of the predecessor, a duty at the rate of four dollars per centum upon such value.

Brother or sister of the father or mother, or descendant of the same, 4 per cent.

Where the successor shall be a brother or sister of the grandfather or grandmother, or a descendant of the brother or sister of the grandfather or grandmother of the predecessor, a duty at the rate of five dollars per centum upon such value.

Brother or sister of the grandfather or grandmother, or descendant of the same, 5 per cent.

Where the successor shall be in any other degree of collateral consanguinity to the predecessor than is hereinbefore described, or shall be a stranger in blood to him, a duty at the rate of six dollars per centum upon such value: *Provided*, That no duty shall be levied in respect of any succession vesting before or subsequent to the passage of this act, where the successor shall be the wife of the predecessor.

Any other degree of consanguinity, or stranger in blood, 6 per cent.

179. That where real estate shall become subject to a trust for any charitable or public purposes, under any past or future disposition, which, if made in favor of an individual, would confer on him a succession, there shall be payable in respect of such real estate, upon its becoming subject to such trusts, a duty at the rate

30 June, 1864, § 136.

Real estate subject to charitable trust under such disposition as would confer succession, to pay a duty at the highest rate.

of six per centum upon the amount or principal value of such real estate.

30 June, 1864, § 134

When successor dies before becoming entitled in possession, but one duty shall be payable, but the duty to be at the highest rate chargeable upon either succession.

180. That where the interest of any successor in any real estate shall, before he shall have become entitled thereto in possession, have passed by reason of death to any other successor or successors, then one duty only shall be paid in respect of such interest, and shall be due from the successor who shall first become entitled thereto in possession; but such duty shall be at the highest rate which, if every such successor had been subject to duty, would have been payable by any one of them.

30 June, 1864, § 135
3 March, 1865, § 1.

Where succession is alienated before the successor becomes entitled in possession, duty to be paid at the same rate and time.

Where title is accelerated by surrender of prior interest, duty to be paid at the time of surrender.

181. That wherever, after the passing of this act, any succession shall, before the successor shall have become entitled thereto in possession, have become vested by alienation, or by any title not conferring a new succession, in any other person, then the duty payable in respect thereof shall be paid at the same rate and time as the same would have been payable if no such alienation had been made or derivative title created; and where the title to any succession shall be accelerated by the surrender or extinction of any prior interests, then the duty thereon shall be payable at the time of such surrender or extinction of prior title.

30 June, 1864, § 140

Contingent incumbrance not to be estimated in valuing a succession.

Where such incumbrance takes effect as an actual burden, a proportionate amount of the duty to be repaid.

182. That, in estimating the value of a succession, no allowance shall be made in respect of any contingent incumbrance thereon; but in the event of such incumbrance taking effect as an actual burden on the interest of the successor, he shall be entitled to a return of a proportionate amount of the duty so paid by him in respect of the amount or value of the incumbrance when taking effect.

30 June, 1864, § 141

No allowance to be made for any contingency by which the estate may pass to another person.

If the estate thus passes, the proper amount to be repaid.

If the property is applied to the payment of the predecessor's debts, the executor to repay the duties from the proceeds.

If the estate is defeated by any person claiming title under the predecessor, such person to be chargeable with the duties refunded.

183. That, in estimating the value of a succession, no allowance shall be made in respect of any contingency upon the happening of which the real estate may pass to some other person; but in the event of the same so passing, the successor shall be entitled to a return of so much of the duty paid by him as will reduce the same to the amount which would have been payable by him if such duty had been assessed in respect of the actual duration or extent of his interest: *Provided*, That if the estate of the successor shall be defeated, in whole or in part, by its application to the payment of the debts of the predecessor, the executor, administrator, or trustee so applying it shall pay out of the proceeds of the sale thereof the amount so refunded: *And provided also*, That if the estate of the successor shall be defeated, in whole or in part, by any person claiming title from and under the predecessor, such person shall be chargeable with the amount of duty so refunded, and such amounts shall be collected in the manner herein provided for the collection of duties.

30 June, 1864, § 147
13 July, 1866, § 9.

Return to be made to assessor within thirty days.

184. That any person liable to pay a tax in respect to any succession shall give notice to the assessor or assistant assessor of his liability to such tax within thirty days from the time when he shall become entitled in possession to such succession or to the receipt of the income and profits thereof, and shall at the same time deliver to the assessor or assistant assessor a full and true account of said succession for the tax whereon he shall be accountable, and of the value of the real estate involved, and of the deductions claimed by him, together with the names of the successor and predecessor and their relation to each other, and all such other particulars as shall be necessary or proper for enabling the assessor or assistant assessor fully and correctly

to ascertain the taxes due; and the assessor or assistant assessor, if satisfied with such account and estimate as originally delivered, or with any amendments that may be made therein upon his requisition, may assess the succession tax on the footing of such account and estimate; but it shall be lawful for the assessor or assistant assessor, if dissatisfied with such account, or if no account and estimate shall be delivered to him, to assess the tax on the best information he can obtain, subject to appeal as hereinafter provided; and if the tax so assessed shall exceed the tax assessible according to the return made to the assessor or assistant assessor, and with which he shall have been dissatisfied, or if no account and estimate has been delivered, and if no appeal shall be taken against such assessment, then it shall be in the discretion of the assessor, having regard to the merits of each case, to assess the whole or any part of the expenses incident to the taking of such assessment, in addition to such tax; and if there shall be an appeal against such last-mentioned assessment, then the payment of such expenses shall be in the discretion of the Commissioner of Internal Revenue.

Assessor if satisfied may assess the tax thereon.

If dissatisfied may assess upon the best information obtainable.

Subject to appeal.

If no appeal taken within the discretion of the assessor, how to assess; expenses in addition to the tax.

Payment of expenses in case of appeal.

185. That it shall be lawful for any party, liable to pay duty in respect of his succession, who shall be dissatisfied with the assessment of the assistant assessor, within thirty days after the date of such assessment, to appeal to the assessor from such assessment, who shall decide on such appeal, and give notice thereof to such party, who, if still dissatisfied, may, within twenty days after notice as aforesaid, appeal from such decision to the Commissioner of Internal Revenue, and furnish a statement of the grounds of such appeal to the Commissioner, whose decision upon the case, as presented by the statements of the assessor or assistant assessor and such party, shall be final.

30 July, 1864, § 149
3 March, 1865, § 1.

Appeal may be taken to the assessor.

Or to the Commissioner.

186. That the Commissioner shall, at the request of any successor, or any person claiming in his right, cause to be made so many separate assessments of the duty payable in respect of the interest of the successor in any separate tracts of real estate, or in defined portions of the same tract, as shall be reasonably required; and in such cases the respective tracts shall be chargeable only with the amount of duty separately assessed in respect thereof.

30 June, 1864, § 146

Com'sioner may cause separate tracts to be separately assessed.

187. That it shall be lawful for the Commissioner, in his discretion, upon application made by any person who shall be entitled to a succession in expectancy, to commute the duty presumptively payable in respect of such succession for a certain sum to be presently paid, and for assessing the amount which shall be so payable he shall cause a present value to be set upon such presumptive duty, regard being had to the contingencies affecting the liability to such duty, and the interest of money involved in such calculation being reckoned at the rate for the time being allowed by the Commissioner in respect of duties paid in advance, and upon the receipt of such certain sum he shall give discharges to the successor accordingly.

30 June, 1864, § 144

Com'sioner may commute duties in certain cases.

188. That where, in the opinion of the Commissioner of Internal Revenue, any succession shall be of such a nature, or so disposed or circumstanced, that the value thereof shall not be fairly ascertainable under any of the preceding directions, or where, from the complication of circumstances affecting the value of a succession, or affecting the assessment or recovery of the duty thereon, the

30 June, 1864, § 143

Com'sioner may compound duties in certain cases.

Commissioner shall think it expedient to exercise this present authority, it shall be lawful for him to compound the duty payable on the succession upon such terms as he shall think fit, and to give discharges to the successor, upon payment of duty according to such composition; and it shall be lawful for him, in any special cases in which he may think it expedient so to do, to enlarge the time for payment of any duty.

30 June, 1864, § 137
13 July, 1866, § 9.

Duty payable when the successor becomes entitled in possession.

189. That the duty imposed by this act shall be assessed in the collection district where the estate is situate, and shall be paid at the time when the successor, or any person in his right or on his behalf, shall become entitled in possession to his succession, or to the receipt of the income and profits thereof, except that if there shall be any prior charge, estate, or interest, not created by the successor himself upon or in the succession, by reason whereof the successor shall not be presently entitled to the full enjoyment or value thereof, the duty, in respect of the increased value accruing upon the determination of such charge, estate, or interest, shall, if not previously paid, compounded for, or commuted, be paid at the time of such determination.

30 June, 1864, § 142

Where a successor has not obtained the whole of his succession when duty becomes payable, he shall be charged on the value obtained.

Secretary of the Treasury may refund duties in certain cases.

190. That where a successor shall not have obtained the whole of his succession at the time of the duty becoming payable, he shall be chargeable only with duty on the value thereof from time to time obtained by him; and whenever any duty shall have been paid on account of any succession, and it shall afterwards be proved, to the satisfaction of the Secretary of the Treasury, that such duty, not being due from the person paying the same, was paid by mistake, or was paid in respect of real estate, which the successor shall have been unable to recover, or of which he shall have been evicted or deprived by any superior title, or that for any other reason it ought to be refunded, the Secretary of the Treasury shall thereupon refund the same to the person entitled thereto, by draft drawn on any collector of internal revenue.

30 June, 1864, § 145.
13 July, 1866, § 9.

Duty to be a lien for five years.

191. That the duty imposed by this act shall be a first charge on the interest of the successor, and of all persons claiming in his right, in all the real estate in respect whereof such duty shall be assessed for five years from the time when such tax shall have become due and payable, unless sooner paid.

30 June, 1864, § 148
13 July, 1866, § 9.

Penalty for neglect to make return or to pay duties.

192. That if any person required to give any such notice or deliver such account, as aforesaid, shall wilfully neglect to do so within the time required by law, he shall be liable to pay the United States a sum equal to ten per centum upon the amount of tax payable by him; and if any person liable to pay any tax in respect of his succession shall, after such tax shall have been finally ascertained, wilfully neglect to do so within ten days after being notified, he shall also be liable to pay to the United States a sum equal to ten per centum upon the amount of tax so unpaid, at the same time and in the same manner as the tax to be collected.

IX.

STAMP DUTIES.

I. INSTRUMENTS.—SCHEDULE B.

30 June, 1864, § 151

Provisions when to take effect.

193. That all laws in force at the time of the passage of this act in relation to stamp duties shall continue in force until the first day of August, eighteen hundred and sixty-four; and on and after the first day of August, eighteen hundred and sixty-four,

there shall be levied, collected and paid, for and in respect of the several instruments, matters, and things mentioned and described in the schedule (marked B) hereunto annexed, or for or in respect of the vellum, parchment, or paper upon which such instruments, matters, or things, or any of them, shall be written or printed, by any person or persons, or party who shall make, sign, or issue the same, or for whose use or benefit the same shall be made, signed, or issued, the several duties or sums of money set down in figures against the same, respectively, or otherwise specified or set forth in the said schedule.

SCHEDULE B.

30 June, 1864, § 151
3 March, 1865, § 1.
13 July, 1866, § 9.

STAMP DUTIES.

	Duty.
Agreement. **AGREEMENT** or contract, other than domestic and inland bills of lading, and those specified in this schedule; any appraisement of value or damage, or for any other purpose; for every sheet or piece of paper upon which either of the same shall be written, five cents	$0 05
Provided, That if more than one appraisement, agreement, or contract shall be written upon one sheet or piece of paper, five cents for each and every additional appraisement, agreement, or contract.	
Bank check. **BANK CHECK**, draft, or order for the payment of any sum of money whatsoever, drawn upon any bank, banker, or trust company, or for any sum exceeding ten dollars drawn upon any other person or persons, companies, or corporations, at sight or on demand, two cents	[0]2
Bill of exchange, (inland.) **BILL OF EXCHANGE**, (inland,) draft, or order for the payment of any sum of money not exceeding one hundred dollars, otherwise than at sight or on demand, or any promissory note, (except bank notes issued for circulation, and checks made and intended to be forthwith presented, and which shall be presented to a bank or banker for payment,) or any memorandum, check, receipt, or other written or printed evidence of an amount of money to be paid on demand, or at a time designated, for a sum not exceeding one hundred dollars, five cents	[0]5
And for every additional hundred dollars, or fractional part thereof in excess of one hundred dollars, five cents	[0]5
Bill of exchange, (foreign.) **BILL OF EXCHANGE**, (foreign,) or letter of credit, drawn in but payable out of the United States, if drawn singly, or otherwise than in a set of three or more, according to the custom of merchants and bankers, shall pay the same rates of duty as inland bills of exchange or promissory notes.	
If drawn in sets of three or more: For every bill of each set where the sum made payable shall not exceed one hundred dollars, or the equivalent thereof, in any foreign currency in which such bills may be expressed, according to the standard of value fixed by the United States, two cents	[0]2
And for every additional hundred dollars or fractional part thereof in excess of one hundred dollars, two cents	[0]2
Bill of lading. **BILL OF LADING** or receipt, (other than charter-party,) for any goods, merchandise, or effects, to be exported from a port or place in the United States to any foreign port or place, ten cents	10
Bill of sale of ship. **BILL OF SALE** by which any ship or vessel, or any part thereof, shall be conveyed to or vested in any other person or persons when the consideration shall not exceed five hundred dollars, fifty cents	50
Exceeding five hundred and not exceeding one thousand dollars, one dollar	1 00
Exceeding one thousand dollars for every additional amount of five hundred dollars, or fractional part thereof, fifty cents	50
Bond. **BOND.**—For indemnifying any person for the payment of any sum of money, where the money ultimately recoverable thereupon is one thousand dollars or less, fifty cents	50
Where the money ultimately recoverable thereupon exceeds one thousand dollars, for every additional one thousand dollars or fractional part thereof in excess of one thousand dollars, fifty cents	50

		Duty.
	BOND for the due execution or performance of the duties of any office, one dollar	1 00
	BOND of any description, other than such as may be required in legal proceedings, or used in connexion with mortgage deeds, and not otherwise charged in this schedule, twenty-five cents	25
Certificate.	CERTIFICATE of stock in any incorporated company, twenty-five cents	25
	CERTIFICATE of profits, or any certificate or memorandum showing an interest in the property or accumulations of any incorporated company, if for a sum not less than ten dollars and not exceeding fifty dollars, ten cents	10
	Exceeding fifty dollars and not exceeding one thousand dollars, twenty-five cents	25
	Exceeding one thousand dollars, for every additional one thousand dollars, or fractional part thereof, twenty-five cents	25
	CERTIFICATE.—Any certificate of damage, or otherwise, and all other certificates or documents issued by any port warden, marine surveyor, or other person acting as such, twenty-five cents	25
	CERTIFICATE of deposit of any sum of money in any bank or trust company, or with any banker or person acting as such—	
	If for a sum not exceeding one hundred dollars, two cents	[0]2
	For a sum exceeding one hundred dollars, five cents	[0]5
	CERTIFICATE of any other description than those specified, five cents	[0]5
Charter-party.	CHARTER-PARTY.—Contract or agreement for the charter of any ship or vessel, or steamer, or any letter, memorandum, or other writing between the captain, master, or owner, or person acting as agent of any ship or vessel, or steamer, and any other person or persons for or relating to the charter of such ship or vessel, or steamer, or any renewal or transfer thereof, if the registered tonnage of such ship or vessel, or steamer, does not exceed one hundred and fifty tons, one dollar	1 00
	Exceeding one hundred and fifty tons and not exceeding three hundred tons, three dollars	3 00
	Exceeding three hundred tons and not exceeding six hundred tons, five dollars	5 00
	Exceeding six hundred tons, ten dollars	10 00
Broker's contract.	CONTRACT.—Broker's note, or memorandum, of sale of any goods or merchandise, real estate, or property of any kind or description, issued by brokers or persons acting as such, for each note or memorandum of sale, ten cents	10
13 July, 1866, § 9.	Bill or memorandum of the sale or contract for the sale of stocks, bonds, gold or silver bullion, coin, promissory notes, or other securities, shall pay a stamp tax at the rate provided in section ninety-nine.	
Conveyance.	CONVEYANCE.—Deed, instrument, or writing, whereby any lands, tenements, or other realty sold shall be granted, assigned, transferred, or otherwise conveyed to, or vested in, the purchaser or purchasers, or any other person or persons by his, her, or their direction, when the consideration or value does not exceed five hundred dollars, fifty cents	50
	When the consideration exceeds five hundred dollars and does not exceed one thousand dollars, one dollar	1 00
	And for every additional five hundred dollars, or fractional part thereof, in excess of one thousand dollars, fifty cents	50
Entry of goods.	ENTRY of any goods, wares, or merchandise at any custom-house, either for consumption or warehousing, not exceeding one hundred dollars in value, twenty-five cents	25
	Exceeding one hundred dollars and not exceeding five hundred dollars in value, fifty cents	50
	Exceeding five hundred dollars in value, one dollar	1 00
	ENTRY for the withdrawal of any goods or merchandise from bonded warehouse, fifty cents	50
Insurance.	INSURANCE, (LIFE.)—Policy of insurance, or other instrument, by whatever name the same shall be called, whereby any insurance shall be made upon any life or lives—	
	When the amount insured shall not exceed one thousand dollars, twenty-five cents	25
	Exceeding one thousand dollars and not exceeding five thousand dollars, fifty-cents	50
	Exceeding five thousand dollars, one dollar	1 00

	Duty	
INSURANCE, (MARINE, INLAND, AND FIRE.)—Each policy of insurance or other instrument, by whatever name the same shall be called, by which insurance shall be made or renewed upon property of any description, whether against perils by the sea or by fire, or other peril of any kind, made by any insurance company, or its agents, or by any other company or person, the premium upon which does not exceed ten dollars, ten cents	10	
Exceeding ten and not exceeding fifty dollars, twenty-five cents	25	
Exceeding fifty dollars, fifty cents	50	
LEASE, agreement, memorandum, or contract for the hire, use, or rent of any land, tenement, or portion thereof, where the rent or rental value is three hundred dollars per annum or less, fifty cents	50	Lease.
Where the rent or rental value exceeds the sum of three hundred dollars per annum, for each additional two hundred dollars, or fractional part thereof in excess of three hundred dollars, fifty cents	50	
MANIFEST for custom-house entry or clearance of the cargo of any ship, vessel, or steamer for a foreign port—		Manifest.
If the registered tonnage of such ship, vessel, or steamer does not exceed three hundred tons, one dollar	1 00	
Exceeding three hundred tons and not exceeding six hundred tons, three dollars	3 00	
Exceeding six hundred tons, five dollars	5 00	
MORTGAGE of lands, estate, or property, real or personal, heritable or movable whatsoever, where the same shall be made as a security for the payment of any definite and certain sum of money lent at the time or previously due and owing or forborne to be paid, being payable; also any conveyance of any lands, estate, or property whatsoever, in trust, to be sold or otherwise converted into money, which shall be intended only as security, and shall be redeemable before the sale or other disposal thereof, either by express stipulation or otherwise; or any personal bond given as security for the payment of any definite or certain sum of money exceeding one hundred dollars, and not exceeding five hundred dollars, fifty cents	50	Mortgage.
Exceeding five hundred dollars, and not exceeding one thousand dollars, one dollar	1 00	
And for every additional five hundred dollars, or fractional part thereof, in excess of one thousand dollars, fifty cents	50	13 July, 1866, § 9.
Upon every assignment or transfer of a mortgage the same stamp tax upon the amount remaining unpaid thereon as is herein imposed upon a mortgage for the same amount: *Provided*, That upon each and every assignment or transfer of a policy of insurance, or the renewal or continuance of any agreement, contract, or charter, by letter or otherwise, a stamp duty shall be required and paid equal to that imposed on the original instrument: *And provided further*, That upon each and every assignment of any lease a stamp duty shall be required and paid equal to that imposed on the original instrument, increased by a stamp duty on the consideration or value of the assignment equal to that imposed upon the conveyance of land for similar consideration or value.		3 March, 1865.
PASSAGE TICKET, by any vessel from a port in the United States to a foreign port, not exceeding thirty-five dollars, fifty cents	50	Passage ticket.
Exceeding thirty-five dollars and not exceeding fifty dollars, one dollar	1 00	
And for every additional fifty dollars, or fractional part thereof, in excess of fifty dollars, one dollar	1 00	
POWER OF ATTORNEY for the sale or transfer of any stock, bonds, or scrip, or for the collection of any dividends or interest thereon, twenty-five cents	25	Power of attorney.
POWER OF ATTORNEY OR PROXY for voting at any election for officers of any incorporated company or society, except religious, charitable, or literary societies, or public cemeteries, ten cents	10	
POWER OF ATTORNEY to receive or collect rent, twenty-five cents	25	
POWER OF ATTORNEY to sell and convey real estate, or to rent or lease the same, one dollar	1 00	
POWER OF ATTORNEY for any other purpose, fifty cents	50	
PROBATE OF WILL, or letters of administration: Where the estate and effects for or in respect of which such probate or letters of administration applied for shall be sworn or declared not to exceed the value of two thousand dollars, one dollar	100	Probate of will.

Exceeding two thousand dollars, for every additional thousand dollars, or fractional part thereof, in excess of two thousand dollars, fifty cents ... 50

Protest.

PROTEST.—Upon the protest of every note, bill of exchange, acceptance, check, or draft, or any marine protest, whether protested by a notary public or by any other officer who may be authorized by the law of any State or States to make such protest, twenty-five cents ... 25

13 July, 1866, § 9.

Receipts for any sum of money, or for the payment of any debt, exceeding twenty dollars in amount, not being for the satisfaction of any mortgage or judgment, or decree of any court, or by indorsement on any stamped obligation in acknowledgment of its fulfilment, for each receipt two cents: *Provided*, That when more than one signature is affixed to the same paper, one or more stamps may be affixed thereto representing the whole amount of the stamp required for such signatures; and that the term money, as herein used, shall be held to include drafts and other instruments given for the payment of money.

Legal docum'ts.

LEGAL DOCUMENTS:

Writ or other original process by which any suit is commenced in any court of record, either of law or equity, fifty cents ... 50

Where the amount claimed in a writ, issued by a court not of record, is one hundred dollars or over, fifty cents ... 50

Upon every confession of judgment or cognovit, for one hundred dollars or over, (except in those cases where the tax for the writ of a commencement of suit has been paid,) fifty cents ... 50

Writs or other process on appeals from justices' courts or other courts of inferior jurisdiction to a court of record, fifty cents ... 50

Warrant of distress, when the amount of rent claimed does not exceed one hundred dollars, twenty-five cents ... 25

When the amount claimed exceeds one hundred dollars, fifty cents. 50

Provided, That no writ, summons, or other process issued by and returnable to a justice of the peace, except as hereinbefore provided, or by any police or municipal court having no larger jurisdiction as to the amount of damages it may render than a justice of the peace in the same State, or issued in any criminal or other suits commenced by the United States or any State, shall be subject to the payment of stamp duties: *And provided further*, That the stamp duties imposed by the foregoing schedule B on manifests, bills of lading, and passage tickets, shall not apply to steamboats or other vessels plying between ports of the United States and ports in British North America.

Affidavits exempt.

Affidavits in suits or legal proceedings shall be exempt from stamp duty.

30 June, 1864, § 159.

Bills of exchange drawn abroad, but payable in the United States, to be stamped before payment.

194. That the acceptor or acceptors of any bill of exchange or order for the payment of any sum of money drawn, or purporting to be drawn, in any foreign country, but payable in the United States, shall, before paying or accepting the same, place thereupon a stamp, indicating the duty upon the same, as the law requires for inland bills of exchange, or promissory notes, and no bill of exchange shall be paid or negotiated without such stamp; and if any person shall pay or negotiate, or offer in payment, or receive or take in payment, any such draft or order, the person or persons so offending shall forfeit the sum of two hundred dollars.

30 June, 1864, § 154.
13 July, 1866, § 9.

Exemptions.

Limited.

195. That all official instruments, documents, and papers issued by the officers of the United States government, or by the officers of any State, county, town, or other municipal corporation, shall be, and hereby are, exempt from taxation: *Provided*, That it is the intent hereby to exempt from liability to taxation such State, county, town, or other municipal corporation, in the exercise only of functions strictly belonging to them in their ordinary governmental and municipal capacity.

30 June, 1864, § 160.
3 March, 1865, § 1.

Papers relating to bounties, &c., exempt.

196. That no stamp duty shall be required on powers of attorney or any other paper relating to applications for bounties, arrearages of pay, or pensions, or to the receipt thereof from time to

time, or upon tickets or contracts of insurance when limited to accidental injury to persons, nor on certificates of the measurement or weight of animals, wood, coal, or hay; nor on deposit notes to mutual insurance companies for insurance upon which policies subject to stamp duties have been or are to be issued; nor on any certificate of the record of a deed or other instrument in writing, or of the acknowledgment or proof thereof by attesting witnesses; nor to any indorsement of a negotiable instrument or on any warrant of attorney, accompanying a bond or note, when such bond or note shall have affixed thereto the stamp or stamps denoting the duty required; and whenever any bond or note shall be secured by a mortgage, but one stamp shall be required to be placed on such papers: *Provided*, That the stamp duty placed thereon shall be the highest rate required for said instruments, or either of them.

Insurance ag'nst accidental injury. Certificates of measurement and weight of animals, wood, coal, or hay. Mutual insurance deposit notes. Certificates of record.

Acknowledgments of deeds, &c.

Bond, mortgage, &c., but one stamp.

197. That it shall not be lawful to record any instrument, document, or paper required by law to be stamped, unless a stamp or stamps of the proper amount shall have been affixed, and cancelled in the manner required by law; and the record of any such instrument, upon which the proper stamp or stamps aforesaid shall not have been affixed and cancelled as aforesaid, shall be utterly void, and shall not be used in evidence.

30 June, 1864, § 152. 13 July, 1866, § 9.

Instrument not to be recorded unless properly stamped.

198. That hereafter no deed, instrument, document, writing, or paper, required by law to be stamped, which has been signed or issued without being duly stamped, or with a deficient stamp, nor any copy thereof, shall be recorded, or admitted, or used as evidence in any court until a legal stamp or stamps, denoting the amount of tax, shall have been affixed thereto, as prescribed by law: *Provided*, That any power of attorney, conveyance, or document of any kind, made or purporting to be made in any foreign country to be used in the United States, shall pay the same tax as is required by law on similar instruments or documents when made or issued in the United States; and the party to whom the same is issued, or by whom it is to be used, shall, before using the same, affix thereon the stamp or stamps indicating the tax required.

30 June, 1864, § 163. 13 July, 1866, § 9.

Instruments heretofore issued without stamps not to be used or recorded until stamps are affixed.

Instruments made abroad.

199. That no instrument, document, writing, or paper of any description, required by law to be stamped, shall be deemed or held invalid and of no effect for the want of the particular kind or description of stamp designated for and denoting the duty charged on any such instrument, document, writing, or paper, provided a legal stamp, or stamps, denoting a duty of equal amount, shall have been duly affixed and used thereon: *Provided*, That the provisions of this section shall not apply to any stamp appropriated to denote the duty charged on proprietary articles, or articles enumerated in schedule C.

30 June, 1864, § 153.

No instrument to be invalid for want of particular stamp, if stamps of proper amount are affixed.

Provisions of this section not to apply to proprietary stamps.

200. That it shall be lawful for any person to present to the collector of the district, subject to the rules and regulations of the Commissioner of Internal Revenue, any instrument not previously issued or used, and require his opinion whether or not the same is chargeable with any stamp duty; and if the said collector shall be of opinion that such instrument is chargeable with any stamp duty, he shall, upon the payment therefor, affix and cancel the proper stamp; and if of the opinion that such instrument is not chargeable with any stamp duty, or is chargeable only with the duty by him designated, he is hereby required to impress thereon a particular stamp, to be provided for that purpose, with such

30 June, 1864, § 162.

Collectors to stamp instruments exempt from duty or subject to certain duty.

words or device thereon as he shall judge proper, which shall denote that such instrument is not chargeable with any stamp duty, or is chargeable only with the duty denoted by the stamp affixed; and every such instrument upon which the said stamp shall be impressed shall be deemed to be not chargeable, or to be chargeable only with the duty denoted by the stamp so affixed, and shall be received in evidence in all courts of law or equity, notwithstanding any objections made to the same by reason of it being unstamped, or of it being insufficiently stamped.

30 June, 1864, § 156.

Mode of cancelling adhesive stamps.

201. That in any and all cases where an adhesive stamp shall be used for denoting any duty imposed by this act, except as hereinafter provided, the person using or affixing the same shall write thereupon the initials of his name and the date upon which the same shall be attached or used, so that the same may not again be used.

Penalty for failure to cancel.

And if any person shall fraudulently make use of an adhesive stamp to denote any duty imposed by this act without so effectually cancelling and obliterating such stamp, except as before mentioned, he, she, or they shall forfeit the sum of fifty dollars:

Proprietors of articles in schedule C may furnish private dies.

Provided, That any proprietor or proprietors of proprietary articles, or articles subject to stamp duty under schedule C of this act, shall have the privilege of furnishing, without expense to the United States, in suitable form, to be approved by the Commissioner of Internal Revenue, his or their own dies or designs for stamps to be used thereon, to be made under the direction and to be retained in the possession of the Commissioner of Internal Revenue for his or their separate use, which shall not be duplicated to any other person.

Mode of cancelling private stamps.

That in all cases where such stamp is used, instead of his or their writing the date thereon, the said stamp shall be so affixed on the box, bottle, or package, that in opening the same, or using the contents thereof, the said stamp shall be effectually destroyed; and in default thereof, shall be liable to the same penalty imposed for neglect to affix said stamp as hereinbefore prescribed in this act.

Penalty for forging or counterfeiting private stamps.

Any person who shall fraudulently obtain or use any of the aforesaid stamps or designs therefor, and any person forging, or counterfeiting, or causing or procuring the forging or counterfeiting any representation, likeness, similitude, or colorable imitation of the said last-mentioned stamp, or any engraver or printer who shall sell or give away said stamps, or selling the same, or, being a merchant, broker, peddler, or person dealing, in whole or in part, in similar goods, wares, merchandise, manufactures, preparations, or articles, or those designed for similar objects or purposes, shall have knowingly or fraudulently in his, her, or their possession any such forged, counterfeited likeness, similitude, or colorable imitation of the said last-mentioned stamp, shall be deemed guilty of a felony, and, upon conviction thereof, shall be subject to all the penalties, fines, and forfeitures prescribed in the preceding section of this act.

30 June, 1864, § 157.

Commis'ner may prescribe other method of cancellation.

202. That the Commissioner of Internal Revenue be, and he is hereby, authorized to prescribe such method for the cancellation of stamps, as substitute for or in addition to the method now prescribed by law, as he may deem expedient and effectual. And he is further authorized, in his discretion, to make the application of such method imperative upon the manufacturers of proprietary articles, or articles included in schedule C, and upon stamps of a minal value exceeding twenty-five cents each.

30 June, 1864, § 155. 13 July, 1866, § 9.

Penalty for forging, counterfeit'g, or misusing stamps or dies.

203. That if any person shall forge or counterfeit, or cause or procure to be forged or counterfeited, any stamp, die, plate, or other instrument, or any part of any stamp, die, plate, or other instrument, which shall have be[en] provided, or may hereafter be provided, made, or used in pursuance of this act, or shall forge, counterfeit, or resemble, or cause or procure to be forged, counterfeited, or resembled, the impression, or any part of the impression, of any such stamp, die, plate, or other instrument as aforesaid, upon any vellum, parchment, or paper, or shall stamp or mark, or cause or procure to be stamped or marked, any vellum, parchment, or paper, with any such forged or counterfeited stamp, die, plate, or other instrument, or part of any stamp, die, plate, or other instrument, as aforesaid, with intent to defraud the United States of any of the taxes hereby imposed, or any part thereof; or if any person shall utter, or sell, or expose to sale, any vellum, parchment, paper, article, or thing, having thereupon the impression of any such counterfeited stamp, die, plate, or other instrument, or any part of any stamp, die, plate, or other instrument, or any such forged, counterfeited, or resembled impression, or part of impression, as aforesaid, knowing the same to be forged, counterfeited, or resembled; or if any person shall knowingly use or permit the use of any stamp, die, plate, or other instrument, which shall have been so provided, made, or used, as aforesaid, with intent to defraud the United States; or if any person shall fraudulently cut, tear, or remove, or cause or procure to be cut, torn, or removed, the impression of any stamp, die, plate, or other instrument, which shall have been provided, made, or used, in pursuance of this act, from any vellum, parchment, or paper, or any instrument or writing charged or chargeable with any of the taxes imposed by law; or if any person shall fraudulently use, join, fix, or place, or cause to be used, joined, fixed, or placed, to, with, or upon any vellum, parchment, paper, or any instrument or writing charged or chargeable with any of the taxes hereby imposed, any adhesive stamp, or the impression of any stamp, die, plate, or other instrument, which shall have been provided, made, or used in pursuance of law, and which shall have been cut, torn, or removed from any other vellum, parchment, or paper, or any instrument or writing charged or chargeable with any of the taxes imposed by law; or if any person shall wilfully remove or cause to be removed, alter or cause to be altered, the cancelling or defacing marks on any adhesive stamp, with intent to use the same, or to cause the use of the same after it shall have been once used, or shall knowingly or wilfully sell or buy such washed or restored stamps, or offer the same for sale, or give or expose the same to any person for use, or knowingly use the same, or prepare the same with intent for the further use thereof; or if any person shall knowingly and without lawful excuse (the proof whereof shall lie on the person accused) have in his possession any washed, restored, or altered stamps, which have been removed from any vellum, parchment, paper, instrument, or writing, then, and in every such case, every person so offending, and every person knowingly and wilfully aiding, abetting, or assisting in committing any such offence as aforesaid, shall, on conviction thereof, forfeit the said counterfeit stamps and the articles upon which they are placed, and be punished by fine not exceeding one thousand dollars, or by imprisonment and confinement to hard labor not exceeding five years, or both, at the discretion of the court.

30 June, 1864, § 158
3 March, 1865, § 1.
13 July, 1866, § 9.

Penalty for issuing instruments without proper stamps.

204. That any person or persons who shall make, sign, or issue, or who shall cause to be made, signed, or issued, any instrument, document, or paper of any kind or description whatsoever, or shall accept, negotiate, or pay, or cause to be accepted, negotiated, or paid, any bill of exchange, draft, or order, or promissory note for the payment of money, without the same being duly stamped, or having thereupon an adhesive stamp for denoting the tax chargeable thereon, and cancelled in the manner required by law, with intent to evade the provisions of this act, shall, for every such offence, forfeit the sum of fifty dollars, and such instrument, document, or paper, bill, draft, order, or note, not being stamped according to law, shall be deemed invalid and of no effect: *Provided*, That the title of a purchaser of land by deed duly stamped shall not be defeated or affected by the want of a proper stamp on any deed conveying said land by any person from, through, or under whom his grantor claims or holds title: *And provided further*, That hereafter, in all cases where the party has not affixed to any instrument the stamp required by law thereon at the time of making or issuing the said instrument, and he or they, or any party having an interest therein, shall be subsequently desirous of affixing such stamp to said instrument, or if said instrument be lost, to a copy thereof, he or they shall appear before the collector of the revenue of the proper district, who shall, upon the payment of the price of the proper stamp required by law, and of a penalty of fifty dollars, and where the whole amount of the tax denoted by the stamp required shall exceed the sum of fifty dollars, on payment also of interest, at the rate of six per centum on said tax from the day on which such stamp ought to have been affixed, affix the proper stamp to such instrument or copy, and note upon the margin thereof the date of his so doing, and the fact that such penalty has been paid; and the same shall thereupon be deemed and held to be as valid, to all intents and purposes, as if stamped when made or issued: *And provided further*, That where it shall appear to said collector, upon oath or otherwise, to his satisfaction, that any such instrument has not been duly stamped at the time of making or issuing the same, by reason of accident, mistake, inadvertence, or urgent necessity, and without any wilful design to defraud the United States of the stamp, or to evade or delay the payment thereof, then and in such case, if such instrument, or, if the original be lost, a copy thereof, duly certified by the officer having charge of any records in which such original is required to be recorded, or otherwise duly proven to the satisfaction of the collector, shall, within twelve calendar months after the first day of August, eighteen hundred and sixty-six, or within twelve calendar months after the making or issuing thereof, be brought to the said collector of revenue to be stamped, and the stamp tax chargeable thereon shall be paid, it shall be lawful for the said collector to remit the penalty aforesaid, and to cause such instrument to be duly stamped. And when the original instrument, or a certified or duly proved copy thereof, as aforesaid, duly stamped so as to entitle the same to be recorded, shall be presented to the clerk, register, recorder, or other officer having charge of the original record, it shall be lawful for such officer, upon the payment of the fee legally chargeable for the recording thereof, to make a new record thereof, or to note upon the original record the fact that the error or omission in the stamping of said original in-

Instruments unstamped invalid.

Title of second purchaser not affected.

Instrum'ts issued without stamps may be subsequently stamped.

Party in interest may present instrument to collector.

Penalty of $50.

Where stamp duty exceeds $50, interest to be paid.

Collector may remit penalty in certain cases.

Subseq'nt stamping may be recorded.

strument has been corrected pursuant to law; and the original instrument or such certified copy or the record thereof may be used in all courts and places in the same manner and with like effect as if the instrument had been originally stamped: *And provided further*, That in all cases where the party has not affixed the stamp required by law upon any instrument made, signed, or issued, at a time when and at a place where no collection district was established, it shall be lawful for him or them, or any party having an interest therein, to affix the proper stamp thereto, or if the original be lost, to a copy thereof; and the instrument or copy to which the proper stamp has been thus affixed prior to the first day of January, one thousand eight hundred and sixty-seven, and the record thereof, shall be as valid, to all intents and purposes, as if stamped by the collector in the manner hereinbefore provided. But no right acquired in good faith before the stamping of such instrument or copy thereof, and the recording thereof, as herein provided, if such record be required by law, shall in any manner be affected by such stamping as aforesaid.

Proviso as to where no collection district was established.

Rights acquired before stamping not affected.

205. That the Commissioner of Internal Revenue be, and is hereby, authorized to sell to and supply collectors, deputy collectors, postmasters, stationers, or any other persons, at his discretion, with adhesive stamps, or stamped paper, vellum, or parchment, as herein provided for, in amounts of not less than fifty dollars, upon the payment, at the time of delivery, of the amount of duties said stamps, stamped paper, vellum, or parchment, so sold or supplied, represent, and may allow, upon the aggregate amount of such stamps, as aforesaid, the sum of not exceeding five per centum as commission to the collectors, postmasters, stationers, or other purchasers; but the cost of any paper, vellum, or parchment shall be paid by the purchaser of such stamped paper, vellum, or parchment, as aforesaid: *Provided*, That any proprietor or proprietors of articles named in schedule C, who shall furnish his or their own die or design for stamps, to be used especially for his or their own proprietary articles, shall be allowed the following commission, namely: On amounts purchased at one time of not less than fifty nor more than five hundred dollars, five per centum; on amounts over five hundred dollars, ten per centum. The Commissioner of Internal Revenue may from time to time make regulations, upon proper evidence of the facts, for the allowance of such of the stamps issued under the provisions of this act as may have been spoiled, destroyed, or rendered useless or unfit for the purpose intended, or for which the owner may have no use, or which through mistake may have been improperly or unnecessarily used, or where the rates or duties represented thereby have been paid in error, or remitted; and such allowance shall be made either by giving other stamps in lieu of the stamps so allowed for, or by repaying the amount or value, after deducting therefrom, in case of repayment, the sum of five per centum to the owner thereof; but no allowance shall be made in any case until the stamps so spoiled or rendered useless shall have been returned to the Commissioner of Internal Revenue, or until satisfactory proof has been made showing the reason why said stamps cannot be so returned: *Provided*, That the Commissioner of Internal Revenue may, from time to time, furnish, supply, and deliver to any manufacturer of friction or other matches, cigar lights or wax tapers, a suitable quantity of adhesive or other stamps, such

30 June, 1864, §161.

Commissioner authorized to sell stamps and allow a commission of 5 per cent.

Commission on private stamps.

Commis'ner may make allowance for stamps spoiled, &c.

Manufacturers of matches may be supplied on credit.

as may be prescribed for use in such cases, without prepayment therefor, on a credit not exceeding sixty days, requiring, in advance, such security as he may judge necessary to secure payment therefor to the Treasurer of the United States, within the time prescribed for such payment. And upon all bonds or other securities taken by said Commissioner, under the provisions of this act, suits may be maintained by said Treasurer in the circuit or district court of the United States, in the several districts where any of the persons giving said bonds or other securities reside or may be found, in any appropriate form of action.

2. PROPRIETARY.—SCHEDULE C.

30 June, 1864, §164

Provisions relating to schedule B applicable to schedule C.

206. That all the provisions of this act relating to dies, stamps, adhesive stamps, and stamp duties shall extend to and include (except where manifestly impracticable) all the articles or objects enumerated in schedule marked C, subject to stamp duties, and apply to the provisions in relation thereto.

SCHEDULE C.

MEDICINES OR PREPARATIONS.

Medicines or preparations.

For and upon every packet, box, bottle, pot, phial, or other enclosure, containing any pills, powders, tinctures, troches, lozenges, sirups, cordials, bitters, anodynes, tonics, plasters, liniments, salves, ointments, pastes, drops, waters, essences, spirits, oils, or other medicinal preparations or compositions whatsoever, made and sold, or removed for consumption and sale, by any person or persons whatever, wherein the person making or preparing the same has, or claims to have, any private formula or occult secret or art for the making or preparing the same, or has or claims to have any exclusive right or title to the making or preparing the same, or which are prepared, uttered, vended, or exposed for sale under any letters patent, or held out or recommended to the public by the makers, venders, or proprietors thereof as proprietary medicines, or as remedies or specifics for any disease, diseases, or affections whatever affecting the human or animal body, as follows: Where such packet, box, bottle, pot, phial, or other enclosure, with its contents, shall not exceed, at retail price, or value, the sum of twenty-five cents, one cent	$0 1
Where such packet, box, bottle, pot, phial, or other enclosure, with its contents, shall exceed the retail price or value of twenty-five cents, and not exceed the retail price or value of fifty cents, two cents	2
Where such packet, box, bottle, pot, phial, or other enclosure, with its contents, shall exceed the retail price or value of fifty cents, and shall not exceed the retail price or value of seventy-five cents, three cents	3
Where such packet, box, bottle, pot, phial, or other enclosure, with its contents, shall exceed the retail price or value of seventy-five cents, and shall not exceed the retail price or value of one dollar, four cents	4
Where such packet, box, bottle, pot, phial, or other enclosure, with its contents, shall exceed the retail price or value of one dollar, for each and every fifty cents or fractional part thereof over and above the one dollar, as before mentioned, an additional two cents.	2

PERFUMERY, COSMETICS, MATCHES, AND CARDS.

Perfumery and cosmetics.

For and upon every packet, box, bottle, pot, phial, or other enclosure, containing any essence, extract, toilet water, cosmetic, hair oil, pomade, hair-dressing, hair restorative, hair dye, tooth-wash, dentifrice, tooth-paste, aromatic cachous, or any similar articles, by whatsoever name the same heretofore have been, now are, or may hereafter be called, known or distinguished, used or applied, or to be used or applied as perfumes or applications to the hair, mouth, or skin, made, prepared, and sold or removed for consumption and sale in the United States, where such packet, box, bottle, pot, phial, or other enclosure, with its contents, shall not exceed, at the retail price or value, the sum of twenty-five cents, one cent.......... 1

Where such packet, box, bottle, pot, phial, or other enclosure, with its contents, shall exceed the retail price or value of twenty-five cents, and shall not exceed the retail price or value of fifty cents, two cents.......... 2

Where such packet, box, bottle, pot, phial, or other enclosure, with its contents, shall exceed the retail price or value of fifty cents, and shall not exceed the retail price or value of seventy-five cents, three cents.......... 3

Where such packet, box, bottle, pot, phial, or other enclosure, with its contents, shall exceed the retail price or value of seventy-five cents, and shall not exceed the retail price or value of one dollar, four cents.......... 4

Where such packet, box, bottle, pot, phial, or other enclosure, with its contents, shall exceed the retail price or value of one dollar, for each and every fifty cents or fractional part thereof over and above the one dollar, as before mentioned, an additional two cents.......... 2

Frict'n matches.

Friction matches, or lucifer matches, or other articles made in part of wood, and used for like purposes, in parcels or packages containing one hundred matches or less, for each parcel or package, one cent.......... 1

When in parcels or packages containing more than one hundred and not more than two hundred matches, for each parcel or package, two cents.......... 2

And for every additional one hundred matches or fractional part thereof, one cent.......... 1

13 July, 1866, § 9.

Wax tapers and cigar lights.

For wax tapers, double the rates herein imposed upon friction or lucifer matches; on cigar lights, made in part of wood, wax, glass, paper, or other materials, in parcels or packages containing twenty-five lights or less in each parcel or package, one cent.... 1

When in parcels or packages containing more than twenty-five and not more than fifty lights, two cents.......... 2

For every additional twenty-five lights or fractional part of that number, one cent additional.......... 1

3 March, 1865, § 1. 13 July, 1866, § 9.

Playing cards.

Playing cards.—For and upon every pack, not exceeding fifty-two cards in number, irrespective of price or value, five cents....... 5

Canned meats, &c.

Canned meats, &c.—For and upon every can, bottle, or other single package, containing meats, fish, shell-fish, fruits, vegetables, sauces, sirups, prepared mustard, jams or jellies contained therein and packed or sealed, made, prepared, and sold, or offered for sale, or removed for consumption in the United States, on and after the first day of October, eighteen hundred and sixty-six, when such can, bottle, or other single package, with its contents, shall not exceed two pounds in weight, the sum of one cent.......... 1

When such can, bottle, or other single package, with its contents, shall exceed two pounds in weight, for every additional pound or fractional part thereof, one cent.......... 1

13 July, 1866, § 13.

No tax upon medicines, &c., compounded according to certain pharmacopœias, &c.

207. That no stamp tax shall be imposed upon any uncompounded medicinal drug or chemical, nor upon any medicine compounded according to the United States or other national pharmacopœia, or of which the full and proper formula is published in any of the dispensatories now or hitherto in common use among physicians or apothecaries, or in any pharmaceutical journal now issued by any incorporated college of pharmacy, when not sold or offered for sale, or advertised under any other name, form, or guise than that under which they may be severally denominated and laid down in said pharmacopœias, dispensatories, or journals as aforesaid; nor upon medicines sold to or for the use of any person, which may be mixed and compounded for said person according to the written receipt or prescription of any physician or sur-

geon. But nothing in this section shall be construed to exempt from stamp tax any medicinal articles, whether simple or compounded by any rule, authority, or formula, published or unpublished, which are put up in a style or manner similar to that of patent or proprietary medicines in general, or advertised in newspapers or by public handbills for popular sale and use, as having any special proprietary claim to merit, or to any peculiar advantage in mode of preparation, quality, use, or effect, whether such claim be real or pretended.

30 June, 1864, § 168.
3 March, 1865, § 1.

Certain articles in schedule C, intended for exportation, may be manufactured in bonded warehouse.

208. That all medicines, preparations, compositions, perfumery, cosmetics, cordials, and other liquors manufactured wholly or in part of domestic spirits, intended for exportation, as provided for by law, in order to be manufactured and sold or removed, without being charged with duty and without having a stamp affixed thereto, shall, under such rules and regulations as the Secretary of the Treasury may prescribe, be made and manufactured in warehouses similarly constructed to those known and designated in treasury regulations as bonded warehouses, class two: *Provided*, That such manufacturer shall first give satisfactory bonds to the collector of internal revenue for the faithful observance of all the provisions of law and the rules and regulations as aforesaid, in amount not less than half of that required by the regulations of the Secretary of the Treasury from persons allowed bonded warehouses.

May be removed without stamps.

Such goods, when manufactured in such warehouses, may be removed for exportation, under the direction of the proper officer having charge thereof, who shall be designated by the Secretary of the Treasury, without being charged with duty, and without having a stamp affixed thereto. Any manufacturer of the articles aforesaid, or of any of them, having such bonded warehouse, as aforesaid, shall be at liberty, under such rules and regulations as the Secretary of the Treasury may prescribe, to convey therein any materials to be used in such manufacture which are allowed by the provisions of law to be exported free from tax or duty, as well as the necessary materials, implements, packages, vessels, brands, and labels for the preparation, putting up, and export of the said manufactured articles; and every article so used shall be exempted from the payment of stamp and excise duty by such manufacturer.

Articles used in such manufacture exempt from duty.

Articles and materials so to be used may be transferred from any bonded warehouse in which the same may be, under such regulations as the Secretary of the Treasury may prescribe, into any bonded warehouse in which such manufacture may be conducted, and may be used in such manufacture, and when so used shall be exempt from stamp and excise duty; and the receipt of the officer in charge, as aforesaid, shall be received as a voucher for the manufacture of such articles.

May be removed from ships or bonded warehouse into warehouse where the same are to be used.

Any materials imported into the United States may, under such rules as the Secretary of the Treasury may prescribe, and under the direction of the proper officer, be removed in original packages from on shipboard, or from the bonded warehouse in which the same may be, into the bonded warehouse in which such manufacture may be carried on, for the purpose of being used in such manufacture, without payment of duties thereon, and may there be used in such manufacture. No article so removed, nor any article manufactured in said bonded

Officer in charge of warehouse to give certificate upon removal.

warehouse, shall be taken therefrom except for exportation, under the direction of the proper officer having charge thereof, as aforesaid, whose certificate, describing the articles by their marks, or otherwise, the quantity, the date of importation, and name of vessel, with such additional particulars as may from time to time be required, shall be received by the collector of customs in cancellation of the bonds, or return of the amount of foreign import duties. All labor performed and services rendered under these regulations shall be under the supervision of an officer of the customs, and at the expense of the manufacturer.

Expenses to be borne by the manufacturer.

209. That lucifer or friction matches, and cigar lights and wax tapers, may be transferred, without payment of duty, directly from the place of manufacture to a bonded warehouse established in conformity with law and treasury regulations, and upon the execution of such transportation bonds or other security as the Secretary of the Treasury may prescribe, said bonds to be taken by the collector in the district from which such removal is made, and may be withdrawn therefrom for consumption after affixing the stamps thereto, as provided by the act to which this act is an amendment, or may be removed therefrom for export to a foreign country without payment of duty or affixing stamps thereto, in conformity with the provisions of the act aforesaid, relating to the removal of distilled spirits, all the rules and regulations and conditions of which, as far as applicable, shall apply to lucifer or friction matches, cigar lights, and wax tapers in bonded warehouse. And no drawback shall in any case be allowed upon any lucifer or friction matches, cigar lights, or wax tapers, upon which any excise duty has been paid, or stamps affixed, either before or after they have been placed in bonded warehouse.

3 March, 1865, § 11.

Matches may be placed in bonded warehouse and exported without payment of duty.

No drawback to be allowed.

210. That any person who shall offer or expose for sale any of the articles named in schedule C, or in any amendments thereto, whether the articles so offered or exposed are imported or are of foreign or domestic manufacture, shall be deemed the manufacturer thereof, and subject to all the duties, liabilities, and penalties imposed by law in regard to the sale of domestic articles without the use of the proper stamp or stamps denoting the tax paid thereon, and all such articles imported, or of foreign manufacture, shall, in addition to the import duties imposed on the same, be subject to the stamp tax, respectively, prescribed in schedule C, as aforesaid: *Provided*, That when such imported articles, except playing cards, lucifer or friction matches, cigar lights, and wax tapers, shall be sold in the original and unbroken package in which the bottles or other enclosures were packed by the manufacturer, the person so selling said articles shall not be subject to any penalty on account of the want of the proper stamp.

30 June, 1864, § 169.
3 March, 1865, § 1.
13 July, 1866, § 9.

Persons offering for sale articles in schedule C to be deemed the manufacturers.

Proviso relating to original and unbroken packages.

211. That if any person, firm, company, or corporation shall make, prepare, and sell, or remove for consumption or sale, drugs, medicines, preparations, compositions, articles, or things, including perfumery, cosmetics, lucifer or friction matches, cigar lights, or wax tapers, and playing cards, and also including prepared mustards, preserved meats, fish, shell-fish, fruits, vegetables, sauces, sirups, jams, and jellies, when packed or sealed in cans, bottles, or other single packages, whether of domestic manufacture or imported, upon which a duty or tax is imposed by law, as enumerated and mentioned in schedule C, without affixing thereto an adhesive stamp or label denoting the tax before mentioned, he or they shall incur a penalty of fifty dollars for every omission to affix such stamp.

30 June, 1864, § 165.
3 March, 1865, § 1.
13 July, 1866, § 9.

Penalty for selling, etc., articles in schedule C without proper stamps.

30 June, 1864, § 166.

Penalty for removing stamps from articles in schedule C.

212. That every manufacturer or maker of any of the articles for sale mentioned in schedule C, after the same shall have been so made, and the particulars hereinbefore required as to stamps have been complied with, who shall take off, remove, or detach, or cause, or permit, or suffer to be taken off, or removed, or detached, any stamp, or who shall use any stamp, or any wrapper or cover to which any stamp is affixed, to cover any other article or commodity than that originally contained in such wrapper or cover, with such stamp when first used, with the intent to evade the stamp duties, shall for every such article, respectively, in respect of which any such offence shall be committed, be subject to a penalty of fifty dollars, to be recovered together with the costs thereupon accruing; and every such article or commodity as aforesaid shall also be forfeited.

30 June, 1864, § 167.
3 March, 1865, § 1.

Forfeiture of articles upon attempt to evade the duty.

213. That on and after the passage of this act, every maker or manufacturer of any of the articles or commodities mentioned in Schedule C, as aforesaid, who shall sell, expose for sale, send out, remove, or deliver any article or commodity, manufactured as aforesaid, before the duty thereon shall have been fully paid, by affixing thereon the proper stamp, as provided by law, or who shall hide, or conceal, or cause to be hidden or concealed, or who shall remove or convey away, or deposit, or cause to be removed or conveyed away from or deposited in any place, any such article or commodity, to evade the duty chargeable thereon, or any part thereof, shall be subject to a penalty of one hundred dollars, together with the forfeiture of any such article or commodity.

30 June, 1864, § 170.

Commiss'r may furnish stamps to certain officers for sale.

214. That in any collection district where, in the judgment of the Commissioner of Internal Revenue, the facilities for the procurement and distribution of stamped vellum, parchment, or paper and adhesive stamps, are or shall be insufficient, the Commissioner, as aforesaid, is authorized to furnish, supply, and deliver to the collector and to the assessor of any such district, and to any assistant treasurer of the United States, or designated depositary thereof, or any postmaster, a suitable quantity or amount of stamped vellum, parchment, or paper, and adhesive stamps, without prepayment therefor, and shall allow the highest rate of commissions allowed by law to any other parties purchasing the same, and

May require bond.

may in advance require of any such collector, assessor, assistant treasurer of the United States, or postmaster, a bond, with sufficient sureties, to an amount equal to the value of any stamped vellum, parchment, or paper, and adhesive stamps which may be placed in his hands and remain unaccounted for, conditioned for the faithful return, whenever so required, of all quantities or amounts undisposed of, and for the payment, monthly, of all quantities or amounts, sold or not remaining on hand. And it shall be the duty of such collector to supply his deputies with, or sell to other parties within his district who may make application therefor, stamped vellum, parchment, or paper, and adhesive stamps, upon the same terms allowed by law, or under the regulations of the Commissioner of Internal Revenue, who is hereby authorized to make such other regulations, not inconsistent herewith, for the security of the United States and the better accommodation of the public, in relation to the matters hereinbefore mentioned, as he may judge necessary and expedient. And the Secretary of the Treasury may from time to time make such regulations as he may find necessary to insure the safe-keeping or prevent the illegal use of all such stamped vellum, parchment, paper, and adhesive stamps.

X.

DRAWBACK.

215. That from and after the date on which this act takes effect, there shall be an allowance or drawback on all articles on which any internal duty or tax shall have been paid, except raw or unmanufactured cotton, crude petroleum or rock oil, refined coal oil, naphtha, benzine or benzole, distilled spirits, manufactured tobacco, snuff, and cigars of all descriptions, bullion, quicksilver, lucifer or friction matches, cigar lights, and wax tapers, equal in amount to the duty or tax paid thereon, and no more, when exported, the evidence that any such duty or tax has been paid to be furnished to the satisfaction of the Commissioner of Internal Revenue by such person or persons as shall claim the allowance or drawback, and the amount to be ascertained under such regulations as shall, from time to time, be prescribed by the Commissioner of Internal Revenue, under the direction of the Secretary of the Treasury, and the same shall be paid by the warrant of the Secretary of the Treasury on the Treasurer of the United States, out of any money arising from internal duties not otherwise appropriated: *Provided*, That no allowance or drawback shall be made or had for any amount claimed or due less than ten dollars, anything in this act to the contrary notwithstanding: *And provided further*, That any certificate of drawback for goods exported, issued in pursuance of the provisions of law, may, under such regulations as may be prescribed by the Secretary of the Treasury, be received by the collector or his deputy in payment of duties under this act. And the Secretary of the Treasury may make such regulations with regard to the form of said certificates and the issuing thereof as, in his judgment, may be necessary: *Provided also*, That no claim for drawback on any articles of merchandise exported prior to June thirtieth, eighteen hundred and sixty-four, shall be allowed unless presented to the Commissioner of Internal Revenue within three months after this amendment takes effect.

30 June, 1864, § 171. 3 March, 1865, § 1. Drawback on certain manufactures exported.

Method of payment.

No allowance to be less than $10.

Certificates of drawback receivable for duties.

Secretary may make regulations.

13 July, 1866, § 9. Proviso of limitation.

216. That upon articles manufactured exclusively from cotton, when exported, there shall be allowed as a drawback an amount equal to the internal tax which shall have been assessed and paid upon such articles in their finished condition, and in addition thereto a drawback or allowance of as many cents per pound upon the pound of cotton cloth, yarn, thread, or knit fabrics, manufactured exclusively from cotton and exported, as shall have been assessed and paid in the form of an internal tax upon the raw cotton entering into the manufacture of said cloth or other article, the amount of such allowance or drawback to be ascertained in such manner as may be prescribed by the Commissioner of Internal Revenue under the direction of the Secretary of the Treasury; and so much of section one hundred and seventy-one of the act of June thirty, eighteen hundred and sixty-four, "to provide internal revenue to support the government, to pay interest on the public debt, and for other purposes," as now provides for a drawback on manufactured cotton, is hereby repealed.

13 July, 1866, § 6. Drawback on articles manufactured of cotton.

Repeals former allowance.

217. That in any port of the United States in which there is more than one collector of internal revenue, the Secretary of the Treasury may designate one of said collectors to have charge of all matters relating to the exportation of articles subject to tax un-

3 March, 1865, § 15. 13 July, 1866, § 20. One collector to be designated to have charge of exportations, where there is more than one in any port.

Officer to be designated by Secretary to superintend.

der the laws to provide internal revenue; and at such ports as the Secretary of the Treasury may deem it necessary, there shall be an officer appointed by him to superintend all matters of exportation and drawback, under the direction of the collector, whose compensation therefor shall be prescribed by the Secretary of the Treasury, but shall not exceed, in any case, an annual rate of two thousand dollars, excepting at New York, where the compensation shall be an annual rate of three thousand dollars. And all the books, papers, and documents in the bureau of drawback in the respective ports, relating to the drawback of taxes paid under the internal revenue laws, shall be delivered to said collector of internal revenue; and any collector of internal revenue, or superintendent of exports and drawbacks, shall have authority to administer such oaths and certify to such papers as may be necessary under any rules and regulations that may be prescribed under the authority herein conferred.

Compensation.

Papers in bureau of drawback to be delivered to collector.

Authority to administer oaths, &c.

30 June, 1864, §172

Penalty for fraudulent claim for drawback.

218. That if any person or persons shall fraudulently claim or seek to obtain an allowance or drawback on goods, wares, or merchandise, on which no internal duty shall have been paid, or shall fraudulently claim any greater allowance or drawback than the duty actually paid, as aforesaid, such person or persons shall forfeit triple the amount wrongfully or fraudulently claimed or sought to be obtained, or the sum of five hundred dollars, at the election of the Secretary of the Treasury, to be recovered as in other cases of forfeiture provided for in the general provisions of this act.

XI.

PENALTIES, FORFEITURES, AND PROCEEDINGS.

30 June, 1864, §15.

Penalty for making fraudulent return.

Or for refusing to appear and produce books.

219 That if any person shall deliver or disclose to any assessor or assistant assessor appointed in pursuance of law any false or fraudulent list, return, account, or statement, with intent to defeat or evade the valuation, enumeration, or assessment intended to be made, or if any person who being duly summoned to appear to testify, or to appear and produce such books as aforesaid, shall neglect to appear or to produce said books, he shall, upon conviction thereof before any circuit or district court of the United States, be fined in any sum not exceeding one thousand dollars, or be imprisoned for not exceeding one year, or both, at the discretion of the court, with cost of prosecution.

30 June, 1864, § 42.

False swearing to be deemed perjury.

220. That if any person, in any case, matter, hearing, or other proceeding in which an oath or affirmation shall be required to be taken or administered under and by virtue of this act, shall, upon the taking of such oath or affirmation, knowingly and wilfully swear or affirm falsely, every person so offending shall be deemed guilty of perjury, and shall, on conviction thereof, be subject to the like punishment and penalties now provided by the laws of the United States for the crime of perjury.

13 July, 1866, § 62.

Bribery of public officers.

221. That if any person or persons shall, directly or indirectly, promise, offer, or give, or cause or procure to be promised, offered, or given, any money, goods, right in action, bribe, present, or reward, or any promise, contract, undertaking, obligation, or security for the payment or delivery of any money, goods, right in action, bribe, present, or reward, or any other valuable thing whatever to any officer of the United States, or person holding any place of trust or profit, or discharging any official function under, or in connexion with, any department of the government

of the United States, after the passage of this act, with intent to influence his decision or action on any question, matter, cause, or thing which may then be pending, or may by law be brought before him in his official capacity, or in his place of trust or profit, or with intent to influence any such officer or person to commit, or aid or abet in committing, any fraud on the revenue of the United States, or to connive at or collude in, or to allow or permit, or make opportunity for the commission of any such fraud, and shall be thereof convicted, such person or persons so offering, promising, or giving, or causing, or procuring to be promised, offered, or given any such money, goods, right in action, bribe, present, or reward, or any promise, contract, undertaking, obligation, or security for the payment or delivery of any money, goods, right in action, bribe, present, or reward, or other valuable thing whatever, and the officer or person who shall in anywise accept or receive the same, or any part, respectively, shall be liable to indictment in any court of the United States having jurisdiction, and shall, upon conviction thereof, be fined not exceeding three times the amount so offered, promised, given, accepted, or received, and imprisoned not exceeding three years; and the person convicted of so accepting or receiving the same, or any part thereof, if an officer or person holding any such place of trust or profit, shall forfeit his office or place; and any person so convicted under this section shall forever be disqualified to hold any office of honor, trust, or profit under the United States.

Accepting bribes

Penalty.

222. That in case any person shall sell, give, or purchase or receive any box, barrel, bag, or any vessel, package, wrapper, cover, or envelope of any kind, stamped, branded or marked in any way so as to show that the contents or intended contents thereof have been duly inspected, or that the tax thereon has been paid, or that any provision of the internal revenue laws has been complied with, whether such stamping, branding, or marking may have been a duly authorized act or may be false and counterfeit, or otherwise without authority of law, said box, barrel, bag, vessel, package, wrapper, cover, or envelope being empty, or containing anything else than the contents which were therein when said articles had been so lawfully stamped, branded, or marked by an officer of the revenue, such person shall be liable to a penalty of not less than fifty nor more than five hundred dollars. And any person who shall make, manufacture, or produce any box, barrel, bag, vessel, package, wrapper, cover, or envelope, stamped, branded, or marked, as above described, or shall stamp, brand, or mark the same, as hereinbefore recited, shall, upon conviction thereof, be liable to penalty as before provided in this section. And any person who shall violate the foregoing provisions of this section, with intent to defraud the revenue, or to defraud any person, shall, upon conviction thereof, be liable to a fine of not less than one thousand nor more than five thousand dollars, or imprisonment for not less than six months, nor more than five years, or both such fine and imprisonment, at the discretion of the court. And all articles sold, given, purchased, received, made, manufactured, produced, branded, stamped, or marked in violation of the provisions of this section, and all their contents, shall be forfeited to the United States.

13 July, 1866, § 16.

Misuse of revenue stamps, &c.

Penalty for.

In case of fraudulent intent.

Forfeiture.

30 June, 1864, § 49.

Provisions hereinafter made for delivery of returns, &c., imposition of fines, &c., apply to all persons, corporations, &c.

223. That all the provisions hereinafter made for the delivery of returns, lists, statements, and valuations, and for additions to the duty in case of false or fraudulent lists or returns, or in case of undervaluation or understatement on lists or returns, or in case of refusal or neglect to deliver lists or returns, and for the imposition of fines, penalties, and forfeitures, shall be held and taken to apply to all persons, associations, corporations, or companies liable to pay duty or tax; and any additions to duties, fines, penalties, or forfeitures hereinafter imposed for failure to perform any duty required to be performed, shall be held and taken to be additional to those hereinbefore provided.

Fines hereinafter imposed addit'nal to those hereinbefore provided.

30 June, 1864, § 48.
13 July, 1866, § 9.

Articles held by any person with intent to defraud the revenue may be seized by certain officers.

224. That all goods, wares, merchandise, articles, or objects, on which taxes are imposed by the provisions of law, which shall be found in the possession, or custody, or within the control of any person or persons, for the purpose of being sold or removed by such person or persons in fraud of the internal revenue laws, or with design to avoid payment of said taxes, may be seized by the collector or deputy collector of the proper district, or by such other collector or deputy collector as may be specially authorized by the Commissioner of Internal Revenue for that purpose, and the same shall be forfeited to the United States; and also all raw materials found in the possession of any person or persons intending to manufacture the same into articles of a kind subject to tax for the purpose of fraudulent[ly] selling such manufactured articles, or with design to evade the payment of said tax; and also all tools, implements, instruments, and personal property whatsoever, in the place or building or within any yard or enclosure where such articles or such raw materials shall be found, may also be seized by any collector or deputy collector, as aforesaid, and the same shall be forfeited as aforesaid; and the proceedings to enforce said forfeiture shall be in the nature of a proceeding in rem in the circuit or district court of the United States for the district where such seizure is made, or in any other court of competent jurisdiction. And any person who shall have in his custody or possession any such goods, wares, merchandise, articles, or objects, subject to tax as aforesaid, for the purpose of selling the same with the design of avoiding payment of the taxes imposed thereon, shall be liable to a penalty of five hundred dollars, or not less than double the amount of taxes fraudulently attempted to be evaded, to be recovered in any court of competent jurisdiction; and the goods, wares, merchandise, articles, or objects, which shall be so seized by any collector or deputy collector, may, at the option of the collector, be delivered to the marshal of said district, and remain in the care and custody of said marshal, and under his control, until he shall obtain possession by process of law, and the cost of seizure made before process issues shall be taxable by the court: *Provided*, That when the property so seized may be liable to perish or become greatly reduced in price or value by keeping, or when it cannot be kept without great expense, the owner thereof, the collector, or the marshal of the district, may apply to the assessor of the district to examine said property; and if, in the opinion of said assessor, it shall be necessary that the said property should be sold to prevent such waste or expense, he shall appraise the same; and the owner thereupon shall have said property returned to him upon giving bond in such form as may be prescribed by the Commissioner of Internal Revenue, and in an

The articles forfeited to the United States.

Forfeiture to be enforced by proceedings *in rem.*

Penalty for fraud $500, or double the amount of duties.

Custody of goods may be given to U. S. marshal.

Perishable property may be appraised and returned to owner, he giving bond for same.

amount equal to the appraised value, with such sureties as the said assessor shall deem good and sufficient, to abide the final order, decree, or judgment of the court having cognizance of the case, and to pay the amount of said appraised value to the collector, marshal, or otherwise, as he may be ordered and directed by the court, which bond shall be filed by said assessor with the United States district attorney for the district in which said proceedings in rem may be commenced: *Provided further*, That in case said bond shall have been executed and the property returned before seizure thereof, by virtue of the process aforesaid, the marshal shall give notice of the pendency of proceedings in court to the parties executing said bond, by personal service or publication, and in manner and form as the court may direct, and the court shall thereupon have jurisdiction of said matter and parties in the same manner as if such property had been seized by virtue of the process aforesaid. But if said owner shall neglect or refuse to give said bond, the assessor shall issue to the collector or marshal aforesaid an order to sell the same; and the said collector or marshal shall thereupon advertise and sell the said property at public auction in the same manner as goods may be sold on final execution in said district; and the proceeds of the sale, after deducting the reasonable costs of the seizure and sale, shall be paid to the court aforesaid, to abide its final order, decree, or judgment.

If bond not given property may be sold at auction.

13 July, 1861, § 14.

Removal or concealment with intent to defraud the revenue cause of forfeiture.

225. That in case any goods or commodities for or in respect whereof any tax is or shall be imposed, or any materials, utensils, or vessels proper or intended to be made use of for or in the making of such goods or commodities shall be removed, or shall be deposited or concealed in any place, with intent to defraud the United States of such tax, or any part thereof, all such goods and commodities, and all such materials, utensils, and vessels, respectively, shall be forfeited; and in every such case, and in every case where any goods or commodities shall be forfeited under this act, or any other act of Congress relating to the internal revenue, all and singular the casks, vessels, cases or other packages whatsoever, containing, or which shall have contained, such goods or commodities, respectively, and every vessel, boat, cart, carriage, or other conveyance whatsoever, and all horses or other animals, and all things used in the removal or for the deposit or concealment thereof, respectively, shall be forfeited; and every person who shall remove, deposit, or conceal, or be concerned in removing, depositing, or concealing any goods or commodities for or in respect whereof any tax is or shall be imposed, with intent to defraud the United States of such tax or any part thereof, shall be liable to a fine or penalty of not exceeding five hundred dollars.

Fine or penalty.

30 June, 1864, § 180.

Debts contracted through the sale of articles, with intent to evade tax, to be void.

226. That if any person liable and required to pay any tax upon any article, goods, wares, merchandise, or manufactures, as herein provided, shall sell, or cause or allow the same to be sold, before the tax to which such article, goods, wares, merchandise, or manufacture is legally liable is paid, with intent to avoid such tax, or in fraud of the revenue herein provided, any debt contracted in the sale of such article, goods, wares, merchandise, or manufactures, or any security given therefor, unless the same shall have been bona fide transferred to the hands of an innocent holder, shall be entirely void, and the collection thereof shall not be enforced in any court. And if any such article, goods, wares, merchandise, or manufacture has been paid for, in whole or in part,

the sum so paid shall be deemed forfeited, and any person who will sue for the same in an action of debt shall recover of the seller the amount so paid, one half to his own use and the other half to the use of the United States.

30 June, 1864, § 179. 3 March, 1865, § 1. 13 July, 1866, § 9.

Collectors to prosecute for fines, penalties, and forfeitures.

227. That, where it is not otherwise provided for, it shall be the duty of the collectors, in their respective districts, and they are hereby authorized, to prosecute for the recovery of any sum or sums that may be forfeited; and all fines, penalties, and forfeitures which may be imposed or incurred shall and may be sued for and recovered, where not otherwise provided, in the name of the United States, in any proper form of action, or by any appropriate form of proceeding, before any circuit or district court of the United States for the district within which said fine, penalty, or forfeiture may have been incurred, or before any court of competent jurisdiction. And where not otherwise provided for, such share as the Secretary of the Treasury shall, by general regulations, provide, not exceeding one moiety nor more than five thousand dollars in any one case, shall be to the use of the person, to be ascertained by the court which shall have imposed or decreed any such fine, penalty, or forfeiture, who shall first inform of the cause, matter, or thing whereby such fine, penalty, or forfeiture shall have been incurred; and when any sum is paid without suit, or before judgment, in lieu of fine, *penlly* [penalty,] or forfeiture, and a share of the same is claimed by any person as informer, the Secretary of the Treasury, under general regulations to be by him prescribed, shall determine whether any claimant is entitled to such share as above limited, and to whom the same shall be paid, and shall make payment accordingly. It is hereby declared to be the true intent and meaning of the present and all previous provisions of internal revenue acts granting shares to informers that no right accrues to or is vested in any informer in any case until the fine, penalty, or forfeiture in such case is fixed by judgment or compromise and the amount or proceeds shall have been paid, when the informer shall become entitled to his legal share of the sum adjudged or agreed upon and received: *Provided*, That nothing herein contained shall be construed to limit or affect the power of remitting the whole or any portion of a fine, penalty, or forfeiture conferred on the Secretary of the Treasury by existing laws. The Commissioner of Internal Revenue shall be, and is hereby, authorized and empowered to compromise, under such regulations as the Secretary of the Treasury shall prescribe, any case arising under the internal revenue laws, whether pending in court or otherwise. The several circuit and district courts of the United States shall have jurisdiction of all offences against any of the provisions of this act committed within their several districts: *Provided*, That whenever in any civil action for a penalty the informer may be a witness for the prosecution, the party against whom such penalty is claimed may be and shall be admitted as a witness on his own behalf. Every person who shall receive any money or other valuable thing under a threat of informing or as a consideration for not informing against any violation of this act, shall, on conviction thereof, be punished by a fine not exceeding two thousand dollars, or by imprisonment not exceeding one year, or both, at the discretion of the court, with costs of prosecution.

Form of proceeding.

Informer's share to be determined after judgment by the court.

Before judgment by the Secretary of the Treasury.

When informer's right accrues.

Existing power to remit not affected.

Commiss'r may compromise cases.

Jurisdiction of circuit and district courts.

Rule of evidence.

Threatening or withholding information.

228. That hereafter in all cases of seizure of any goods, wares, or merchandise which shall, in the opinion of the collector or deputy collector making such seizure, be of the appraised value of three hundred dollars or less, and which shall have been so seized as being subject to forfeiture under any of the provisions of this act, or of any act to which this is an amendment, excepting in cases otherwise provided, the said collector or deputy collector shall proceed as follows, that is to say: He shall cause a list containing a particular description of the goods, wares, or merchandise seized to be prepared in duplicate, and an appraisement of the same to be made by three sworn appraisers, to be selected by him for said purpose, who shall be respectable and disinterest[ed] citizens of the United States residing within the collection district wherein the seizure was made. The aforesaid list and appraisement shall be properly attested by such collector or deputy collector and the persons making the appraisement, for which service said appraisers shall be allowed the sum of one dollar and fifty cents per day each, to be paid as other necessary charges of collectors according to law. If the said goods shall be found by such appraisers to be of the value of three hundred dollars or less, the said collector or deputy collector shall publish a notice, for the space of three weeks, in some newspaper of the district where the seizure was made, describing the articles and stating the time, place, and cause of their seizure, and requiring any person or persons claiming them to appear and make such claim within thirty days from the date of the first publication of such notice: *Provided,* That any person or persons claiming the goods, wares, or merchandise, so seized, within the time specified in the notice, may file with such collector or deputy collector a claim, stating his or their interest in the articles seized, and may execute a bond to the United States in the penal sum of two hundred and fifty dollars, with sureties, to be approved by said collector or deputy collector, conditioned that, in case of condemnation of the articles so seized, the obligors will pay all the costs and expenses of the proceedings, to obtain such condemnation; and upon the delivery of such bond to the collector or deputy collector, he shall transmit the same, with the duplicate list or description of the goods seized, to the United States district attorney for the district, who shall proceed thereon in the ordinary manner prescribed by law: *And provided also,* That if there shall be no claim interposed, and no bond given within the time above specified, the collector or deputy collector, as the case may be, shall give ten days' notice of the sale of the goods, wares, or merchandise, by publication, and at the time and place specified in said notice shall sell the article so seized at public auction, and after deducting the expense of appraisement and sale he shall deposit the proceeds to the credit of the Secretary of the Treasury. And within one year after the sale of any goods, wares, or merchandise, as aforesaid, any person or persons claiming to be interested in the goods, wares, or merchandise so sold may apply to the Secretary of the Treasury for a remission of the forfeiture thereof, or any of them, and a restoration of the proceeds of the said sale, which may be granted by the said Secretary upon satisfactory proof, to be furnished in such manner as he shall prescribe: *Provided,* That it shall be satisfactorily shown that the applicant, at the time of the seizure and sale of the goods in question, and during the intervening time,

13 July, 1866, § 63.

Proceedings on seizure of goods valued at $300 or less.

Appraisement.

Fees.

Notice of sale.

Claimant may give bond.

Proceedings thereon.

Sale in default of claim or bond.

Application for remission.

was absent out of the United States, or in such circumstances as prevented him from knowing of such seizure, and that he did not know of the same; and also that the said forfeiture was incurred without wilful negligence or any intention of fraud on the part of the owner or owners of such goods. If no application for such restoration be made within one year, as hereinbefore prescribed, then, at the expiration of the said time, the Secretary of the Treasury shall cause the proceeds of the sale of the said goods, wares, or merchandise to be distributed according to law, as in the case of goods, wares, or merchandise condemned and sold pursuant to the decree of a competent court.

When proceeds to be distributed.

13 July, 1866, § 15.

Search warrant may be issued.

229. That the judge of any circuit or district court of the United States, or any commissioner thereof, may issue a search warrant, authorizing any internal revenue officer to search any premises, if such officer shall make oath in writing that he has reason to believe, and does believe, that a fraud upon the revenue has been or is being committed upon or by the use of said premises.

13 July, 1866, § 67.

Suit or prosecution against internal revenue officer, &c., in State court.

230. That in any case, civil or criminal, where suit or prosecution shall be commenced in any court of any State against any officer of the United States, appointed under or acting by authority of the act entitled "An act to provide internal revenue to support the government, to pay interest on the public debt, and for other purposes," passed June thirtieth, eighteen hundred and sixty-four, or of any act in addition thereto or in amendment thereof, or against any person acting under or by authority of any such officer on account of any act done under color of his office, or against any person holding property or estate by title derived from any such officer, concerning such property or estate, and affecting the validity of this act or acts of which it is amendatory, it shall be lawful for the defendant, in such suit or prosecution, at any time before trial, upon a petition to the circuit court of the United States in and for the district in which the defendant shall have been served with process, setting forth the nature of said suit or prosecution, and verifying the said petition by affidavit, together with a certificate, signed by an attorney or counsellor-at-law of some court of record of the State in which such suit shall have been commenced, or of the United States, setting forth that, as counsel for the petitioner, he has examined the proceedings against him, and carefully inquired into all the matters set forth in the petition, and that he believes the same to be true; which petition, affidavit, and certificate shall be presented to the said circuit court if in session, and if not, to the clerk thereof, at his office, and shall be filed in said office, and the cause shall thereupon be entered on the docket of said court, and shall be thereafter proceeded in as a cause originally commenced in that court; and it shall be the duty of the clerk of said court, if the suit were commenced in the court below by summons, to issue a writ of certiorari to the State court, requiring said court to send to the said circuit court the record and proceedings in said cause; or if it were commenced by capias, he shall issue a writ of habeas corpus cum causa, a duplicate of which said writ shall be delivered to the clerk of the State court, or left at his office, by the marshal of the district, or his deputy, or some person duly authorized thereto; and thereupon it shall be the duty of the said State court to stay all further proceedings in such cause, and the said suit or prosecution, upon delivery of such process, or leaving

May be removed to United States circuit court.

Proceedings therefor.

the same as aforesaid, shall be deemed and taken to be moved to the said circuit court, and any further proceedings, trial, or judgment therein in the State court shall be wholly null and void. And if the defendant in any such suit be in actual custody on mesne process therein, it shall be the duty of the marshal, by virtue of the writ of habeas corpus cum causa, to take the body of the defendant into his custody, to be dealt with in the said cause according to the rules of law and the order of the circuit court, or of any judge thereof in vacation. All attachments made and all bail and other security given upon such suit or prosecution shall be and continue in like force and effect as if the same suit or prosecution had proceeded to final judgment and execution in the State court; and if, upon the removal of any such suit or prosecution, it shall be made [to] appear to the said circuit court that no copy of the record and proceedings therein in the State court can be obtained, it shall be lawful for said circuit court to allow and require the plaintiff to proceed de novo, and to file a declaration of his cause of action, and the parties may thereupon proceed as in action originally brought in said circuit court; and, on failure of so proceeding, judgment of nolle prosequi may be rendered against the plaintiff, with costs for the defendant: *Provided*, That an act entitled "An act further to provide for the collection of duties on imports," passed March second, eighteen hundred and thirty-three, shall not be so construed as to apply to cases arising under an act entitled "An act to provide internal revenue to support the government, to pay interest on the public debt, and for other purposes," passed June thirtieth, eighteen hundred and sixty-four, or any act in addition thereto or in amendment thereof, nor to any case in which the validity or interpretation of said act or acts shall be in issue: *Provided further*, That if any officer appointed under and by virtue of any act to provide internal revenue, or any person acting under or by authority of any such officer, shall receive any injury to his person or property, for or on account of any act by him done, under any law of the United States, for the collection of taxes, he shall be entitled to maintain suit for damage therefor in the circuit court of the United States, in the district wherein the party doing the injury may reside or shall be found. And all property taken or detained by any officer or other person under authority of any revenue law of the United States shall be irrepleviable, and shall be deemed to be in the custody of the law, and subject only to the orders and decrees of the courts of the United States having jurisdiction thereof. And if any person shall dispossess or rescue, or attempt to dispossess or rescue, any property so taken or detained as aforesaid, or shall aid or assist therein, such person shall be deemed guilty of a misdemeanor, and shall be liable to such punishment as is provided by the twenty-second section of the act for the punishment of certain crimes against the United States, approved the thirtieth day of April, anno Domini one thousand seven hundred and ninety, for the wilful obstruction or resistance of officers in the service of process.

Defendant in actual custody.

Attachments & bail.

Construction of "force act."

Remedy for internal revenue officer, &c.

Property in custody to be irrepleviable.

231. That the fiftieth section of an act passed June thirtieth, eighteen hundred and sixty-four, entitled "An act to provide internal revenue to support the government, to pay interest on the public debt, and for other purposes," is hereby repealed: *Provided*, That any case which may have been removed from the courts of

13 July, 1866, § 68.

Repeal of §50 of act of June 30, 1864.

Cases to be remanded to State court unless.

any State under said fiftieth section to the courts of the United States shall be remanded to the State court from which it was so removed, with all the records relating to such cases, unless the justice of the circuit court of the United States in which such suit or prosecution is pending shall be of opinion that said case would be removable from the court of the State to the circuit court under and by virtue of the sixty-seventh section of this act.

Attachment, bail, &c.

And in all cases which may have been removed from any court of any State under and by virtue of said fiftieth section of said act of June thirtieth, eighteen hundred and sixty-four, all attachments made, and all bail or other security given upon such suit or prosecution, shall be and continue in full force and effect until final judgment and execution, whether such suit shall be prosecuted to final judgment in the circuit court of the United States, or remanded to the State court from which it was removed.

13 July, 1866, § 69.

Writ of error in criminal proceeding. How defendant may be released.

232. That whenever a writ of error shall be issued for the revision of any judgment or decree in any criminal proceeding where is drawn in question the construction of any statute of the United States, in a court of any State, as is provided in the twenty-fifth section of an act entitled "An act to establish the judicial courts of the United States," passed September twenty-fourth, seventeen hundred and eighty-nine, the defendant, if charged with an offence bailable by the laws of such State, shall not be released from custody until a final judgment upon such writ, or until a bond, with sufficient sureties, in a reasonable sum, as ordered and approved by the State court, shall be given; and if the offence is not so bailable, until a final judgment upon the writ of error.

Such cases to have precedence.

Writs of error in criminal cases shall have precedence upon the docket of the Supreme Court of all cases to which the government of the United States is not a party, excepting only such cases as the court, at their discretion, may decide to be of public importance.

XII.

MISCELLANEOUS PROVISIONS.

13 July, 1866, § 60.

Internal revenue officers to make statement of fees, &c., when required.

233. That every internal revenue officer, whose payment, charges, salary, or compensation shall be composed, either wholly or in part, of fees, commissions, allowances, or rewards, from whatever source derived, shall be required to render to the Commissioner of Internal Revenue, under regulations to be approved by the Secretary of the Treasury, a statement under oath setting forth the entire amount of such fees, commissions, emoluments, allowances or rewards of whatever nature, or from whatever source received, during the time for which said statement is rendered;

False statement to be deemed perjury.

and any false statement knowingly and wilfully rendered under the requirements of this section, or regulations established in accordance therewith, shall be deemed wilful perjury, and punished on conviction thereof, as provided in section forty-two of the act of June thirty, eighteen hundred and sixty-four, to which this act is an amendment;

Penalty for neglect, &c., to make statement when required.

and any neglect or omission to render such statement when required shall be punished on conviction therefor by a fine of not less than two hundred dollars nor more than five hundred dollars, in the discretion of the court.

13 July, 1866, § 66.

Special commissioner of the revenue.

234. That the Secretary of the Treasury is hereby authorized to appoint an officer in his department who shal be styled "Special Commissioner of the Revenue," whose office shall terminate in

four years from the thirtieth day of June, eighteen hundred and sixty-six. It shall be the duty of the Special Commissioner of the Revenue to inquire into all the sources of national revenue, and the best methods of collecting the revenue; the relations of foreign trade to domestic industry; the mutual adjustment of the systems of taxation by customs and excise, with the view of insuring the requisite revenue with the least disturbance or inconvenience to the progress of industry and the development of the resources of the country; and to inquire, from time to time, under the direction of the Secretary of the Treasury, into the manner in which officers charged with the administration and collection of the revenues perform their duties. And the said Special Commissioner of the Revenue shall from time to time report, through the Secretary of the Treasury, to Congress, either in the form of a bill or otherwise, such modifications of the rates of taxation or of the methods of collecting the revenues, and such other facts pertaining to the trade, industry, commerce, or taxation of the country, as he may find, by actual observation of the operation of the law, to be conducive to the public interest; and, in order to enable the Special Commissioner of the Revenue to properly conduct his investigations, he is hereby empowered to examine the books, papers and accounts of any officer of the revenue, to administer oaths, examine and summon witnesses, and take testimony; and each and every such person falsely swearing or affirming shall be subject to the penalties and disabilities prescribed by law for the punishment of corrupt and wilful perjury; and all officers of the government are hereby required to extend to the said Commissioner all reasonable facilities for the collection of information pertinent to the duties of his office. And the said Special Commissioner shall be paid an annual salary of four thousand dollars, and the travelling expenses necessarily incurred while in the discharge of his duty; and all letters and documents to and from the Special Commissioner relating to the duties and business of his office shall be transmitted by mail free of postage. And section nineteen of an act entitled "An act to amend an act entitled 'An act to provide internal revenue to support the government, to pay interest on the public debt, and for other purposes,' approved June thirtieth, eighteen hundred and sixty-four," approved March third, eighteen hundred and sixty-five, be, and the same is hereby repealed.

Duties of.

Authorized to administer oaths, &c.

False swearing perjury.

Facilities to be extended to special commissioner.

Salary.

Travelling expenses.

Franking privilege.

Repeal of section 19, March 3, 1865.

235. That if, for any cause, at any time after this act goes into operation, the laws of the United States cannot be executed in a State or Territory of the United States, or any part thereof, or within the District of Columbia, it shall be the duty of the President, and he is hereby authorized, to proceed to execute the provisions of this act within the limits of such State or Territory, or part thereof, or District of Columbia, so soon as the authority of the United States therein shall be re-established, and to collect the taxes, duties, and licenses in such States and Territories, under the regulations prescribed in this act, so far as applicable; and where not applicable, the assessment and levy shall be made, and the time and manner of collection regulated, by the instructions and directions of the Commissioner of Internal Revenue, under the direction of the Secretary of the Treasury.

30 June, 1865, § 46.

Duty of the President in States and Territories where the act cannot be executed.

13 July, 1866, § 71.

Internal revenue acts to be published in German newspapers.

236. That it shall be the duty of the Commissioner of Internal Revenue to have this act, and the acts to which it is amendatory, published in at least one German newspaper in each of the States of the Union where such paper may be published.

30 June, 1864, § 182.

The word State to include Territories and District of Columbia.

237. That wherever the word State is used in this act, it shall be construed to include the Territories and the District of Columbia, where such construction is necessary to carry out the provisions of this act.

13 July, 1866, § 70.

When to take effect.

Inconsistent provisions repealed.

Remain in force for certain purposes.

238. That this act shall take effect, where not otherwise provided, on the first day of August, eighteen hundred and sixty-six, and all provisions of any former act inconsistent with the provisions of this act are hereby repealed: *Provided, however*, That all the provisions of said acts shall be in force for collecting all taxes, duties and licenses properly assessed or liable to be assessed, or accruing under the provisions of acts, the right to which has already accrued or which may hereafter accrue under said acts, and for maintaining and continuing liens, fines, penalties, and forfeitures incurred under and by virtue thereof, and for carrying out and completing all proceedings which have been already commenced, or that may be commenced, to enforce such fines, penalties, and forfeitures, or criminal proceedings under said acts, and for the punishment of crimes of which any party shall be or has been found guilty: *And provided further*, That whenever the duty imposed by any existing law shall cease in consequence of any limitation therein contained before the respective provisions of this act shall take effect, the same duty shall be, and is hereby, continued until such provisions of this act shall take effect; and where any act is hereby repealed, no duty imposed thereby shall be held to cease, in consequence of such repeal, until the respective corresponding provisions of this act shall take effect: *And provided further*, That all manufactures and productions on which a duty was imposed by either of the acts repealed by this act, which shall be in the possession of the manufacturer or producer, or of his agent or agents, on the day when this act takes effect, the duty imposed by any such former act not having been paid, shall be held and deemed to have been manufactured or produced after such date; and whenever by the terms of this act a duty is imposed upon any articles, goods, wares, or merchandise, manufactured or produced, upon which no duty was imposed by either of said former acts, it shall apply to such as were manufactured or produced, and not removed from the place of manufacture or production, on the day when this act takes effect. And the Commissioner of Internal Revenue, under the direction of the Secretary of the Treasury, is authorized to make all necessary regulations and prescribe all necessary forms and proceedings for the collection of such taxes and the enforcement of such fines and penalties for the execution of the provisions of this act.

Commissioner to make necessary regulations.

3 March, 1865, § 16.

Inconsistent provisions repealed.

Remain in force for certain purposes.

239. That all provisions of any former act inconsistent with the provisions of this act are hereby repealed: *Provided, however*, That no duty imposed by any previous act, which has become due or of which return has been or ought to be made, shall be remitted or released by this act, but the same shall be collected and paid, and all fines and penalties heretofore incurred shall be enforced and collected, and all offences heretofore committed shall be punished, as if this act had not been passed; and the Commissioner of Internal Revenue, under the direction of the Secretary

of the Treasury, is authorized to make all necessary regulations and to prescribe all necessary forms and proceedings for the collection of such taxes and the enforcement of such fines and penalties for the execution of the provisions of this act.

Commissioner to make necessary regulations.

240. That the following acts of Congress are hereby repealed, to wit: The act of July first, eighteen hundred and sixty-two, entitled "An act to provide internal revenue to support the government and to pay interest on the public debt," except the one hundred and fifteenth and one hundred and nineteenth sections thereof; and excepting, further, all provisions of said act which create the offices of Commissioner of Internal Revenue, assessor, assistant assessor, collector, deputy collector, and inspector, and provide for the appointment and qualification of said officers. Also, the act of July sixteenth, eighteen hundred and sixty-two, entitled "An act to impose an additional duty on sugars produced in the United States." Also, the act of December twenty-fifth, eighteen hundred and sixty-two, entitled "An act to amend an act entitled 'An act to provide internal revenue to support the government and to pay interest on the public debt,' approved July first, eighteen hundred and sixty-two." Also, the act of March third, eighteen hundred and sixty-three, entitled "An act to amend an act entitled 'An act to provide internal revenue to support the government and to pay interest on the public debt,' approved July first, eighteen hundred and sixty-two, and for other purposes," excepting the provisions of said act which create the offices of deputy commissioner and cashier of internal duties and revenue agents, and provide for the appointment and qualification of said officers. Also, the twenty-fourth and twenty-fifth sections of the act of July fourteenth, eighteen hundred and sixty-two, entitled "An act increasing temporarily the duties on imports, and for other purposes." Also, the second section of the act of March third, eighteen hundred and sixty-three, entitled "An act to prevent and punish frauds upon the revenue, to provide for the more certain and speedy collection of claims in favor of the United States, and for other purposes," so far as the same applies to officers of internal revenue. And, also, the act of March seventh, eighteen hundred and sixty-four, entitled "An act to increase the internal revenue, and for other purposes," together with all acts and parts of acts inconsistent herewith: *Provided*, That all the provisions of said acts shall be in force for levying and collecting all taxes, duties and licenses properly assessed or liable to be assessed, or accruing under the provisions of former acts or drawbacks, the right to which has already accrued or which may hereafter accrue, under said acts, and for maintaining and continuing liens, fines, penalties, and forfeitures incurred under and by virtue thereof, and for carrying out and completing all proceedings which have been already commenced or that may be commenced to enforce such fines, penalties, and forfeitures, or criminal proceedings under said acts, and for the punishment of crimes of which any party shall be or has been found guilty: *And provided further*, That no office created by the said acts and continued by this act shall be vacated by reason of any provisions herein contained, but the officers heretofore appointed shall continue to hold the said offices without reappointment: *And provided further*, That whenever the duty imposed by any existing law shall cease in consequence of any limitation therein contained before the respective provisions of this act

30 June, 1864, § 173.

Repeal of former acts.

Provisions to remain in force for collecting taxes already accrued, &c.

Offices not to be vacated by reason of this act.

Former duties to continue until corresponding provisions of this act take effect.

shall take effect, the same duty shall be, and is hereby, continued until such provisions of this act shall take effect; and where any act is hereby repealed, no duty imposed thereby shall be held to cease, in consequence of such repeal, until the respective corresponding provisions of this act shall take effect: *And provided further*, That all manufactures and productions on which a duty was imposed by either of the acts repealed by this act, which shall be in the possession of the manufacturer or producer, or of his agent or agents, on the day when this act takes effect, the duty imposed by any such former act not having been paid, shall be held and deemed to have been manufactured or produced after such date; and whenever by the terms of this act a duty is imposed upon any articles, goods, wares, or merchandise manufactured or produced, upon which no duty was imposed by either of said former acts, it shall apply to such as were manufactured or produced and not removed from the place of manufacture or production, on the day when this act takes effect: *And provided further*, That no direct tax whatsoever shall be assessed or collected under this or any other act of Congress heretofore passed, until Congress shall enact another law requiring such assessment and collection to be made; but this shall not be construed to repeal or postpone the assessment or collection of the first direct tax levied, or which should be levied, under the act entitled "An act to provide increased revenue from imports, to pay interest on the public debt, and for other purposes," approved August fifth, eighteen hundred and sixty-one, nor in any way to affect the legality of said tax or any process or remedy provided in said acts, or any other acts, for the enforcement or collection of the same in any State or States and Territories and the District of Columbia; but said first tax, and any such process or remedy, shall continue in all respects in force, anything in this act to the contrary notwithstanding.

Articles manufactured before the passage of the law.

No further direct tax to be collected until ordered by Congress.

Proceedings to continue for the collection of the first tax imposed by act of August 5, 1861.

30 June, 1864, §174.

Commissioner may make necessary regulations.

241. That the said Commissioner of Internal Revenue, under the direction of the Secretary of the Treasury, is authorized to make all such regulations, not otherwise provided for, as may become necessary by reason of the alteration of the laws in relation to internal revenue, by virtue of this act.

APPENDIX.

[PUBLIC RESOLUTION No. 59.]

JOINT RESOLUTION imposing a special income duty.

Joint resolution.

Be it resolved by the Senate and House of Representatives of the United States of America in Congress assembled, That, in addition to the income duty already imposed by law, there shall be levied, assessed, and collected on the first day of October, eighteen hundred and sixty-four, a special income duty upon the gains, profits, or income for the year ending the thirty-first day of December next preceding the time herein named, by levying, assessing, and collecting said duty of all persons residing within the United States, or of citizens of the United States residing abroad, at the rate of five per centum on all sums exceeding six hundred dollars, and the same shall be levied, assessed, estimated, and collected, except as to the rates, according to the provisions of existing laws for the collection of an income duty, annually, where not inapplicable hereto; and the Secretary of the Treasury is hereby authorized to make such rules and regulations as to the time and mode, or other matters, to enforce the collection of the special income duty herein provided for, as may be necessary: *Provided,* That in estimating the annual gains, profits, or income, as aforesaid, for the foregoing special income duty, no deductions shall be made for dividends or interest received from any association, corporation, or company, nor shall any deduction be made for any salary or pay received.

Special income duty of 5 per cent. to be levied and collected October 1, 1864.

Secretary of the Treasury authorized to make rules, &c.

No deductions for dividends, interest, &c.

Approved July 4, 1864.

[PUBLIC RESOLUTION No. 79.]

JOINT RESOLUTION to prevent the further enforcement of the Joint Resolution (No. 77) approved July 4, 1864, against officers and soldiers of the United States, who have been honorably discharged, so as to relieve them from the further payment of the special five per cent. income tax imposed thereby.

Whereas, by the resolution (No. 77) of Congress approved July 4, 1864, a special income tax of five per cent. on all incomes exceeding six hundred dollars was directed to be assessed and collected, and was enforced generally upon all citizens accessible to the revenue officers, but was not enforced against all our soldiers in the field in the active service of the country; and whereas, since the surrender of the insurrectionary armies and the disbanding and return of the federal soldiers to their homes, said tax is being, with manifest hardship, assessed and collected of them in many parts of the country: Therefore,

Be it resolved by the Senate and House of Representatives of the United States of America in Congress assembled, That said special tax so imposed shall not be further enforced against said officers or soldiers lately in the service of the United States, and who have been honorably discharged therefrom, and that the Secretary of the Treasury direct the proper observance of the resolution by all revenue officers.

Approved July 28, 1866.

---

30 June, 1864, §58.

Secretary of the Treasury shall appoint inspectors.

Commis'er shall prescribe form of oath and fees.

Penalty of $100 for refusal to admit inspectors, &c.

242.* That there shall be appointed by the Secretary of the Treasury, in every collection district where the same may be necessary, one or more inspectors of spirits, refined coal oil or other oil, tobacco, cigars, and other articles, who shall take an oath faithfully to perform their duties, in such form as the Commissioner of Internal Revenue shall prescribe, and who shall be entitled to receive such fees as may be fixed and prescribed by said Commissioner, to be paid by the owner or manufacturer of the articles inspected, gauged, or proved. And any manufacturer of spirits, refined coal oil or other oil, tobacco, cigars, or other articles which may by law be required to be inspected, who shall refuse to admit an inspector upon his premises, so far as it may be necessary for the performance of his duties, or who shall obstruct an inspector in the performance of his duties, shall forfeit the sum of one hundred dollars, to be recovered in the manner provided for other penalties imposed by this act.

---

* Omitted from its proper place.

INDEX.

B.

G.

10

www.ingramcontent.com/pod-product-compliance
Lightning Source LLC
LaVergne TN
LVHW021358110826
845150LV00007B/1701

* 9 7 8 1 4 2 5 5 1 3 3 8 2 *